FROM RELIGIOUS EXPERIENCE

TO A RELIGIOUS ATTITUDE

Loyola Pastoral Series
Lumen Vitae Studies

From religious experience to a religious attitude

Edited by A. Godin, S.J.

Chicago 1965

Loyola University Press

Distributed in Canada by
PALM PUBLISHERS, LTD., *Montreal*

© 1965 Loyola University Press

Printed in the United States of America

Library of Congress Catalog Card Number: 65-12553

IMPRIMI POTEST John R. Connery, S.J., Provincial of the Chicago Province, September 27, 1964. NIHIL OBSTAT John B. Amberg, S.J., *Censor deputatus*, September 29, 1964. IMPRIMATUR Most Reverend Cletus F. O'Donnell, J.C.D., Vicar General, Archdiocese of Chicago, September 30, 1964. THE NIHIL OBSTAT AND THE IMPRIMATUR ARE OFFICIAL DECLARATIONS THAT A BOOK OR PAMPHLET IS FREE OF DOCTRINAL OR MORAL ERROR. NO IMPLICATION IS CONTAINED THEREIN THAT THOSE WHO HAVE GRANTED THE NIHIL OBSTAT AND IMPRIMATUR AGREE WITH THE CONTENTS, OPINIONS, OR STATEMENTS EXPRESSED.

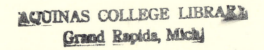

American Preface

From Religious Experience to a Religious Attitude brings together twelve significant studies in religious psychology. In addition to nine studies that have previously appeared in *Lumen Vitae*, the book includes three new studies: "Religious Expression and Mental Deficiency," by Henri Bissonnier; "The Idea of God: Its Evolution between the Ages 11 and 19," by Pierre Babin; and "Religious Knowledge among Pupils of Secular and Religious Catechists: A Comparative Study," by Jean-Jacques Larivière. All the articles have been re-edited for American readers.

Contents

Introduction

This volume of Studies in Religious Psychology is intended primarily for teachers of religion who desire serious information on religious psychology, and are not afraid to face rigorous thinking and observations obtained with some scientific precision. We have not avoided, therefore—especially when presenting positive research—certain allusions to questions of method; for example, the regroupings of free associations from the stimulus word 'God,' by J.-P. Deconchy in his study on religious semantics. We publish the detailed description of a procedure of comparison ('pairing'), used by J.-J. Larivière in applying his test of religious knowledge, and a statistical analysis ('scalability') which permits R. Goldman to fix an age threshold in questions of relative comprehension of the Bible. These technical articles are always found difficult by teachers who have not done specialized studies. Nevertheless, the editor thinks that these methods of analysis must sooner or later be used in catechetical research, if teachers are to control not only the authenticity of the Christian message, but also the efficacy of its transmission.

We hope that this volume will be equally welcome to psychologists of religion and to those who teach, often in spite of scanty preparation, the elements of religious psychology in catechetical schools or institutes. Psychologists, if they are really 'scientific,' will criticize us for publishing results insufficiently validated, works less exacting as to method, or for bringing forward theoretical expositions which are too marked by a preoccupation with Christian education.

But many psychologists of religion have become aware of the relative uselessness of researches, even though statistically valid, whose object is often ill-defined, the 'items' poorly formulated, and the aim devoid of religious pertinence. They want contact with theologians, phenomenologists, and teachers of religion to settle their parameters of research, to formulate their hypotheses or construct their objective tests better; in short, to improve their chances of arriving at significant results and not only at correlations statistically

significant. An encouraging sign of this new state of mind is
the Symposium at Cornell in 1961, which assembled qualified
representatives of four disciplines: psychologists, sociologists,
theologians, and educators (from three religions).[1] Whenever
the Academy of Religion and Mental Health assembles its
best scientific workers and publishes their contributions and
discussions, it calls for the defining of projects for research,
with the collaboration of theologians and psychologists, although it has not been tried on any precise point.[2] In the
present state of the psychology of religion, it is still extremely
rare to find a scientifically adequate research whose results
can be commented on from the theological or educational
standpoint,[3] or which has a basic hypothesis of real religious
pertinence. In this volume we hope the readers, especially the
psychologists, will recognize the religious and Christian validity of the questions raised by R. H. Thouless and L. B. Brown
on the opportuneness (distinct from the efficacy[4]) of certain
prayers, as well as those raised by C. Van Bunnen on the symbolic grasp of a biblical story and by our research, in collaboration with M. Hallez, on parental images connected with
the idea of divine paternity.

In a word, this series of Studies in Religious Psychology
has sought to consider both these sets of readers: teachers and

---

[1] We gave a detailed review of the Cornell Symposium in *Lumen Vitae*, XVI
(1961), 741-46. The works have been published in *Review of Recent Research* and
*Research Plans in the Field of Religion, Values and Morality and Their Bearing on
Religious and Character Formation*. Religious Education Association, New York.

[2] Especially in the volume *Research in Religion and Health* (Proceedings of the
Fifth Academy Symposium, 1961). New York 1963. See the long appendix to the
previous volume, *Religion, Culture and Mental Health* (Proceedings of the Third
Academy Symposium, 1959). New York 1961.

[3] We think this is due to the separation for fifty years, in the religious domain,
of positive psychologists (except a few psychiatrists and psychoanalysts) from
phenomenologists (even if they claim to be psychologists as is frequent in Germany).
Traces of this separation are found in *Religion und Erlebnis*, edited by J. Rudin.
Olten-Freiburg, Walter Vg., 1963. In this study only a few pages are devoted to observation (children and pathological cases), and the most interesting thoughts are not
accompanied by any attempt to verify their 'representativity' in a population.

[4] Of this basic antinomy of Christian prayer, no modern psychologist has probably spoken better than Father L. Beirnaert, "La prière de demande dans notre vie
d'homme"; in *Expérience chrétienne et psychologie*. Paris 1964. pp. 333-54.

psychologists. It lives by their collaboration; it hopes they will end by reading each other's works, and perhaps meet together and be mutually enriched through dialogue.

Two Reactions to the Positive Psychology of Religion

It cannot be denied that while there is a growing interest in psychological research, there is also, among religion teachers and some theologians, a certain apprehension which is expressed by latent or explicit opposition. Psychology, taken as a science, is one of the attempts of modern man to discover the components of his destiny and to increase his liberty by further control of the factors which influence his experiences, especially the basic ones imposed on him by blind necessity. Experience of the sacred and of various 'sacralities' (mystical beliefs, ritual practices, mysticism) will be more and more the subject of scientific research and critical thought.[5] Hence a movement largely attracted towards 'secularization,' the chief articulations of which appear in the study by A. Vergote.

Does a myth still act as a myth when it is recognized and analyzed as such? Is the mystical experience still lived as mystical when it is reduced to states of consciousness capable of being reproduced, as W. H. Clark suggests, by "the grace" of certain drugs? Yes, perhaps, provided the whole difference can be discerned between something sacred imposed, passively endured, and something sacred actively assumed and recognized, that is to say, the distinction between *experience* and *attitude* which serves as title to this book. But we understand the resistance, expressed also in a constant fluctuation between the two views on the psychology of religion, between the two sorts of eagerness which inspire the efforts, expectations, and joys of those who labor at it.

---

[5] In a difficult but penetrating essay in the *Encyclopédie de la Psychologie* (Paris 1962. II, 124-28), Abbé J. C. Osouf describes the inevitable dawn of secularization apparent when the searcher applies the scientific aim to his own religion (not only to that of others, as ethnologists and some old-time missionaries have done.) Osouf sees the problem as that of two languages (religious and scientific) which invigorate each other provided they remain faithful to their common source: the mediation of symbols.

Two Trends in the Psychology of Religion

Two trends run through the psychology of religion to our own day. The first, interested in mysticism, seeks to describe the manifestations and psychological effects of religion, even of grace, when man seeks to conform his conduct to it. The other trend, more modest in its object, chiefly seeks to settle the nature and extent of the sociopsychic conditionings which form the substructure, stable and largely fixed by the dispositions in which liberty gradually opens out to God's call: pre-existing groundwork, obstacle, or modality of expression. Precise knowledge of the laws, constant, or factors that govern this field of energy, which a Thomist philosopher would call "the dispositive material cause" of our religious acts, is no small help to the Christian towards understanding better and better the originality of the divine offer of an 'adoptive son-ship,' to prepare for it with greater lucidity, and to help others more efficiently to perceive its demands while responding to it. Of this second trend we have tried to indicate the status and basic principles as a positive, that is, a strictly scientific psychology of religion.[6] We shall say no more here of these methodological principles.

The existence of these two trends—as in the past, this series of volumes will welcome representatives of both—invites reflection on a certain eagerness to be found in each. At first sight, we might perhaps say that in both cases it is an eagerness to know. Beneath the diversity of methods and matter, there appears a double type of knowledge and a profound difference (if not divergence) in aspirations, which could easily be missed, in their most legitimate qualities, by representatives of the other trend. Since this more or less latent or admitted eagerness directs the interests, observation, and sometimes the interpretations which authors or research workers inclined to either of these spirits put forward, it may be useful to disclose the twofold component, in order to ensure better dialogue between our collaborators and our readers.

---

[6] *Child and Adult before God* (Lumen Vitae Studies in Religious Psychology). Brussels 1961. pp. 15-16.

Eagerness To Share

A first group of research workers incline towards observation of rather rare experiences of privileged subjects, or at least of exceptional moments in the religious life: mystical states, conversions, individual descriptions of unusual behaviors. Many, when they are Christians, declare definitely that the psychology of religion must seek to recognize the expressions or signs of divine grace, to describe the states of conscience or behaviors which bear the marks of such religious experiences, even to consider their effect, which would otherwise be inexplicable.

Since they often admit, either hastily or regretfully, that they are not seeking to build up a real science, their psychological observations and interpretations seem rather to be guided by an eagerness for a communion or share in these states or privileged moments. Hence their repeated insistence on the necessity for the psychologist himself being "in a state of grace" (sometimes in the psychological sense, sometimes in the theological sense) in sympathetic consonance with the phenomenon observed: mystical aspects of behavior, attentive ear for the interior phenomenon, attitudes of prayer, and so forth.

Hence also their propensity to declare that in order to be really useful to religious education, religious psychology must also present observation of spiritually privileged children, or even exceptional, or should at least observe with attention and reverence the moments or acts which particularly mark their religious development. By thus describing subjects especially advanced or "gifted," rare but eventually typical reactions, lofty spiritual moments with "example" value, the followers of this tendency think that the psychology of religion attains its true object, becoming capable of directly helping teachers, perhaps even theologians, to better discern concretely the end of their efforts and the object of their science: union of God with man achieved in the concrete, empirically perceptible even when the subject is still physically and psychologically a child.

While seeking to satisfy this eagerness to track spiritual growth, to observe, describe, or assist it as spiritual, this psy-

chology of religion encounters two temptations against which
it must constantly strive so as not to yield to them.

The first is an inclination to interpret as "effects of grace,"
states of conscience, edifying reactions, or convincing observations, because they enter into the network of exigencies
theoretically considered as "criteria of grace." The interpretation is all the more easily in danger of being illusory when
it concerns children, since they are largely (and even entirely,
at first) under the influence of the conditionings of their edu-
cative setting, which tends to arouse behaviors in conformity
with the "criteria of grace," or at least what are considered
such in a given culture, a special epoch, or setting. To confuse
effects of conditioning and expressions of liberty opening to
grace (or rather interpreting manifestations observed as effects of the latter) would easily lead towards a theological
intellectualism, but slightly psychological, and soon disappointing for any eagerness to share in the spiritual growth of
the individuals observed. Setting aside attribution to a causality of grace (though how can that be distinguished, with children, from well-organized psycho-educational causalities?),
these interpretations would not be very different from those
established by Jung, starting from religious archetypes, the
gnostic tendency of which has been pointed out several times.

The second temptation would be to stop at a juxtaposition
of biographies (exemplary lives, sudden conversions) or anec-
dotes (unusual behaviors, remarkable traits) which, not being susceptible to any generalization, do not constitute a
science, and are only of a very relative use in pastoral work
or in home or school education.[7] The desire to discover certain
"constants of grace" (which some take to be mental or cultural models) can, on its side, weaken the psychological tendency to encounter concretely, and to share psychologically
the life of the possible convert or growing child, seen as being

---

[7] We do not mean to deny the great interest of saints' lives or descriptions of
exemplary moments in educational perspective as such. The latter, as we see it, includes (unlike psychological perspective) a function of witness calling for a process
of identification with concrete models, of whom the prototype and supreme exemplar
is obviously Jesus Christ, 'exemplary' cause of grace, whose divine nature and sancti-
fying action escape, by right as in fact, psychological science as such.

individually open to grace. Besides, observer or teacher could always wonder (for want of a precise and scientific knowledge of the setting whence the observation is drawn) whether they have not merely found what they themselves have planted unwittingly or unconsciously. They thus find again the painful and rending contradiction between a need of communion and the wish for objective verification that inspires any scientific thought.

The religious psychologist, legitimately desirous of sharing the development of the life of grace in order to perceive its movement better, would do well in any case to remember that Christian growth at every age, but particularly in childhood or at moments of conversion, is not first a state of mind but a work: the gradual realization of the freedom open to God's gift, progressive acceptance of an adoptive sonship, the recognition of which is made in faith, starting from the word of the Gospel, and the vitality of which is expressed in charity by the network of relations which the Spirit arouses in us with the living Church.[8] If observable behaviors can be considered as "signs" of grace, it is at the level of interpretation of a symbolic type, of prudential (not strictly scientific) judgment which perceives these behaviors in the light of faith.

Eagerness To Purify

Representatives of the other trend in the psychology of religion have also learned to moderate their eagerness to share, or rather to direct its energy towards slightly different ends. What counts for them is to reach a better understanding of the psychosocial conditionings which constitute the basic terrain from which liberty wrests itself to meet God's gift, and towards which it returns to express the gift by living in it. These psychologists, if Christians, hope that by perceiving more and more the play of natural mechanisms which govern the blossoming of secular religiosity, they may gradually offer

---

[8] Father Pierre Watté has published under the title "Pacifications intérieures," *Christus* 41 (1964), 59-76, a shrewd and penetrating study on the dynamisms implied in a peace which is both a gift (in the faith in Jesus Christ) and a task to perform (active effort of pacification in one's own soul and one's environment): "And it is the task which will often allow us to perceive the gift."

the teacher (and the theologian) an indirect assistance towards asserting the originality of the Christian message better, towards recognizing the exceptional value of certain privileged spiritual developments, and going more safely through this mutation or conversion which at every age is called for by the word of Christ our Saviour heard in the recesses of man's soul, which it alone can achieve.[9]

The aim they assign to this scientific psychology of religion is more modest: not the discernment of the effects of grace, but rather the more and more precise and rigorous knowledge of the natural and cultural influences within which the eventual opening to grace takes place. However keen their eagerness to share may be, as teachers and Christians, they have learned to use it first as eagerness to purify, an eagerness which stresses the discovery of all that is, in primitive and affective religiosity, merely an instinctive cry and not yet acquiescence with the word. Eagerness to discern, consequently, and to liberate from basic conditionings, not to escape from them by some kind of scientific miracle, but on the contrary, gradually and patiently to register in them the expressions of their Christian faith and charity becomes a task never achieved.

The danger for this psychology of religion, its special temptation as scientific psychology, is also twofold.

On one hand, it may think it has exhausted the object of religion because it has discovered certain conditions of appear-

---

[9] We find it rather alarming to see the need to share turn the attention of audiences made up of teachers or average Christians so easily towards the marvelous, the sacred, signs of grace chiefly looked for in children or primitive peoples (that is, less developed intellectually). They are much less impressed by the forms, otherwise austere, of the action of grace at work in tumultuous adolescents, cultured adults, critical or discouraged elderly people. A text about the revelation made "to little ones, hidden from the wise and prudent" is more of a screen than a proof, if it is true that these "little ones" in the Gospel have only an indirect relation to mental, cultural, or physical age, and that the kingdom of heaven is also for "those who are like them"— which raises a delicate question of adult psychology, based on symbolic expression and spiritual analogy. In practice, a certain share in the childish expressions of religion is 'easy,' in the sense that it hardly forces us to come out of ourselves, to feel ill at ease in meeting a personality truly "other" than ourselves. For the child is always alive within us, but the man also must be Christianized, respected, loved, and scientifically understood.

ance and development in a given setting, and for the majority, to be more interested in statistical norms than in privileged subjects or exceptional moments. Great followers of this psychology have often yielded to this reductionist rationalism (for example, Freud, in clinical psychology, and many psycho-statistical works published in America).

On the other hand, it neglects the second moment in lived religion, when liberty, having opened out towards the living God, comes back to embody and express this experience, full of both joy and pain, attracting yet tormenting, in acts of ritual and behaviors which, observed from outside, often resemble socially conditioned forms of religious life. The ambiguity of these expressive behaviors and symbolic signs of lived religion has often discouraged psychologists from giving them the attention they deserve, or taking interest in questions of 'meaning.'[10] The confusion between the impression, passively received, of a socially and culturally imposed religiosity, and the expression, freely introduced, of a personal religion remains the chief obstacle encountered by scientific religious psychology, an obstacle difficult to situate correctly,[11] in the plane of thought, and especially difficult (if not impossible) to overcome in the psychological observation of young children. Let us illustrate through the use of two examples in this volume.

---

[10] Even as qualified an advocate of scientific religious psychology as W. Keilbach, "Die empirische Religionspsychologie als Zweig der Religionswissenschaft," *Archiv für Religionspsychologie*, VII (1962), 13-30, tends to separate from positive psychology questions of 'meaning.' No doubt he intends to reserve to philosophy the arbitration relative to 'objective' truth. But can we accept that the psychologist, when observing religious behaviors, is not interested in knowing whether they have, at least for the subject expressing them, a religious meaning?

[11] We must ask phenomenologists to think correctly over this relation between impression and expression, between 'theopathy' and 'theophany' in the religious domain. An important work in this line is G. Morel, S.J., *Le sens de l'existence selon S. Jean de la Croix.* Paris 1960. 3 vols. The relations between consciousness and expression, purifying negativity and inadequate expressivity, are seriously examined on the basis of mystical experience itself, enlightened by modern dialectics. We still have to ask how these dialectic movements are expressed in manifestations or religious institutions which can be empirically observed. Probably by a system of "psychological antinomies," as Thomas O'Dea suggests in an article very close to the operational possibilities of a scientific research, "Five Dilemmas in the Institutionalization of Religion," *Journal for the Scientific Study of Religion,* I (1961), 30-41.

Discussion

On the level of experience which can be observed, why should God's action be more active and perceptible in Michel (aged 8) who, at the end of a crisis, becomes sensitive to the silence of prayer in a group and ceases to disturb the catechist's lesson,[12] than in Yvon (aged 9), who slowly spells out on his sheet of free associations: "Creates the earth—has created us—does not forsake us—forgives us—good," assuredly a remarkable series for a child of his age.[13]

The fact that a psychologist can, in both cases, detect traces of a certain psychic conditioning in no way prevents a believing observer from interpreting these behaviors on the Christian plane, evaluating them as expressions of a more or less achieved Christian maturity. Nevertheless, we venture to add two reflections here:

1 The evaluation of Yvon's answer as an exceptional expression of Christian maturity (by statistically established norms) and as unusually good (either in comparison with the norms from older children or by a theological criterion) is a more useful and valuable observation for teachers than describing the event, no doubt ineffable, which took place in the psychological conscience of Michel, and which altered his perceptible behavior afterwards. In fine, Michel's behavior, however encouraging for his teacher and her eagerness to share, has no 'example' value for the other children; neither has Yvon's answer. In this sense, neither of these two observations is directly useful educationally. And yet, the background from which Yvon's answer arises is directly enlightening for teachers. From accurate knowledge of this background and the laborious work it presupposes, they are enabled to detect other exceptional cases expressing Christian maturity, unpredictable in the settings where these educators teach.

2 The fact that both the observations of Michel and Yvon are looked upon as expressions of Christian maturity does not easily permit a conclusion of the special action of God, nor an

---

[12] Observation by M. Fargues, commented on by P. Ranwez. See page 71 of this volume.

[13] Sheet of free associations prepared by Abbé J. P. Deconchy. See page 120.

assertion that it is more active in the first case than in the second.[14] One of the interesting aspects of P. Ranwez' article is that it states, as the criteria for discerning an action of grace, the demands theoretically set down by the theologians and the difficulty of satisfying them in psychological observations of the behavior of children. Comparison is not useless, nor the balance sheet negative. But it requires, we think, a clearer distinction between a prudential and intuitive judgment passed on Christian maturity shown through this childish behavior (a delicate matter but perhaps accessible, using the precautions accurately stated by P. Ranwez) and the possibility of constructing a real knowledge of the psychological action of grace from these childish ways of behavior, at an age when liberty is barely emerging from its mass of conditionings.

Besides, this second possibility (considered by some to be unrealistic) is not required to achieve the essential aim of a scientific psychology of religion.[15] It would fully deserve this name when it analyzes the psychic determinisms at work in any conduct culturally defined as religious.

---

[14] The plane of expression is, in reality, the only one on which the psychologist can evaluate religious or Christian maturity. On this subject there is a most accurate statement by Father P. Babin in a recent book *Dieu et l'adolescent*. Paris 1963. "What can the word *adult* on the spiritual plane mean (for the psychologist)?" he asks. Having dismissed illusory solutions, he concludes that it can only mean "conscience and liberty through which the life of faith is expressed." To be qualified as exceptional, an observation needs knowledge of the background (normal or average) from which it springs; that is, from many other systematic observations, made as far as possible under the same conditions. In comparing expressions the psychologist can judge the degree of Christian maturity, but (as most psychologists of the second tendency think) not the special action of divine grace.

[15] In a debate on *Psychologie et religion* (Paris 1960), Father Michel-Marie de la Croix considers that it is difficult to attribute scientifically the quality 'religious' to a privileged psychic experience. "For the Christian," he adds, "could not expect from psychology the revelation of a new way of access to God. We believe that God has spoken to us through his Son once for all." Every formally Christian experience, therefore, appears as a 'de-centration' and active share in that revelation. A contemporary of Christ, 'enlightened by the Father' (Matthew XV, 17)—that is, in faith—could have a direct and immediate knowledge through participation and connaturality of his divine character. But every expression of Christian maturity, derived from it and capable of observation by others, would call for an operation of symbolic type in order to be recognized, even on the plane of intuitive knowledge; an active synthesis between this expression perceived as 'sign,' and understood according to what it signifies.

And yet, by practicing interpretation of religious behaviors only from psychosocial conditionings and statistical means, the Christian psychologist would deprive himself of a full understanding of his objects of investigation. The longitudinal study of individual cases (exceptional or not) and attentive examination of privileged moments, and of answers other than average (above, below, or abnormal) also seem to us necessary for the psychologists' work, and more in the psychology of religion than elsewhere. In this volume works of this kind will be found by H. Bissonnier, analyzing pecularities of religious expression among backward children, by W. H. Clark and P. Ranwez already quoted, and up to a certain point in the interview method adopted by the psychosociologist J. Brothers.

Conclusion

To sum up, the two trends of eagerness which seem to influence the two present currents in religious psychology appear to be partially opposed and yet complementary.

The eagerness to make the Christian and religious attitude more free and pure, as regards conditionings which mark its outset toward the sacred and the divine transcendence, supports the demand for a more and more accurate search into these determinisms, and justifies increasingly close psychosocial hermeneutics. The psychoanalytical understanding and statistical method, in the analysis of individual and cultural factors, are its most efficient levers at present.[16]

By the words *psychosocial hermeneutics* we intend to recognize the contribution of the phenomenologist Paul Ricoeur, who in France has studied the complementarity of these two tendencies with the most penetration. He concluded a confer-

---

[16] The difficulty of uniting them in research has been vigorously stressed by Dr. M. Gitelson in a close analysis on eagerness to share and objectivity in psychoanalysis, "On the Present Scientific and Social Position of Psychoanalysis," *International Journal of Psycho-Analysis*, 8 (1963), 521-27. See the various reactions aroused by this discourse in the same review, 8 (1963), 384-86. Worth reading also is an article by Joseph Havens, "The Participant's vs. the Observer's Frame of Reference," *Journal for the Scientific Study of Religion*, 1 (1961), 79-87.

ence on settling the aim of a psychology of religion as a science with these words:

> Reflection implies an archeology and an eschatology of conscience; it requires a de-mystification, which psychoanalysis develops, of the false conscience . . . of religion in the measure that it is the projection of an archaic destiny both ancestral and childish. But I understand this de-mystification as only one side of a restoration of the signs of the Sacred, which are the prophecy of conscience . . . (and) of which the eschatological signification can never be totally turned into knowledge and into gnosis . . . The progressive order of symbols is not indifferent to the regressive order of phantasms; when plunging into archaic mythologies of the unconscious, new signs of the Sacred arise. The eschatology of conscience is always a creative repetition of its archeology.[17]

The transition from an experience of the sacred initially 'impressed' upon the emotional life, towards a religious attitude seeking to 'express' itself by consecrating some fragment of the world, demands the mediation of symbolism (myths, rites, and sacrifices). Psychologically to observe and evaluate this transition requires careful examination of the ever changing relation between religion as an institution and religion as a personal commitment, between God as seen by the group and God as progressively conceived within the mind and heart. This relation, I am afraid, remains ambiguous and ambivalent as long as it does not encounter God who reveals himself, and is not grounded on the mediating symbols through which he chooses to meet us in a living religious community.

A. Godin, s. j.
Professor of the Psychology of Religion
International centre Lumen Vitae *(Brussels)*

---

[17] Paul Ricoeur, "Herméneutique et réflexion"; in *Demitizzazione e Imagine.* Rome 1962. pp. 19-34.

1

Theoretical Perspectives

Religious Experience

by Reverend A. VERGOTE

Professor of the Psychology and Philosophy of Religion
at Louvain University [1]

The study of religious phenomena and the history of religions alike make us aware of an innate capacity on the part of mankind to experience the Divine. Together with the sense of beauty, with all the manifestations of love and with ethical values, reverence for the sacred figures among the basic dimensions of man.

The Experience of the Sacred in Nature.

Man's sense of the sacred seems less apparent in our day. It is very widely affirmed that God no longer makes His voice heard to contemporary man, at least through nature. He has withdrawn Himself, men say, and nature no longer puts man vividly in mind of his Maker. Nature, by dint of a process which first made itself felt at the time of the Renaissance, becomes, as it were, secularized, and with that secularization a purtfying process is also no doubt linked. BERNANOS has written that silence is one of God's qualities. But, if God is no longer perceptible to the heart of man, how can man any longer receive supernatural illumination ? If man's intellect no longer sees God reflected in His works, how will he be able to bring into contact with each other the present world, which experience makes known to us, and the Word of God Who is founding the new order ? In order that man may

---

1. The Rev. Antoine VERGOTE was born at Courtrai in 1921. He won doctorates in both Theology and Philosophy at Louvain University. In 1954 he was appointed Conference Master and in 1962 Professor at the same University. He lectures on Religious psychology and on philosophy. A member of various psychological, philosophical and psycho-analytic societies, he has published numerous articles on: The Fourth Gospel, The Psychology of Aristotle and St. Thomas, Freud and psycho-analysis, Religion and the problem of anxiety, The psychological Sources of Contemporary Atheism, and « Psychological Conditions of Adult Faith » (*Lumen Vitae*, 1960, 4, 623-34). — Address : 4, rue Marie-Thérèse, Louvain, Belgium (Editor's note).

be responsive to the Word that is outside time, is it not necessary that the world that is inside time should symbolize God and that His immanent Word, if we are to become at least dimly aware of Him, should be revealed through nature ? If indeed God seems absent from the world of nature and if, in the pervading atmosphere of our civilization, all trace of Him is effaced by the critical and technological spirit of the day, it is hard to see how the Church's message can ever be conveyed to the contemporary world. Or may we hope that, on the contrary, in the midst of this silence, the Church's voice will now sound forth all the more clearly because she has now rid herself of all bio-cosmic mysticism ?

Our present object, however, is not to reply to the theological problem constituted by the question of the continuity or otherwise of these two different aspects of religion : that of natural religious experience and that of the Transcendent Word. We have rather expressed our fear that a Divine Word which would make God descend into a natural world devoid of supernatural content, may be smothered in that religious void which the critical civilization of the day has surrounded mankind.

Let us consider, therefore, on the one hand, just what this much-published idea of the secularization of the cosmos stands for ; and on the other hand, whether there are not other religious experiences on which faith in the God of the prophets and of Christ our Lord could base itself. The surprising success of the works of Teilhard de Chardin is not to be accounted for by any considerations of a literary or scientific order, but merely by its religious significance. Whatever may be thought of this attempt to make the Presence of the Incarnate Word commensurate with the dimensions of the universe, men in search of God have found in Teilhard's ideas a key enabling them to open the way to tracing God's Presence in His works in the world of sense and time, even approaching thereby the God of Jesus Christ. « If so many souls have been touched by Father TEILHARD DE CHARDIN, this is perhaps above all because he found a way of making the universe a temple once more. » [1] This seems to show that after all, modern man is accessible to the appeal to find through his sense perceptions an approach to the God of the Gospels. If our interpretation of the extraordinary attention given to Teilhard de Chardin is correct, this does not necessarily imply that there is any truth in the theological thesis which postulates a radical cleavage between the natural order and revelation, for it does not prejudge the

1. Jean LACROIX, *Le sens de l'athéisme moderne*, p. 28, Paris, 1958.

question of the distance between the God who inhabits the temple of the universe and the God present on the Cross and in the Resurrection. But this approach, should it be held permissible, would argue a certain permanence in religious experience. It would run counter in some degree to the theory that would limit such experience to men of primitive culture under cosmo-biological influence. Teilhard's vision of nature is in fact a product of scientific culture, and is thus very definitely distinguishable from any experience of immediate union with nature. Nevertheless it is equally far from being a mere scientific theory about the universe. Its predominantly evolutionist character awakens so ready an affective response in the mind of modern man because it puts forward, in scientific terms, the conviction of basic unity between every individual or civilization and the current of vital energy which is their motive power. Is not Nature, we are asked, in its profoundest essence, precisely that *physis*, [1] that inexhaustible creative life, that surge of cosmic sap, which courses through, and nourishes, each individual and each collective group ?

Thorough psychological investigation would be necessary in order to put to the test the various ideas which are widespread today in regard to religious experience and the absence of God in our modern civilization. Such studies as have already been carried out on the subject are fragmentary and incomplete. Nor do the following pages claim to furnish an adequate reply to the question of religious experience and its relationship to the Christian standpoint. They do, however, aim at singling out certain essential concepts and at providing some positive data which may serve to modify and correct the pastoral and theological impressions quoted.

I. THE PHENOMENOLOGY OF RELIGIOUS EXPERIENCE

1. *The term « experience »* is one of the most ambiguous that exists. In English it normally means all the knowledge resulting from the exercise of the faculties (e.g. « experience » of a profession or of a given social circle...) Used in a scientific sense, « experience, » whether interior or exterior, means the acquirement of genuine knowledge furnished by the world considered as external to the mind : the concept thus expresses the empirical sum of one's

---

1. Cf. M. HEIDEGGER, « *Vom Wesen und Begriff der* ΦΥΣΙΣ, *Aristotle, Physics*, B. 1 », in *Il Pensiero* (Ediz. Cisalpino, Milano-Varese), III (1958), N. 131-156, 255-289.

total knowledge. Again in psychology and in philosophy the term « experience » expresses the fact of feeling something, in so far as this fact is considered not merely as a transitory phenomenon but as one that extends one's ideas or invades one's mind. »[1]

The title of William JAMES' book *The Varieties of Religious Experience* uses the word « experience » in this sense. James describes religious experience as the religious tendencies of man in so far as he is conscious of them : « religious feelings and religious impulses. »[2] James had evolved a theory of religious sentiment which fitted into his special psychiatric conception of man's conscious and subliminal self. In the same way, R. OTTO, in his book *The Idea of the Holy*, worked out a philosophy of irrational knowledge which is a development of a particular aspect of Kantian philosophy.

We must be careful, both in regard to James and to Otto, to distinguish between their philosophical and psychological prepossessions, on the one hand, and on the other, their basic purpose which is to bring out clearly the affective or « experiential » side of religion. We may think that this accentuation of the affective nature of religion is exaggerated. Those used to a dogmatic religion, based on revelation, tend to mistrust a religion too much based on feeling, and that for several reasons : there is a danger of confusing emotion and reality; minds are apt suddenly to be led captive by the surge of rationalism which has permeated such large tracts of western philosophical thought ; lastly, the upheaval connected with pietism and modernism ended by rendering suspect the psychology of religious experience in which theological concepts are reduced to their psychological content. Contemporary philosophy has none the less compelled us to recognize, underneath the language of concepts, that amalgam of preconceptual and experiential ideas to which Reason finally gives explicit clarification, and to which the human Will, by freely accepting them, gives spiritual value.

Contemporary philosophy moreover has, on its side, made clear to us the *osmosis* which links feeling and mind, and it is trying to work out the laws of this inflow of affectivity into the intellect. It is in any case not at all surprising that religion, being above all else an attitude to existence, and a relationship with others, should plunge its roots into what Kant calls « *Gemüt*, » that is, into affec-

---

1. A. LALANDE, *Vocabulaire technique et critique de la philosophie*, Paris, 1947, pp. 309-310.
2. Mentor Book, New York, 1958, p. 22.

tivity, and that it should therefore be experience before being choice or attitude.

We understand then by religious experience, that immediate, to a large extent « pathic » grasp of the sacred, that immediate contact with the realm of the Divine. We are deliberately refraining here from touching upon the subject of Christian experience. It is indeed true that the revealed Truths of Christianity, the Person of Christ, the Grace of the Spirit, the Fatherhood of God, are in some degree objects of experience. Faith is not merely rational assent. It finds an echo in our affective selves, and this gives it its psychological strength and amplitude. St. Thomas of Aquinas tells us that man is pushed towards the assent he gives to the Faith by a « quasi-instinct. » Christian experience can then be studied in its widest sense, as has been done by J. MOUROUX. [1] That is not, however, what we have in mind, and we feel grave doubts as to the possibility of making a genuine psychological study of Christian experience considered as a whole. None the less, it seems to us to be of pressing importance to enquire how, and in what degree, a religious experience forms part of human existence, and what are its relations with the supernatural act of faith.

2. *The comparative history of religion* has shown us how extraordinarily manifest and fruitful in results religious experience has been in the civilization that preceded our own. This awareness of the sacred permeated the whole of social and cultural existence. Basing himself upon the philosopher D.M. EDWARDS, J. WACH remarks with great justice : « The Sacred is not so much a fourth value to be added to the Good, the True and the Beautiful as the womb whence these values spring, their form and their common source. In other words, religion is not merely a branch of a tree, it is its very trunk. Thus the analysis of a given culture involves the examination of the theological doctrines, the myths or the rites, which serve as clues to the nature of the religious beliefs of those concerned. And not only this : it means our making ourselves acquainted by close research with the true atmosphere of the time, and giving careful study to the general attitude towards religion expressed in the life of the cultural period taken as a whole. » [2]

This anthropologist's opinion states the problem accurately : in those civilizations that are described as primitive, all social and individual activities are permeated with, and linked together by,

---

1. *The Christian Experience*, London and New York, Sheed and Ward, 1955.
2. *Sociologie et Religion*, Paris. 1955.

an overriding and fundamental awareness of religion. The existence
of the religious instinct is indeed the prime factor in all primitive
religion. At the same time it seems as though we were here faced
with an embryonic cultural life destined to thrust itself outward
in new directions by means of different outspringing branches of
culture, all nourished with its own sap. In other words, if religious
experience is identified with this common trunk, is it not fated,
in the dynamic course on which it is launched by collective and
individual history, to be later transformed into branches of profane
culture ? Is religious experience then in fact primitive, not only in
the sense of its being that primary and lasting phenomenon of
which philosophers speak, but also in the sense of its being a pre-
mature growth and thus something of a provisory character only ?
In that case it would, in the nature of things, be bound to disappear, and there would be no reason for surprise if it were not
found in men of our generation.

An analysis, based on « phenomenology, » of religious experience
cannot decide these questions and authors who draw from the
history of religion the conclusion that religious experience is constant among men and co-extensive with humanity commit the basic
error of misunderstanding the essentially *historical* character of humanity. A religious experience is a special landmark in the field
of human perception. It is not a platonic idea. It can be transient,
like certain kinds of mental awareness, and we know also that it
is a closed book to a considerable number of our contemporaries
who have never been preoccupied by the question of religion. And,
in so far as men of our time are affected by religious feeling, does
the effort to bridge the gulf between human nature and the Invisible, the Divine Source of all being, inspire the same idea of
something « tremendum et fascinosum, » the same sentiments of
mixed attraction and revulsion which it used to evoke ? Does the
sense of the Numinous still depend on the symbolic presence of
unseen, transcendent things which, while being themselves absent,
are nevertheless rendered present to the imagination by the power
of the symbols ?

Without wishing to prejudge the result of positive study, we
must admit that theological considerations incline us to postulate
the potential presence of religious experience in all men. Indeed,
experience is needed to effect that fissure whereby alone the Word
of God can enter into a human subject. One can in fact see no
way in which God's Word would be accessible to man unless it
made itself heard in the realm of the possible, that realm in which
we are faced by the paradoxical reality of Something that is both

infinitely near and infinitely far away. Nothing short of the direct grasp of an ultimate value, that of salvation, would seem to reveal a way whereby God can become accessible and approachable through history. In other words, for the theologian, religious experience forms part of the *praeambula fidei* which are necessary if the act of faith is to be really a human act and not merely the parrot-like recital of a formula in radical discord with the general tenor of life.

We do not then identify religious experience with Christian experience. For us, *religious experience* is constituted by *that irresistible religious urge which places man in face of that mystery of the world-complex in which he is merged*, which challenges him and leads him to look into the question of the reason of his existence. The object aimed at in religious experience is salvation, the attainment of the Divine ; man is drawn towards religion by the paradoxical experience, both of the strangeness of this world and of the hidden closeness of its Great Original which is his. Under what form, and by what means does the religious experience make itself felt amongst our contemporaries ? Nothing short of a psychological investigation could teach us this. We do not claim to have achieved that end, but we offer some preliminary observations which may be of use.

II. PRESENT-DAY FORMS OF RELIGIOUS EXPERIENCE

1. *The Symbolic Presence of the Divine in Nature.*

Nature was for pagan religions the predestined place where the Divine made itself present through symbols. The sense of the sacred was closely connected with the world of nature. Thus the whole universe was seen instinctively as a single cosmic reality indwelt by the sacred. This however was particularly concentrated in those elements which symbolize the mystery of origins and the world behind the veil : springs of water, mountains, storms. Human acts moreover are not entirely neutral any more than are the forces of nature. They are directly connected with the Divine reality. Again, everything is seen as theophanic and separate from the profane world because all is connected with the Divine. The sacred is thus directly present in the stone, in the tree, in theophanic rites. There is interpenetration, if not fusion, between the cosmic and the sacred.

All stones are not, of course, theophanic. Distinctions are made between some stones and others which, either because of their connexion with ritual, or of their unusual shape, are considered to be sacred. But, even so, these are but points in which the sacred reality diffused through the whole of nature is as it were concentrated. The dichotomy of the sacred and the profane, essential to the religious relationship as such, is not effaced, and all objects in nature are incorporated in the Divine. Were it otherwise, there would be no grounds for speaking of certain things as sacred, or of their symbolic connexion with the supernatural. But if there be rupture between the two zones, this is not because of their essential heterogeneity, but rather in virtue of a choice which localizes the sacred reality diffused throughout nature in certain particularly symbolic objects : « Everything which is unusual, singular, novel, perfect or monstrous becomes a receptacle for magico-religious powers, and, according to circumstances, an object for veneration or fear, in accordance with the twofold reaction constantly evoked by what is sacred. » [1]

Modern culture has accentuated the autonomy of the individual person, and has rescued it from immersion in the cosmos. The sacred has also been freed from the vital need to inhere in the world of nature. Nature has become at most the symbolic reflex of another zone which outstrips it completely, the zone of the sacred, now promoted to transcendental dimensions. Thus nature is emptied alike of what is human and of what is sacred, and human religion easily becomes estranged from human nature. When the conception of what is sacred was still submerged in the depth of the bio-cosmic world, man had direct access thereto. All his activities were impregnated with this sacred reality diffused throughout the cosmos : agriculture, hunting, sex-life, illness and death. A person who has been loosed from these cosmic preconceptions is faced with the difficult tasks of raising himself to a transcendental religious life. In this vertical relationship, nature can still play its part as a symbolic connecting link. But does it in fact fulfil this function effectively for present-day civilization ?

An investigation which we have carried out with the help of a group of psychologists, in different *milieux*, has furnished us with some illuminating facts in regard to people thus culturally conditioned, and to their type of religious experience.

---

1. MIRCEA ELIADE, *Traité d'histoire des religions*, Paris, Payot, 1949, p. 25.

G. STICKLER [1] interviewed 60 unskilled Italian working women in three factories at Genoa and Milan, of an average age of 21, of whom 32 per cent practise their religion regularly, 40 per cent sometimes, 28 per cent never. Here are the terms employed by the women interviewed (with a number indicating how often):

AID (22), CREATOR (10), PROVIDENCE (9), FRIEND (7), COMFORT (7), PROTECTION (6), CONSOLATION (5), MAJESTY (3), GOODNESS (3), COURAGE (3), LOVE (3), FATHER (3), GUIDE (2), REMORSE (1).

Several of the above words, as used by the women in question, were identical in meaning,[2] so that *in the context* we have here been able to draw up, out of a total of 84 spontaneous evocations, the following table of frequencies:

God — *aid, providence, protection, father* — 40 times.
God — *comfort, consolation, courage* — 13 times.
God — *creator, majesty, power (in nature)* — 13 times.

There existed then, among these women, a certain sensibility towards nature, regarded as an expression of « the power of their Creator » (this is the term they used spontaneously) and sometimes as a sign of His goodness towards men. At least this is the attitude expressed by thirteen among them.

« To see the mountain scenery, the sea and the sunset.... and to think about God, that is all one thing. » (19 years old).
« When I am in the mountains, I feel God as Creator always, when I see certain very beautiful sights.... but I don't « think, » it comes as an « inspiration to my heart. » (18 years old).
« When I go to church, when I take part in worship, I easily feel filled with devotion. I feel God's Presence more strongly then, as I do in the silence of nature. It is above all a feeling of respect towards God which then takes hold of me. » (22 years old).
The following experience, though it pays tribute to the Lord's goodness, regards it as a distant goodness which does not involve a personal

---

1. *Contribution à l'étude objective de l'attitude envers Dieu* (Mémoire de Licence en Psychologie-inédit-Louvain, 1963, pp. 16-24 et 127-128). The only question introducing these interviews was as follows : « I wish that you would recall some fact or event in your life (either a sad or a happy event) when you really felt that God existed, that was intervening in some way in your life and that He therefore meant at that moment or from then onwards, something very real to you. »
2. Thus : the *friendship* of God is sometimes felt rather as *consolation* in times of moral trial.

relationship : « If I contemplate nature, I sometimes think that it is God who has created these things. Then I feel that He is infinitely better than I am, but still very far away from me. » (21 years old).

This sensitiveness to nature may arouse a feeling of fear and of justified culpability in the face of Divine power : « I have always been very alive to the beauty of nature which makes me think of God, but what affects me most is a tempest, a storm.... there one truly feels the power of God.... I still sometimes think that it is an expression of His anger with men. » (17 years old).

We have quoted the above interviews because they show a religious sensibility very similar to that with which phenomenology and the history of religions have made us familiar. It is an affective relationship which contacts directly in nature those elements of beauty, of serenity, of joy and of power which reflect the nature of God present in the cosmos. In God are concentrated all those qualities felt by man in whom nature finds an echo. This God is the source of this outflow of Divine qualities which nature makes visible. To some extent this view of God is a pre-Christian one. We shall come back later to the divergencies that have been noted between the Christian attitude to the mysterious God of history and the God whose subjects acclaim Him as the Super-natural Indweller of the natural world.

2. Withdrawal
from the « Primary » Divine Presence.

A systematic investigation with the aid of a table indicating the attitudes of various groups towards religion [1] reveals, in regard to this type of experience, a definite superiority on the part of these working women over the other groups (students, boys and girls, of secondary schools, approximately American high-school) particularly over the university students. Those items which express astonishment and fear in the face of a power so infinitely superior to mankind are more frequent amongst the women workers. This attitude has no connexion with age and is conditioned simply by the level and type of intellectual formation. University members in particular take up such a distant attitude towards nature as to neutralize completely its significance on the plane of religious symbolism. « It is only through subsequent reflexion that I associate God with nature. » « The position is that I generally feel admira-

---

1. G. Stickler, o.c., pp. 127-128.

tion for scenery without overmuch thought of God. » Or it may even be that nature, objectified, judged in the light of science and measured in accordance with an ideal of ethical justice, appears to provide evidence against the existence of a God who is Just and Good.

Thus, intellectual formation doubly dissociates man from nature and removes from the latter its symbolic power to evoke the God to whom we pray. First it emphasizes the independence of the different grades of existence. Nature becomes a *spectacle* for men, and his contemplation of natural phenomena is no longer imbued with that primitive feeling of awe which associated nature instinctively with a mysterious Beyond.

Nature has become just nature, and no more than that, and is only retrospectively connected with God by men who none the less admit that He is its Creator. Secondly, man confirmed in his autonomy sometimes goes further than nature in the *demands* he makes of human society and of God : namely the demands of justice and goodness. This ends in revolt more often than in the past. R.H. THOULESS [1] has described the relationship of religious experience with nature : « The idea that God expresses Himself in the beauty of nature implies an optimistic attitude towards the external world. For the extrovert, healthy in mind and body, and not very much concerned with ultimate moral problems, this attitude is natural. He is aware of no contradiction when he sees nature as the Face of God. » We emphasize the instinctive sense of unity between primitive man and nature, and we should say that the reflective character of modern man, especially the intellectual type, is not necessarily a loss : it is the acquisition of autonomy in regard to nature, and the affirmation of the fact that nature is dominated by laws.

Let us conclude our enquiry into this first factor of experience. Among certain workers nature still evokes spontaneously the vision of God. Among students from technical schools as well as universities, this religious sentiment is far less present. This fact suggests to us a possible hypothesis : contrary to what is so often repeated, it is not industrial life as such which quenches or transforms that type of religious experience ; it is the instruction given to those who receive a technical education which so profoundly modifies man's relationship to nature. It is this that confirms the human subject in his autonomy in regard to nature, and dissociates the latter from its divine source.

---

1. *An Introduction to the Psychology of Religion*, Cambridge, 1956, p. 35.

3. *The Emergence*
of « Secondary » Religious Points of View.

This evolution is not necessarily an evil. We must judge this
element of experience in the light of all the component parts of the
experience, thereafter taking into account, in its totality, the resulting
attitude towards God.

Besides this we should enquire whether the human subjects most
affected by a rational mode of thinking are not capable of attaching
a retrospective symbolic value to a nature which has re-acquired
its own autonomy. In this way they may be inventing a new concept of the sacred, which will restore to nature its symbolical religious status in a more biblical context, freed from its bio-cosmo-
sacral and pre-Christian complexities. An investigation of the views
of older persons, representing various trends of Christian thought,
would here be particularly welcome.

If, in the eyes of so many of our educated contemporaries, God
is no longer present in nature, neither is He frequently or instinctively present in their experiences of joy and happiness, and rarely,
at least according to the replies resulting from our enquiry, in
affairs of the heart. Even if He be known under the name of the
God of Love, these experiences of happiness and love have even
less of that primary religious quality than have their relations with
nature, and this applies to the majority of members of all circles.
God is not « primarily » very present to them either in their joys
or their sorrows. [1]

The results of our enquiries are not, however, univocal on this point.
Among the Italian women workers there are exceptional cases (about
5 per cent among them) who do spontaneously associate God with their
experiences of human love. « I think of God and feel Him near to me
in the affectionate caresses of my mother ; then I thank God to have
given me life.... I am a true believer ; very little is needed to make me
happy. » (20 years old). « God is present in my love for a young man.
He helps me in the difficulties which I have on his account with my
parents. In the very affection I have for him I feel an emotion, a certain
sense of elevation, which makes me think of God. » (20 years old).

This evidence is further strengthened and clarified by what we
were told one day by a young man of 31, with a university degree,
brought up as a Christian, who after years of complete unbelief
had, though in a somewhat vague manner, become a believer again.

---

1. G. STICKLER, *o.c.*, p. 15.

He was very much in love with a girl, and on the occasion of one of his first meetings with her, seated beside her at a station where he was seeing her off, he twice experienced brief moments of an intense lucidity : the indefinable feeling that life could not pass away, that it must last, that it formed part of an imperishable, a transcendent, reality. Was this experience by an intellectual, expressed in quasi-metaphysical language, not this same experience of God through love ? We have reason to believe, not as a result of systematic enquiry, but through personal avowals, that many young mothers go through this religious experience, at least the first time that they give birth to a child ; and that by this means they realize something of the mystery of life and love which is beyond their grasp, and are thus raised above their ordinary human condition.

4. « Primary » Experience and Attitude.

The following question was put to 180 boys and girls of Belgian grammar schools in order to obtain the expression of their views : « Do you ever think of God at times when no one has spoken of Him to you ? »[1]

The following table gives some of their answers, with percentages :

31 per cent : in moral difficulties.
15   »   »   : in material difficulties.
11   »   »   : in happy circumstances.
 7   »   »   : in moments of happiness or joy.
 7   »   »   : in the beauty of nature.
 4   »   »   : in success.

What are we to make of these replies ? Happy circumstances are nearly always evoked in the same words as painful circumstances and *after* them.

Thus : « I think of God at difficult moments or, on the other hand, when all goes well. » (Boy, 15 years old). « When I am in difficulties or when I am happy. » (Boy, 17 years old). « In painful moments and in moments of great joy. » (Girl, 16 years). « Above all, when I am unhappy ; sometimes also when I am very happy and want to give thanks. » (Girl, 17 years).

---

1. G. BARELLI, *Contribution à l'étude objective de l'attitude envers Dieu* (Thèse de Licence), Louvain, 1963, p. 9.

We may wonder whether this religious reaction corresponds to a primary experience or to a secondary reflexion due to a religious indoctrination. One gets the impression that the subjects in question instinctively think of God in times of need and that, in confessing this, they take fresh stock of themselves and go on to associate joy too with God. This association might well signify a sense of gratitude in someone who realizes that his first religious reaction was lacking in nobility and failed to correspond to the religious attitude towards life which had constantly been impressed upon him or her.

This spontaneous reaction is certainly sincere; but does it also in fact occur at the time of the experience recorded ? The sincerity of the verbal replies given by those questioned does not necessari'y mean that in fact their reaction at the time was as stated, i.e., that they thought of God at joyful moments. There is probably a *hiatus* between the first reaction of the mind and the good impulse, and yet again between the good impulse and the putting into effect of this Christian attitude.

We here make use of the term « attitude » because it expresses precisely *the secondary character of the religious reaction which follows upon a happy experience.* [1] We believe that this association « happiness-God » is rarely experienced. Once anyone has achieved such an association it can become a recognition of God's presence and a feeling of gratitude. But then this feeling will have a per-manence which will take from it its emotional and experiential character. We believe that, in cases where the attitude of a person is strongly imbued with integral religious culture, God will have become for His own sake a source of permanent contentment, and this contented feeling will be reinforced by every joyful experience.

It is however significant that, in the few texts which deal with the experience of human love, the religious reaction appears in its primary experiential character. Here the experience of joy is not preceded by that of need or trouble. We see here that love is seen as the grateful welcome of another's gift. It is always felt to be a grace. In love, one is the recipient of the benevolence of others. In other joys, on the contrary, the person feeling the joy is at first « concentred all on self. » Yet it remains true to say that it is above all the consciousness of his need that makes everyone turn instinc-tively to God. When in vital need or in sorrow, he feels himself

---

1. We deal more fully with this matter in our article : « De l'expérience à l'attitude religieuse » which will shortly appear in *Archiv für Religionspsychologie*, Volume VIII (should appear at the end of 1964).

delivered into the hands of a power immeasurably his superior and for whose help he appeals. His own helplessness makes him realize his dependence and his need to have recourse to an All-powerful and All-loving Being. We have already studied the significance of these religious experiences.

If we are to accept the popular view, material distress or moral misery (guilt or loneliness) are the prime factors in determining men to seek religion. In thus having recourse to God, man experiences the reality of God's protection. Often however, the apparent lack of response to his demands arouses in him a reaction of revolt and incredulity. This alone serves to indicate the questionable value of those instinctive religious urges which derive solely from an existential experience of misery.

Conclusions.

The demand for help which, in his necessities, man addresses to God has beyond doubt always been at once his most fundamental religious experience, and that to be viewed with most reserve. It is true that, when he makes an appeal, man can come into direct communication with God. But is it yet God to whom he is appealing ? Or rather, is it already God ?... If this request is in fact addressed to a God Who is recognized as such, it is strange that its non-fulfilment should be met with so much indignation ! It reminds us of Eckart's dictum that things man gratuitously takes for God are often idols.

The presence of God in the elements of nature and in the experience of happiness is recognized but little in those whose views we have been examining. This observation confirms the widely held theory that in our civilization nature is secularized. This does not mean that, in the case of a religious-minded person, nature could not become anew, as it were, the symbolic reflexion of the transcendent God. If God is really present everywhere to the truly religious, everything will have the power of calling Him to mind and of making Him perceptible to the senses. To speak here and now of religious experience, however, means something very different from speaking of it in connexion with civilizations which have not yet broken away from « sacralised » nature.

The question of religious experience has often been placed in a false light because those who dealt with it took as their model societies which had not yet reached this stage of maturity. The problem of religious experience cannot be solved unless account is taken of the profound change which has affected the link between man and nature. One would have to consider here the presence of symbolic structures in the organization of families, as also certain institutions and myths which have sprung up within our industrialised society.

Undoubtedly man is still trying to find the ultimate meaning of life, to find salvation, and therein lies the essential source of his religious feeling. Perhaps it may even be true that, for a majority, there has been no experiential preparation for their faith other than this thirst for salvation. This makes itself felt all the more strongly amongst our contemporaries in view of the fact that nature has for so many of them lost its close relationship with the Divine Invisible it was once thought to veil.

Will this preoccupation with the ultimate meaning of life be by itself enough to make modern man accessible to the historical word of Revelation which replaces myths by a ringing appeal from God ? Man seeks life, communion and peace with himself in a renewed innocence. He is likewise trying to find out the ultimate meaning of a world in which he is more and more engrossed — not the natural world which surrounds him, but the world now in process of formation, which he prays that God will cause to develop and bring to fruition. Those who have become aware of this new relationship towards the world will welcome any indication that its future could be in the direction of a journey towards God.

Is not this the attitude towards religion of modern man ? the desire, alike existential and based on history, alike rebellious and hopeful, to find God in the pursuit of all his vital activities ? This God is no longer regarded as a Sacred Something, sensibly and diffusedly present : the God sought today does not so much manifest His Presence as make Himself an object of desire.

Mysticism as a Basic Concept in Defining the Religious Self

by Walter Houston CLARK

Andover Newton Theological School, Newton Centre (U.S.A.) [1]

At the Root of Christianity.

For several centuries Protestants and freethinkers have been predicting the demise of the Catholic Church. The only thing that keeps it alive — so the argument runs — is its marvelous organization, together with a shrewd and Machiavellian sense for policy and political manipulation. Yet the Church obstinately refuses to cooperate with such prophecies, and the revival of ecumenism initiated by Pope John has not only dismayed some of the Church's more inveterate critics, but has turned former enemies into friends. Protestant theological seminaries in the United States have held joint faculty meeting with Catholic Schools, while in Boston, a province which that stalwart Puritan, Cotton Mather, used to con-

---

1. Walter Houston CLARK was born in 1902 in Westfield, N.J., U.S.A. He majored in Chemistry at Williams College, where he received his B.A. At Harvard University he received his A.M. (Literature), Ed. M. (Psychology), and Ph.D. (Psychology and History and Philosophy of Education). For nearly 20 years he taught English and Bible at Lenox School (Massachusetts) for Boys. In 1945 he went to Bowdoin College as Instructor in Psychology, then in 1947 to Middlebury College as Associate Professor of Psychology and Education. From 1951 to 1962 he was Dean and Professor of Psychology at the Hartford School of Religious Education at Hartford Seminary Foundation, and in 1962 accepted his present post as Professor of Psychology of Religion at Andover Newton Theological School, in Newton, Massachusetts. He has published a historical and psychological study of the Moral Re-Armament movement: *The Oxford Group* (N.Y.: Bookman Associates, 1951); and *The Psychology of Religion* (N.Y.: Macmillan, 1958) was reviewed in *Lumen Vitae*, 1961, 2, p. 326. He was a Founder of the Society for the Scientific Study of Religion, is a Past President of the American Association of Schools of Religious Education, and is now Chairman of the Committee on Research of the Religious Education Association of the U.S.A. and Canada. — Address: 750 Commonwealth Avenue, Newton Center 59, Mass., U.S.A. (Editor's note).

sider his own,[1] Cardinal Cushing is almost as beloved by Protestants as he is by his own flock. After the death of the late Pope,
a memorial service held for the latter in Boston's Protestant Episcopal
Cathedral was crowded to the very stairways, and many were unable
to get in at all. Things have changed over the last three hundred
years. Such do not seem to be the signs of an institution that is
moribund, much less dead.

Quite naturally Catholics and non-Catholics find different explanations for such a phenomenon. Also scholars from different
disciplines, each with his own viewpoint, will approach the problem
from different angles. Doubtless each will add a grain of truth at
the same time that, partly blinded by the necessary restrictions of
his own point of view, he will oversimplify reality in order to make
some sense out of it. Therefore it is out of a profound sense of his
limitations that the present writer, as a Protestant and a psychologist
of religion, advances the suggestion that it is more through its
persistent nourishing of the mystical life, through the Mass and
other institutions, that the Church has been able to maintain over
the centuries that flame of vitality which, though at times it may
have flickered, nevertheless never has gone out. This observation
constitutes just one reason, among others, why it is important to
examine the mystical consciousness in the attempt to describe the
larger universe of the religious.

Mysticism and Psychology.

Certainly mysticism cannot be ignored either by those responsible
for the well-being of religious institutions, whether Catholic or non-
Catholic, or by those concerned with the religious nurture of the
young. The psychologist of religion must consider it as he seeks to
define and describe his area of study. If he is to pretend that his
discipline is in any sense a science, he remembers that the first
step in the systematizing of any field is to order one's observations
and so describe them that they can be studied scientifically. One
can never hope to be as exact in describing the field of religion
as in describing the world of nature because religion is so much
less tangible. Consequently, there is much dispute among even
experts in the field as to what religion really is. This is an unhappy
state of affairs for a would-be-science. But since there is little that
can be done about it, the next best thing is for each student to

---

1. (1663-1728) : a clerical leader in Massachusetts Bay Colony at a time when
Quakers were exiled while interest even in the Church of England was considered the equivalent of treason.

define what he takes to be religion so that others may know to what phenomena his conclusions may pertain. It is with this ultimate aim in mind, that I concern myself with mysticism. It seems to me to be the essential principle underlying the religious consciousness.

American psychologists have spent a kind of fifty-year sojourn in Egypt in bondage to the behaviorists. This has paid exceedingly meager dividends from the point of view of learning anything very important about personality. Fortunately, many of the behaviorists themselves have become seduced by Freudianism sufficiently to enrich their superficial obsession with mere human behavior through the insights of Freudian subjectivism. This has even led, by devious paths, to some tentative return to the concept of the self, first popularized in the psychology of William James. This development is a happy omen for psychologists of religion. However, they will be in no position to exploit this development without descriptions of the religious self to act as guidelines. There are a few American psychologists who have approached the problem. For example, G.W. ALLPORT in his perceptive book *Becoming* [1] speaks of what he calls *the proprium*, the luminous core of the personality that must be activated for any kind of single-minded, passionate pursuit such as religion. This idea has been well used by Orlo STRUNK, Jr. in his little volume *Religion : A Psychological Interpretation*, [2] which constitutes the best discussion of the religious self that we appear to have. But it is still desirable to describe much more exactly the religious self as opposed to other aspects of the self, so far as this is possible. Here it is important to recognize that religion has many forms, and almost any of these forms might be seized on by somebody and made the essential principle of the religious life and so the core concept of the religious self. Each approach will doubtless have something to commend it, and it must be understood that no one can pretend to be definitive in this controversial field. But in this article I propose to argue the case for mystical experience, not as an all-inclusive category that will cover all aspects of the religious self, but as its core concept.

Religious Experience.

Most forms of what passes for religious behaviour are not clearly to be distinguished from secular experience. William James included

---

1. New Haven; Conn.: Yale University Press, 1955.
2. New York: Abingdon Press, 1962.

in religion any human activity that was directed toward a « religious
object. » This is one way of defining religion. I propose to differ
in that I am saying that *there must be something unique in the
quality of the experience itself that makes it religious*. This quality
is the mystical. One may give all his time and energy to the business affairs of a church, but unless this service is not in some way
enlightened by *a sense of the Beyond*, a mystical encounter with
God, then it is hard to see how it is psychologically different from
the handling of a secular business. A theologian with an extreme
acuteness of intellect may give his life to the intellectual consideration of the attributes of God, but unless he himself has had
some immediate experience of God, it is hard to see how his intellectual pursuit is psychologically different from that of a secular
philosopher who spends his time, say, in a consideration of the
attributes of the State. It is the fact that most theologians are
redeemed through some firsthand knowledge of God himself that
their works become religious and reflect true Wisdom rather than
the mere playing with ideas. Otherwise, they can be thought of as
religious only in a very secondary or even tertiary sense, and not
in the essential sense in which I am now speaking. [1]

But in mysticism we have an experience that is unique and is
consistently reported as qualitatively different from all other human
experiences. It is found wherever religion is found, sometimes in
very primitive form, but nevertheless still different and unique.
It has even been reported by atheists and agnostics, for example
by Arthur KOESTLER. He was a dedicated Communist and therefore an atheist when he underwent not indeed a Christian mystical
experience but one that involved genuine mysticism. He was in
one of Franco's prisons expecting execution when he sustained the
remarkable experience he recounts in the chapter « The hours by
the window » in his autobiographical *The Invisible Writing*. [2] The
episode initiated his period of disenchantment with Communism,
and he left the movement for good about two years later. Such
experiences of cosmic unity are nearly always identified as in some
way religious whether or not the subject uses the terminology of
any particular faith to describe what he has undergone. They are
usually felt in some way to be a direct apprehension of Truth,
though this may not be identified verbally as God.

---

1. For a discussion of this point see W.H. CLARK, *Psychology of Religion*.
N.Y. : Macmillan, 1958, Chapter 1, or Orlo STRUNK, Jr., *op. cit.*
2. Boston : Beacon Press, 1955.

The Core of Mysticism.

Psychologists will find one of the most recent and valuable titles containing a careful comparative and phenomenological description of mysticism to be *Mysticism and Philosophy* [1] by the Princeton University philosopher W.T. STACE. He has gathered his data carefully from a wide variety of cultures and faith traditions in all centuries. While not all scholars would necessarily agree with him at every point, he has listed common characteristics in what he calls « the universal core » of mysticism. He divides mystical experience into two types, « extrovertive mysticism, » the lesser of the two, in which unity is sensed, but outward reality nevertheless maintains the separateness of objects ; and « introvertive mysticism, » in which all differentiation dissolves into one unity. In describing introvertive mysticism, Stace lists : 1) The unitary consciousness ; 2) Timelessness and spacelessness; 3) Sense of objectivity or reality; 4) Blessedness, peace ; 5) Feeling of the holy, sacred, or divine ; 6) Sense of paradoxicality ; 7) Alleged by mystics to be ineffable. These characteristics, the universal core of mystical experience, which he says is natural and non-creedal, he distinguishes from the various interpretations of mysticism, which will differ from faith to faith. God, for example, tends to be much more sharply distinguished in the Judeo-Christian and Mohammedan faiths than He is in Buddhism. This does not mean, however, that the latter is atheistic — at least in the usual sense — as many Western writers have claimed.

Parenthetically we may ask whether the characteristics listed by Stace are not very similar to those described by A.H. MASLOW or Marghanita LASKI, [2] both of whom mention mystical experience but neither of whom sees mysticism as more than a part of a much larger whole, a special kind of « peak experience » or « ecstasy. » There is no doubt that there is a close kinship between mystical experience and deeply creative experiences of a different kind, such as the ecstasies of a poet or an artist, or even certain kinds of mathematical or scientific illumination. LASKI discusses sexual love as a source of ecstasy. However, it would seem that secular forms of ecstasy may often be psychologically identical with mysticism. At the very least, the mystic is the poet or the artist of the religious life, so that what distinguishes a profound experience with

1. Philadelphia : Lippincott, 1960, especially Chapter 2.
2. MASLOW, *Toward a Psychology of Being. Princeton*, N.J. : Van Nostrand, 1962. — LASKI, *Ecstasy: A Study of Some Secular and Religious Experiences.* Bloomington, Ind. : University of Indiana Press, 1961.

the mark of religion may be its *interpretation*, which is to say its *theology*. Thus, in the last analysis, it would be the experiencer who would determine what religion is. This, of course is one way to approach religion, but it is not the one I am proposing. There is not space for me to discuss this complex problem further. I will return to Stace's characteristics.

I have verified these seven characteristics among contemporary mystics who have been willing to supply me with information about their religious experiences, notably by a counselee whose experience illustrates all of the seven features. Her first mystical experience occurred and was described before Stace's book appeared and so was not influenced by it. The event led to a sharp change in her values and eventually to her resigning a professorship in order to prepare herself for a religious vocation. One can also find some of these features suggested in a case where the mysticism developed under non-directive therapy described by Carl ROGERS as « The case of Mrs. Oak. » [1] Another case in an incorrigible criminal will be found briefly described in the first chapter of STANDAL and CORSINI's *Critical Incidents in Psychotherapy.* [2] These cases support the contention of Stace that mystical experience is unique and wholly different from any ordinary human experience. In this way mysticism seems to fit our requirement that whatever our basic concept of the religious self is, it should be well differentiated from non-religious approaches to the self.

These three cases also illustrate another frequent concomitant of mystical experience inasmuch as all three exhibited radical and profound changes in values and behavior. Churches teach that this is the normal and to-be-expected accompaniment of the making of any faith commitment — or even when this is made for us, as in Baptism. However, social scientists have had a great deal of difficulty detecting any close correspondence between church affiliation and superior ethical behavior — at least apart from some kind of shattering confrontation with the Divine that also brings one face-to-face with oneself and involves profound commitment. [3] This kind of confrontation or solution of one's problem of identification is often brought about through mystical experience. I question whether any profound experience identified as religious is wholly without some mystical feature, whether acknowledged by the individual or not.

---

1. ROGERS, C.R. and DYMOND, R.F., *Psychotherapy and Personality Change.* Chicago: U. of Chicago Press, 1954.
2. Englewood Cliffs, N.J.: Prentice Hall, 1959.
3. See, for example, THORNDIKE, E.L., *Your City*, N.Y.: Harcourt, Brace, 1939, or WARNER, W. Lloyd, *Democracy in Jonesville*, N.Y.: Harpers, 1949.

Mysticism and Scientific Psychology.

In spite of this tremendous power to change personality, most psychologists, at least in America, have been almost wholly without curiosity about the place of mysticism in personality. One can scan the index of textbook after textbook, both in the general field of psychology and that of personality without finding a single reference to mystical experience. Freud and depth psychology will usually be given very generous treatment, but any remarks about mysticism, if made at all, are apt to be disparaging. Yet Aldous HUXLEY has called mysticism the only method yet discovered for « the radical and permanent transformation of personality. » [1]

Doubtless much of this neglect is due to the desire of psychologists to be considered scientists, and it must be admitted that mystical experience makes a very elusive subject for the pursuit of scientific studies. Scientists have a predilection for data either that they already pretty well understand, or that gives clear indications of yielding its secrets to scientific methodology, or that fits into scientific theory. Insecure as to their status as scientists, psychologists particularly are apt to eschew any study that does not promise clear-cut results. It is largely for this reason that they have wasted so much time and money in their obsessive interest in the superficial aspects of personality. Aside from suggestive speculations of Jungian oriented psychologists, there are few theories to explain these sometimes amazing mystical transformations.

Perhaps the most satisfying that I have come across are the theories developed by Dr. Henry ELKIN, a psychotherapist of New York City. [2] He sees the self developing from the primordial, undifferentiated state of unified bliss that constitutes the world as it must appear to the newly born child, at least until an unkind reality rudely interrupts the bliss. This original state of mind becomes the prototype of mystical experience and in some sense is reawakened in the mystical ecstasy of the adult. From this state there develops, perhaps aided by the terrifying experience of the infant's finding himself helpless and dependent, first a generalized sense of the world that lies beyond himself, to him the *wholly other*, and then gradually, as features of this *other* detach themselves from the amorphous mass of his perceptions, he begins to sense the *differentiated other*. This then becomes his phenomenological world of objects and people. Along with this is developed his attitudes and emotions.

---

1. *Grey Eminence*, N.Y.: Meridian Books, p. 306.
2. « On the origin of the self », *Psychoanalysis and the Psychoanalytic Review*, 45, (4) (Winter) 1958-1959, pp. 57-76.

Depending on whether he has been treated with love by those who care for him or merely manipulated as if he were an object to be used, he learns to react toward others in a similar way. The world may be a home in which he finds his place through fellowship and love, or, on the other hand, a place where other people are to be exploited.

Mystical experience in the adult according to Elkin, then, is in some sense a re-awakening of the primordial state. Partly it is a sort of regression in which the individual may risk psychosis through fixation at this infantile level, and also perhaps through releasing dangerous primordial urges or complexes sleeping in the unconscious. But because the individual takes with him in his strange voyage back to infancy the whole apparatus of the painfully acquired development which has made him an adult, the mystical experience of unity differs in important ways from the original experience of the infant. Often the mystics spontaneously have referred to their experience as a « re-birth. » This suggests that in some way the individual has an opportunity to re-experience his development. Brought up to exploit others so that any kind of trust or love relationship is practically impossible, the mystic may so cogently feel his unity with that of all mankind that suddenly he finds within himself that which seems to him *a miraculous new power to relate to others.* No longer is his cooperation with society based on a shrewd sense of give and take with the hope of getting the best of the bargain himself. For the first time in his life he may so cogently have realized his identity with all mankind that compassion and love are possible for him, and he becomes capable of identifying with a fellowship or community instead of being only the reluctant member of a collectivity. For such a one the Church becomes the Blessed Community instead of merely the means of securing celestial favors. Something like this seems to have occurred within the psyche of the rebellious and wretched criminal already alluded to in the reference to Standal and Corsini. It is in this way that at least the dim outlines of the psychical processes appear that can explain the sudden and radical transformations of personality that often follow on a profound mystical experience.

An Objection.

But it may be objected that the mystical consciousness is too unusual an occurrence to be useful as the core concept of the religious self. Is this not too much of a Medieval phenomenon to serve a purpose suited to modern religious life ? In answer we can make two replies.

First, if we discover only a few cases in which mystical experiences mediate these transforming changes in human nature, we can suspect the possibility that this can take place in all. The changes that took place in Socrates, St. Teresa of Avila, Blaise Pascal, or even in Carl Rogers' Mrs. Oak took place at a deep level of personality. Elkin's theories suggest that in such cases the memory traces of early infancy are involved. If this is so, when the mystic speaks of « re-birth, » or Jesus tells Nicodemus that he must return to his mother's womb, they may not be speaking quite so symbolically as we usually assume. And if mysticism depends in any important way on the infant's experience following birth, it may very well be a universal potentiality within the reach of all.

Second, we may see an analogy to the esthetic which will strengthen the case for the universality of this potentiality. No matter how scarce true artists in the creative sense are, we know that it would be a very twisted and inhuman personality in whom some preference for the beautiful were wholly absent, even though it might be nothing more than a preference for green grass over the asphalt pavements of a dirty inner city. In much the same way, if we only look for it, and though some people have to be taken off their guard to disclose it, we can sense some primitive concern for the spiritual and mystical in almost everyone. The Communists seem to have had a signal lack of success in suppressing all religion in their country, and their shrill tirades on the evils of religion sound suspiciously like protesting too much. Then there is the fact that we all can sense a strange kind of power behind the personality of a true mystic, and also our natures « reverberate » in moving ways to the words of mystics, as with PLATO's Allegory of the Cave in *The Republic*, the poetry of *the Book of Job*, or CHRIST's words to Nicodemus.

A New Incentive for Research.

It would seem that we have additional confirmation of this speculation in the researches with LSD and other psychedelic substances, which seem to uncover hidden reaches of the psyche. With considerable consistency subjects of experiments report that the drugs do not seem so much to *produce* such experiences as to *uncover* or *release* them. People, on recovering from the effects of the drugs are not so apt, as with alcohol, to say, « I was not myself ! » as to declare, « I was never so completely myself ! » If this is the case, then it is of considerable significance that so often the drugs mediate either genuine mystical experience in many people, or something so very similar that the two cannot be distinguished.

In a doctoral study at Harvard (Divinity School) not yet published, Dr. Walter PAHNKE seems to have demonstrated pretty conclusively that the psychedelic psilocybin, administered under the proper conditions, will release experiences matching to a considerable degree the features listed by Stace in his description of the universal core of mysticism. [1] At the same time subjects report a strangely heightened and vitalized understanding of many religious terms and writings that had been largely meaningless to them before. If we grant the cogency of these points, we may wonder whether it is not the fact that in the West, as compared to the East, mysticism has been relatively ignored and depreciated so that its natural vitality has been repressed, or has tended to wither away for the lack of cultivation. This being true, perhaps even the Catholic Church may be neglecting its birthright. Such reflections help us to explain the poverty of mystical experience in what passes for religion in the world around us.

There are bound to be people who will raise the question whether an experience stimulated by a drug properly can be called religious. Here again we run into the problem of definition. Of course any person has the right to define a drug mediated experience as non-religious. Presumably the grounds would be that such an experience is « artificial, » and therefore not of supernatural origin. However, it may be argued that the attempt to mediate religious experience through the use of music, architecture, instruction, fasting, or ritual is just as artificial, if not more so, as the ingestion of the products of naturally growing plants created by God. Furthermore never do we see the drugs acting alone producing the alleged religious experience. Other variables include the preparation of the subject, the setting, the follow-up, and the inner personality structure of the subject himself. The drugs are simply an auxiliary which, used carefully within a religious structure, *may* assist in mediating an experience which, aside from the presence of the drug, cannot be

---

1. The title of the thesis by Dr. Walter N. PAHNKE is *Drugs and Mysticism: An Analysis of the Relationship Between Psychedelic Drugs and Mystical Consciousness.* It will be available at the Harvard University Library, Cambridge 38, Massachusetts, U.S.A., though restricted for five years. Before this time persons may write : Dr. Pahnke at 277 West 14 Place, Chicago Heights, Illinois, for permission to obtain a microfilm of the thesis.

Research in the field of psychotherapy and personality with the psychedelics is well reviewed in an article by S.M. UNGER, 'Mescaline, LSD, Psilocybin, and Personality Change' in *Psychiatry: Journal for the Study of Interpersonal Processes,* Vol. 26, No. 2, May 1963. A quarterly, *The Psychedelic Review* has recently begun publication, Box 223, Cambridge 38, Massachusetts, U.S.A. at $ 5.00 a year, $ 1.50 a single copy. The *Review* has a list of reprints of important articles in this field available through its office, at reasonable prices.

distinguished psychologically from mysticism. Studies have indicated that, when the experience is interpreted transcendentally or religiously, chances are improved for the rehabilitation of hopeless alcoholics and hardened criminals. [1] Even though observations like these mean that the psychologist can learn a little more of the religious life, in no sense does it ultimately become any less of a mystery. Though man may sow and till, winds may blow and the rains fall, nevertheless it is still God that gives the increase.

We have already spoken of the lack of curiosity among psychologists about mysticism. It is for this reason that we must depend on philosophers and theologians rather than on psychologists for most of the useful modern descriptions of the phenomena. Professor R.C. ZAEHNER, the Catholic scholar at Oxford in his comparative studies of religion has given mysticism considerable attention and has written a book on it. [2] The clearest and probably the best of these writers is W.T. STACE, already mentioned, while a more subjective writer, though notable in other ways, is the well known German theologian, Rudolf OTTO, whose work, *Das Heilige (The Idea of the Holy)* is a modern classic. Eduard SPRANGER, the German philosopher, in *Lebensformen (Types of Men)*, uses mysticism as the central concept of his description of the religious type. The value of such systematic and exact descriptions is that they will assist the psychologist in studying mysticism and will even aid him in devising scales by which to measure its extent and intensity.

Based on Spranger's typology we have the ALLPORT-VERNON-LINDZEY *Study of Values*, [3] which includes religion as one of its six dimensions. However, it departs somewhat from Spranger's concept of religion by slighting its mystical aspect.

PAHNKE, in his study of the effects of psilocybin already mentioned, devised rough scales to measure not only the quality but the intensity of mystical experience. The task was made easier for him largely through the carefulness of Stace's descriptions. There is room for much more precise measuring instruments, but Pahnke has shown, despite criticism that mystical experience, being ineffable, cannot be measured, that the task can be accomplished. Also the fact that Pahnke seems to have demonstrated that the psychedelic substances do in fact release mystical experience points to the possibility of producing mystical experience under near labo-

---

1. See UNGER, *op. cit.*, also T. LEARY and W.H. CLARK, « Religious Implications of Consciousness Expanding Drugs. » *Religious Education*, Vol. 58, No. 3 (May-June), 1963.
2. *Mysticism.* Oxford: Oxford University Press, 1957.
3. Published by Houghton Mifflin, Boston, Massachusetts.

ratory conditions and this promises to make the production of a
scale much easier. A scale, in its turn, should be a helpful instrument
to psychologists of religion in studying the nature of the mystical
consciousness and its consequences. To what extent does mysticism
change personality for the better ? On the other hand, is it a dangerous experience, as is sometimes claimed ? To what extent does
it involve elements from the unconscious and at what layers ? With
what other psychological phenomena is it associated ? These are
some of the questions that come to mind, the answers to which
a scale might facilitate.

Examples of questions that might be used in a scale with respect to
a religious experience are :
Did you find your perception of distinctions between objects weakened ?
*Did you experience a feeling of oneness or unity with God or the
Universe ?*
Did you feel the experience to have been sacred ?
Do you feel unable to describe your experience adequately to others ?
*When you try to explain your experience, do you feel inclined to use
contradictory expressions ?*
The subject could then be allowed several choices in his answers such
as « intensely, » « to some degree, » « very slightly, » « cannot tell, »
« definitely not. » With a number of questions and five or six gradations
allowed for reply to each question, a number of degrees of quantification
can be secured. Although the investigator should realize that a scale in
this field must be of necessity rough, it can still be of use for a more
precise and scientific study of religious phenomena.

Conclusion.

In the meantime the idea that mysticism may be used as a basic
concept in defining the religious remains a proposal ; it is simply
a way of organizing our ideas about the religious consciousness,
but it seems to have definite advantages : 1) It is the best differentiated state of mind available that can be defined psychologically
as a religious experience ; 2) It is not confined to any one religious
tradition but is a central concept in many, including Catholic
Christianity ; 3) It involves personality at a deep enough level so
that personality changes of a radical nature can be ascribed to it ;
and 4) There is good reason to believe that the potentiality for
mysticism is innate. For these reasons mysticism is important and
deserves to be studied much more widely by psychologists, psychotherapists, religious educators, and religious scholars in general.

Discernment of Children's Religious Experience

by Pierre RANWEZ, S.J.

International Centre for Studies in Religious Education, Brussels [1]

The aim of the Christian teacher is to create such conditions round the child that its freedom, sought by grace, can be used without too many hindrances. He wants to see the child, enlightened by adapted instruction and instructed in moral behaviour, turn to God in faith and fidelity.

Can the teacher control the results of his efforts ?

As regards *religious knowledge*, yes. Especially with children of school age, it is possible to control fairly precisely whether the matter taught has been assimilated. Every teacher of religion — like any teacher of secular subjects — will test whether he has been understood. To do this, he will break his discourse and ask questions, sometimes he will use dialogue, he will find out whether the lessons have been properly studied, and will examine still further by what are called intellectual questions.

This first stage will soon be passed. *Very revealing tests* can be applied with method, without reaching controls which are strictly scientific. Madame FARGUES, with a group of teachers and psychologists, has drawn up a set of questions which can help the teacher to gauge the pupil's progress and the value of the lessons. [2] The questions assure three advantages : control of the essential points

---

1. At a time when a new edition of a book by P. RANWEZ that has become classic for religious training at home is being published — *Ensemble vers le Seigneur*, Brussels, Lumen Vitae Press (in English, *Together toward God*, Newman Press, 1959) — we are glad to publish this article by the author in a field in which fantasy can be as harmful as the impossible quantification of a pseudo-science. — Address : 184, rue Washington, Brussels 5, BELGIUM (Editor's note).

2. « *Tests* » *collectifs de catéchisme*. Vol. I, Sèvres, Soc. d'éditions, 1954 : vol. II, Paris, Ed. du Cerf, 1951.

of the message ; thanks to re-groupings and indirect questions the child must express his own thought and not merely repeat phrases by heart ; the teacher is urged to improve his instruction by perceiving the weaknesses shown by the answers.

A third category of controls has been planned : *scientific controls* bearing on special points, such as, degrees of knowledge of one subject at different school grades ; interpretations of religious pictures or stories diversified according to factors which can be checked, etc. Several numbers and special issues of LUMEN VITAE on religious psychology contain most useful studies on different ways of investigation and their application. [1] These shou'd be referred to before starting a research into religious knowledge and mentalities. [2]

The title of this article suggests yet another question. Can we discern the awakening of faith and the progress of grace in a child ? This is the problem we approach here.

Anxious to teach a small child to pray, or uncertain when a child may approach the holy Table or the sacrament of Penance for the first time, parents wish to know whether dialogue has begun between their little one and God. They want to reach *a judgment of spiritual maturity*. Is it impossible ? Are they not seeking to capture what cannot be captured ?

To throw light on this difficult question, we will go forward in two stages. In the first, we will try to state what adult experience can be of the progress of grace within him, or which is the same thing, by what signs can he perceive God's action in his soul. From the conclusions obtained, we will ask, in our second section, whether these signs exteriorly visible can manifest interior experience, especially in the child.

I. IS IT POSSIBLE TO EXPERIENCE
THE PROGRESS OF GRACE IN ONESELF ?

First of all, we must ask whether the progress of grace can, in some way, come under experience. Can the subject be conscious of the spiritual event in which he profits, and is in part, active ?

---

1. Specially vol. XII (1957) 2; Vol. XVI (1961) 2 (reprinted as separate volumes : *Research in Religious Psychology* and *Child and Adult Before God*).

2. Inquiries among children of equal aptitude taught by different methods would make interesting studies; in this way, it could be discerned which were the best methods concerning some specific point.

Having studied several theologians [1] and spiritual writers, we are drawn towards stating the following positions :

1) By the gift of a mystical grace God can gratify a soul with the intuition of the supernatural, and even of God. On this last point, Father MARÉCHAL in particular could be read.

2) Nothing prevents us from thinking that, in a non-mystic Christian life, transitory favours bring brief illumination.

3) In a non-mystic Christian life,

a) the supernatural origin of an act does not usually appear
— if one aspect exclusively of this act is examined (for example, a lively feeling of consolation);
— if the act is examined in its total structure, but isolating it from the mass of previous and of consequent acts (here, however, we must qualify our negation);

b) the supernatural origin of an act, or a mass of acts, can appear if taken in their total structure, and in the context of the acts preceding and ensuing. In this case, the supernatural origin appears not uniquely at the end of discursive reasoning, but both from a mass of signs whose value can be assessed as a whole, and from counter proofs and confirmations supplied by reflection.

4) The traits marking the action of God would be chiefly the following :

a) the newness of a spiritual state, appearing both dependent on the will and « bestowed, » with positive characteristics differing from the negative ones of the previous state ;

b) an attraction towards God developing in a context of recollection and interior unification ;

c) a corresponding turning away from what is contrary to God (detachment from self and from the world), with a readiness to serve others ;

---

1. We mention especially : J. MARÉCHAL, S.J., *Etudes sur la psychologie des Mystiques* (2 vols., Bruges, Desclée De Brouwer, 1938²); J. MOUROUX, *The Christian Experience* (London and New York, Sheed and Ward, 1955); R. VANCOURT, *La phénoménologie de la foi* (Tournai, Desclée, 1953); F. GRÉGOIRE, *Questions sur l'expérience religieuse* (Louvain, Public. Universitaires, cours polycopié, 1957); Y. CONGAR, *La foi et la théologie* (Tournai, Desclée, 1962); M. NÉDONCELLE, *Prière humaine, prière divine* (Paris-Bruges, Desclée De Brouwer, 1962); K. RAHNER, S.J., « De l'expérience de la grâce », dans *Ecrits théologiques*, Tome III (Paris-Bruges, Desclée De Brouwer, 1963).

d) an atmosphere of joy and peace, deep and almost indefinable.[1]

In spite of this, these signs should be controlled by exterior signs which remain always supreme :

— orthodoxy and fulfilment of the commandments ;

— agreement with hierarchical authority and communion of charity with the ecclesial community and fellowmen.

From these premises we can consider an *act of conversion* as particularly significant, seen in the light of behaviour before and after. When speaking of conversion we are not thinking of a unique or quasi unique act in a life, but of the acts usually numerous in a Christian destiny, which begin a fresh stage in the religious journey.

In the concrete, we can chiefly consider the experience of conversion in the context of prayer. This is not separate from the rest of life, it animates and is carried along by it. The exercise of prayer usually leads the Christian to an absolutely original experience. *In fact, it achieves an act whose structure demands the existence of Him who is addressed.* This action is humanly absurd, since the one addressed is invisible, dumb and apparently powerless. But this absence, silence and powerlessness are only actual at one level of experience. At another level, the subject experiences a sovereign presence, response and power. Let us see how.

The usual experience of prayer can be described thus. When all the immediately perceptible elements should end in the interior evidence of the uselessness of prayer (which often happens) ; when the absence, silence and seeming powerlessness of God should plunge the subject into distaste and weariness (which again often happens, so that many turn away from prayer), deep experience contradicts what superficial experience seems to impose. The assiduous soul perceives that in the measure that prayer penetrates its life, it is filled with peace and a certain joy. We must explain carefully. Many Christians, while living virtuous lives, do not gain this experience because their prayer, rare, or very intellectual, or very sensitively « consoled, » does not permit them to capture this revealing contrast between the apparent absurdity of prayer and the coherence of Christian behaviour, between the dark aridity of prayer and a certain penetrating and invading peace, between desolation and a distant light.

---

1. Cf. Sum. theol. Iᵃ IIᵃᵉ. quest. CXII, a. 5, c. « A thing can be known conjecturally, by means of certain signs. In this way, we can know we possess grace, when we are conscious that our delight is in God, that we despise worldly things, that we have not to reproach ourselves of a serious sin. It is in this sense that we may understand the words of the *Apocalypse* : « To him who overcomes, I will give hidden manna, which no one knows but him who receives it. ». He who receives it knows this by the experience of a certain sweetness (consolation), which he who does not receive it does not experience.

The less ordinary experience is that the soul finds an interior newness even in prayer. A new aptitude awakens, an evidence appears, an
act of engagement and of abnegation takes place (an act seeming both
free and « bestowed »), joy penetrates the soul. This experience, which
places the soul in conformity with the Christian values, rarely brings
its immediate proof with it. But this developes in the weeks, months and
years to come. It can happen that the intervention supposed as divine,
is only a human re-action, a fleeting feeling. But if transformation in
life becomes lasting, if the interior renewal continues, this confirms
the authenticity of the initial impulse. It can be recognized also by
several signs, well known to spiritual writers :

— a certain suddenness; the invasion of unexpected light and strength; [1]

— the simultaneous consciousness of freedom and of a gift ; we mean
the consciousness of an act more deliberate than usual, although this
act appears exteriorly as bestowed ;

— a deep peace perhaps in spite of superficial agitation ; peace which
may be accompanied with a feeling of interior strength, in spite of
apparent difficulties ;

— all these signs are accompanied by the fitting in of the light and
strength received with the progress and other values guaranteed by the
Church.

Concerning spiritual experience, Saint BERNARD has written a
masterly page (translated in *L'expérience chrétienne*, p. 351, by
J. MOUROUX).

« I admit that I too have been visited by the Word — I speak as a madman
— several times even. And although he has entered my soul several times I
never felt his coming. I felt that he had come, I remember that he was there;
sometimes even I felt he was about to come, but his actual coming, or his
going, never. From whence he came into my soul, whether did he go on leaving,
nor yet how did he enter or leave — even now I admit I do not know, as
it is written : « Thou knowest not whence he is nor whither he goes. » Nor is
this surprising since it is of him that it is said « Thou shalt not know the path
of his steps... » You will ask how I knew that he was present, since his ways
are undiscernible. He is *alive* and *powerful*; as soon as he came within me, he
roused my sleeping soul; he stirred, touched and wounded my heart which was
weak and hard as stone. But when he has entered, the Word and Spouse has
never made his entrance known by any sign, neither by his voice, his countenance, or by his footfall. He did not reveal himself to me by any movement;
none of my senses perceived his secret coming; only in my heart I knew his
presence; by the flight of vices, the subduing of passions, I recognized the power

---

1. Cf. *Spiritual Exercises* of Saint IGNATIUS, 2nd. rule for a fuller discernment of spirits. « It is reserved to God alone to accord His consolation, without
any other cause accounting for it. For it is the special power of the creator
to penetrate within His creature, to direct it entirely towards the love of Himself, to draw it towards Him and to transform it... »

of his strength; by the examination and disavowal of my hidden sins, I wondered at the depth of his wisdom; by the slight progress of my life, I experienced his gentle bounty; by the renewal and conversion in my deepest soul — of the inner man — I caught a glimpse of the beauty of his face, and seeing all this as a whole, I trembled before this excess of greatness. »

II. IS IT POSSIBLE
TO DISCERN THE WORKINGS OF GRACE IN A CHILD ?

Regarding what has been said, the *adult*'s testimony of his interior experience will be enlightening. Exterior observation could only provide subsidiary revelation with important zones of imprecision and uncertainty.

Before seeking by what means it would be possible to discern and evaluate the movement of a child's religious life, let us ask whether there really is such a life, and therefore personal religious experience.

1. *Has a Child any Religious Life and Personal Experience ?*

With the tiny child, still incapable of the least free act, the life of grace exists in the sense that God is present, living and ready within him. The depth of his being is sanctified (the very substance of his soul), thanks to the intervention of God his Saviour, and his faculties are equipped for supernatural action. But the moment has not yet come for this gift of God to be used by deliberate choice. The child, impregnated with grace, can only perform supernatural acts when he is able to achieve a human act as such, that is, a conscious and deliberate act. It is necessary then for freedom to force a passage through the determinisms which imprison it. This will be intermittent at first and barely perceptible. The first free act, however small it may be, can therefore be a formidable event in a human being's destiny. This first act could be very perfect as regards religious quality, even if from the human standpoint, it appears deficient compared to an adult act. In fact, if the child accepts God's gift in the full measure of which he is actually capable, it can be said that he gives all to God. From the human point of view, obviously, the poverty of such acts appears in several ways ;

— the human act of a child's awakening freedom is only fleeting;

— being still incapable of reflection, the child's act is but imperfectly conscious ;

— since the child is still almost entirely submerged in instinctive and hereditary determinisms, besides being affectively, intellectually and materially dependent on the people around him, the emergence of freedom is hardly outlined ; it will more often consist in a certain acquiescence rather than in an original creation.

The next point must be carefully noted.

The religious and moral behaviour of a child is not structured on the same lines as that of the adult. With the latter, morally healthy acts are normally constructed according to certain rules clearly defined. Good acts correspond to certain abstract norms. There is nothing of that kind with the child. He has no moral code yet in use. If a mass of rules were given him too soon, he would use them wrongly. His behaviour is moral in the measure alone that it is the expression of the authentic elan of his being towards Some One for whom his reverence, admiration and love have been awakened. And yet this act — usually transitory, barely conscious, and apparently vague from the moral point of view — can be a religious act.

We may presume that a child of about three who can respond with a smile to his mother's love, can do more and better than an automatic action ; we may presume that a first impression of his budding personality has succeeded. We think the child is virtually open to God from this moment. Once his soul can feel a first movement of admiration or love, the ardor surging from the depth of his being soars past the reality immediately within his vision or his grasp. He seeks God without knowing it. It is time to mention Him.

Recalling memories of his fifth or sixth year, Julian GREEN relates the following [1] :

« From these years gone by, I retain the memory of a moment of ecstasy such as I have never known since. Should we mention such things or conceal them ? At this moment then, I raised my head towards the window, and looked out at the dark sky lit up by a few stars. How can I describe what is beyond the power of words. That moment was perhaps the most important in my life, and I do not know what to say about it. I was alone in a dark room, looking at the sky, and I felt what I can only call an ardor of love. I have loved since, but never quite like that, without knowing that I was doing it. Somehow I knew He was there, looking at me and loving me too. How did this thought dawn in my mind ? I do not know. I was sure Some One was there, speaking to me without words. With that I have said everything. Why must I write that I never found in any human discourse what I was allowed to feel then for about ten seconds, when I could hardly put three intelligible words together, and did not realize my own existence ? Why am I obliged to set down that for years I forgot that moment, the torrent of days and nights almost obliterating it from

1. *Partir avant le jour*, p. 16. Grasset, 1963. Translated from the French.

my memory ? Would I had remembered in hours of trial ! Why has its recollection come back to me now ? What does all that mean ? »[1]

2. Are the Child's First Religious Acts Conscious ?

The child is incapable of reflection ; the religious acts we have alluded to, scarcely emerge from the shadowy zone in which the child's consciousness sleeps. A fortiori the child is absolutely incapable of explaining his still vague experiences. And yet, while unable to relate his experience and incapable of real reflection, the child is conscious in the depth of his soul, and can express this in a certain way.

3. Are the Child's First Religious Acts Perceptible ?

Speaking above of adult religious experience, we noted the traits revealing God's action. Besides a certain change in contrast with the former state, we stressed, according to the doctrine of St. Thomas :

— an attraction towards God, developing in a context of recollection ;

— an urge to turn away from what is contrary to God (detachment from self and from the world);

— a climate of peace and joy.

These three signs, fundamentally ambiguous, can appear in a child :

— a certain taste for silence and manifestation of an aptitude for interior attention (first orientation towards contemplation);

— the sense of disinterestedness and gratuitousness (pleasure in giving or sharing) ;

— a certain joy and interior gaiety...

Nevertheless, it is chiefly in the act of conversion, and especially in the context of prayer, that we place the most characteristic and frequent religious experience. Does this exist in a child and is it

---

1. In another of his books, *Le bel aujourd'hui* (Paris, Plon), written between 1955-1958, J. GREEN relates : « When only a child, I loved the word firmament. It seemed full of light. My first purely religious feeling, as far as I remember, was at the age of five or six... I was in my parents' room, rue de Passy. It was quite dark, but through the window I could see thousands of stars sparkling in the sky. It was the first time, as far I know, that God spoke to me directly, in that vast confused language which words can never express. »

discernible ? Rather than reason in the abstract, we will quote several examples from among many, and then see what conclusions a teacher and experienced psychologist draws from such observation.

4. *Examples of Children's Religious Experience.*

a) *Personal Souvenirs.*

Hagiography is not silent in the case of children. We will give but one example.

Pierre FAVRE notes in his *Mémorial* that when aged about 7 he sometimes felt special moments of devotion, and that « from that time on, the Lord and Spouse of his soul sought to take possession of its very depths. » This intimacy with God continued to grow. « When about 12, » the holy man wrote, « impulses of the Holy Spirit prompted me to offer myself to God's service, so much so that one day during the holidays, when I was in the field where I helped to look after the flocks, filled with joy and a great desire for purity, I promised the Lord God to observe chastity all my life. » [1]

The awareness of the growth of their vocation has led many priests or religious to trace it to their earliest youth. Here is one testimony :

« I never felt the least pressure, not even from those who rejoiced at my vocation... my parents ; nor from God, who respects wills, even those He wishes to draw to His service ; but... in reality, it was God who called me, not I who chose. I never heard this call as a voice of course, not even an interior one (or I do not remember it) ; if I said : « I want to be a priest, » it was not the same as saying : « I want to be an airman. » I meant : I will become a priest, because God wishes it and urges me to it. For me, there was this very clear vision of faith from the beginning. Later on, I often felt this difference which separated me from companions who remained in doubt over their future for a long time. For me, this question was settled as far back as I can remember, and never suffered any eclipse, but grew in tenacity. Of course I did not realize from the start what the priesthood really meant. I was not capable. But I cannot see any break in the continuity of the spontaneous reactions of a child of four or five who said he wanted to become a priest, and the conviction which only increased with time. This makes me reject the opinion that there can be no authentic vocation in even very small children. In whatever way it is perceived, if Vocation is a call following a *divine* choice, there is no need for the subject to have a detailed knowledge straightaway of what the call means. » [2]

---

1. Blessed Pierre FAVRE, *Mémorial*, Coll. Christus, Translated and commented by M. de Certeau, S.J., 1960, Desclée De Brouwer (456 pages), p. 108.
2. Testimony of a Jesuit in C. BLANADET, *A votre appel, Seigneur*. Testimonies of priests on their vocation. Rodez, Secrétariat d'Action Catholique, 1956, p. 87.

This last example reveals a spiritual event almost imperceptible to start with, but developing with time and a strong connection with the entirety of the subject's religious destiny, and provides an undeniable character of authenticity. The same sign appears in the case of Pierre Favre, besides a more apparent immediate evidence, in the joy that flooded the child's soul when he made his vow of chastity.

b) *Observations.*

ANTOINETTE (to change her name) is four or five years old. She is eaten up by jealousy for her little brother. Her whole inner horizon seems to be darkened by this persistent passion. One day, her father, coming home from a journey, brings her a lovely box of assorted sweets. The child is dazzled by this marvellous present. She suddenly feels prompted to share these beautiful mouthfuls. She follows the impulse, generously gives away her riches, and from this very act is immediately cured of her jealousy.

Here we can detect the criterion of gratuitousness and dis-. interestedness, the significance of which was often stressed by Father RAHNER.

Like many children of her age, Josiana (a borrowed name for her), five years old, rejects religious suggestions. She does not want to pray. When spoken to of God, she objects that she cannot see Him. Voluntary or not, an obstacle exists. One evening it disappears. Mummy told the story of Abraham being called by God. She left on the table, the Bible Picture-book illustrated by Marbœuf, where we see God's pilgrim setting out from his country. Josiana has listened to the story. She opens the picture-book and looks long at the illustration, and then announces : « That keeps you quiet. » Something must have happened, for her interior resistance to prayer softens. From that day she has consented to pray, and does so with a recollection in complete contrast to her previous behaviour.

MARIE CLAIRE is six. It is difficult to know, as with most small children, whether the sense of God has been roused within her. One evening an unusual thing happens. « Mummy, » she declares, « You must tell me something about God. » Taken by surprise, Mummy hesitates a moment. « You will have to be very quiet, » she suggests. « Yes, talk to me, I am very quiet. » Marie Claire settles herself down, and the two smaller ones sit down too. Mummy tells the story of Moses who saw God in a burning bush. Marie Claire listens as never before. Mummy feels that some interior event is on the way, and tries to aid the work of grace. The story finished, all kneel down and Mummy suggests prayer of adoration and thanksgiving. When Mummy rises, Marie Claire stays kneeling for a minute and then goes to the children's room to get ready for bed. A little later, when Mummy goes to say good-night to her, she finds the child in bed, beaming for joy. « I've drawn the story of Moses, » she declares showing her mother a naïvely-coloured drawing. After a silence, she added : « This time, Mummy, you really made me think of God. » Mummy gives her a kiss and prepares to put out the light. « Leave the light a little while, I would still like to pray a little. » The child knelt down for a moment, then got back into bed. The precious drawing went under her pillow. « I will keep it a little while, then I will give it to you. »

To have real significance, the above example should be accompanied with information on the child's behaviour before and after it. By itself it is open to several interpretations ; but there are signs of awakening interior attention, the budding of a spiritual joy and a certain sense of gratuitousness.

5. *Some Bibliographical Paths.*

Stories of children's experiences are to be found in many child biographies, notably in the publications of the Eucharistic Crusade by Fathers BESSIÈRES, MARMOITON and PERROY. These biographies were particularly numerous around 1930.

Very helpful stories will be found in *Nos enfants devant le Seigneur* (Tours, Mame, 1959) by Madame FARGUES. In her little book *Père et mère à l'image de Dieu*, Paris, Le grain de sénevé, Mademoiselle DINGEON studies several cases in detail. The review *L'Anneau d'or* prints several enquiries into child religious life. We point out especially : Xavier LEFEBVRE, *La vie religieuse du jeune enfant, compte rendu d'enquête*, No. 89 (Sept.-Oct. 1959), pp. 401-413. By the same author : *La vie religieuse du jeune enfant, conclusions d'une enquête*, No. 95 (Sept.-Oct. 1960), pp. 413-425. Paul and Renée MONJARDET, *Sens chrétien de la mort*, No. 95 (Sept.-Oct. 1960), pp. 383-396. On this subject, see also the little book by Madame FARGUES, *L'enfant devant le mystère de la mort*, Paris, Fleurus, 1963. Again in *L'Anneau d'or*, Étienne LAMURE, *L'enfant et la prière, compte rendu d'enquête*, No. 109 (Jan-Feb. 1963), pp. 44-58. The testimonies of priests and religious sometimes throw light on the workings of grace during the first years of life, among others : C. BLANADET, *A votre appel, Seigneur ! Témoignages de prêtres sur leur vocation.* Rodez, Secrétariat d'Action Catholique et Maison du livre, 1956. By the same author : *Risquer sa vie pour Dieu ! Témoignages de religieuses sur leur vocation*, ibid. 1955. Testimonies of converts sometimes reveal some aspects of childhood's first religious awakenings, as for example, « *J'étais entrée dans le mystère de l'Église* » by Elsa STEINMANN in « *J'ai rencontré le Dieu vivant* » by M. NÉDONCELLE and R. GIRAULT, Paris, Éd. de la Revue des jeunes, 1952 (pp. 187-195). The memoirs of an Orthodox monk, the

Archimandrite SPIRIDON, *Mes missions en Sibérie* (edited in Paris, Ed.
du Cerf) contain astounding pages on his early years, with unrivalled
pages on the mystical and contemplative aptitudes of childhood. The
Swiss psychologist, Pierre BOVET has written a book on child religious
psychology, *Le sentiment religieux et la psychologie de l'enfant.* 2nd
edition, Neuchâtel, 1951. Besides a bibliography, the author himself
relates some very interesting facts on the religious life of children.
Finally, there is a book, not new, which was a real novelty in its day :
F. GELLÉ, *La grâce à dix ans. Essai de discernement et d'éducation de la
grâce chez les jeunes enfants.* Paris, Beauchesne, 1912. A book for consultation also could be that by J.-M. TIMON-DAVID, *Traité de la confession des enfants et des jeunes gens.* Marseilles, 1865, 15th. re-edition,
Paris, Fleurus, 1954.

6. *Observation Reported by Madame* FARGUES.

I am sure Madame FARGUES will pardon me if I quote considerable passages from a most remarkable study. It is a chaptei
entitled : *Deux petits garçons s'éveillent.* [1] The writer relates the
conversion of two children. First, she points out the range and
significance of the observations made. Here are the essential passages
of this study :

« I have already said how risky it is to speak as a psychologist of religious
awakening with these children, since the theologian does not help the psychologist much. I will therefore speak as a teacher...
I will not insist on the perfect behaviour of our little band when we take
them to pray in the chapel; to me, this silence, gravity and recollection could
be considered the result of suitable human education, nothing more; for all that,
it is not just nothing. We catechists open the door thus, for the Spirit to
breathe when He wills. These children would probably never have given these
signs of readiness if they had been neither prepared nor set in motion for
praying together.
Did the Spirit breathe ? Usually we cannot tell, since everything could
possibly be explained by suggestion or conformism, as well as by the aptitude,
normal and natural in little people, to be captivated by what is holy.
Twice at any rate, the Spirit passed, and each time a child was converted.
Each manifestation lasted about a minute and was hardly noticeable. But foi
me, it was absolutely certain...
CHRISTIAN and MICHEL came from very de-Christianized localities, living
irregularly from all points of view. They were both eight, physically and intellectually well developed, nothing of the deficient, psychopathic or difficult
temperament, but from their locality, standard of life, and above all, an
alarming lack of home training, they were « tough, » even very tough...

1. This study appeared first in the review *Vérité et Vie* (Strasbourg) no. 24,
then in the book by Madame FARGUES, *Nos enfants devant le Seigneur.* Tours,
Mame, 1959, 272 p. In the last chapter she studies several cases of child sanctity.

Both wanted to assist at catechism right from the start, and came fairly regularly.

Michel started from zero from the religious stand-point. Christian had been to a small catechism class occasionally, and had grasped a few Gospel facts and religious words: Our Lady, heaven, hell, etc., which did not seem to have made any impression on him.

The first day, Christian looked boldly at me, while his eyes seemed to say: « I shall give you a bad time. »

The writer then describes the first lessons : exercises in bodily control, visits to the chapel, learning of God in admiring the beauty of his works, learning of Christ and the book of His word.

« One day, after about two months, the question of conscience came up; we explained experiences of interior life, sorrow after a fault, happiness after a good deed... Two or three... reflected seriously, and remembered occasions when their conscience had spoken to them. CHRISTIAN was one.

The text for the day was made from passages of Psalm 138, « Lord, Thou knowest me... » in seven couplets. They were each told to choose the phrase they liked and understood best... Christian chose : « Before the words are on my lips, Thou knowest, Lord, what I want to say. »

That day, I did not lead the religious exercise in the chapel. I simply gave the children a few directions, chiefly negative. They were to walk slowly as usual, but they need not keep together. They were not to go right up to the altar. They could stand or kneel, as they liked, since today each one could talk to God as he wished, for as long as he liked, whispering his very own prayer.

I went in softly behind them, without their being aware of an adult presence. I watched them go in together in procession, spread out in front of the altar and remain standing as they usually did. I mention this to show how group-dependent and unfree they still were. At least their anarchy remained under control; they stood there a moment in silence, motionless, imitating each other in general good-will. Then I saw one of them kneel down — it was Christian; I saw him slowly bow his head and remain thus for a long moment — it seemed long because of the dead silence (but I did not look at my watch).

The others imitated him and knelt down too.

That was all.

Then they came out as quietly as they had gone in. I do not remember who gave the signal, or whether Christian followed it or continued praying a few seconds more. I chiefly remember that kneeling down and that slow inclination of the head. And I know that from that day, God was Some One for Christian. From then, we could remind him that he was under God's eyes (one had to be discreet about it, of course), invite him to pray, to offer up some effort. For example, instead of confiscating a small toy which he kept taking out of his pocket, I trusted him : « If you promised Our Lord not to play with that, would you keep your promise ? » The day I suggested this act of heroism, he promised quite sincerely. At the end of the lesson, I asked him whether he had kept his promise... He had nearly kept it... but not quite. Here was a convert, though not a saint.

MICHEL's case was still more striking, because it was Michel — the type of child who wants to be troublesome, accepts no restraint, will not make any effort. He was not ungifted and could be easily interested. When badly behaved, or not behaved at all, an anarchist, he was at least psychically healthy. When his interest was aroused, intelligent questions and answers followed. No trace

of spiritual training... There cannot be one straight road from the atheist world
to the Christian world, an abyss separates them. Our paths at catechism — the
parables, gestures, music, admiration — lead to the edge of the abyss; once
there, you must jump.

Michel jumped — but on the last day only. The story of Christian repeated
itself. To an onlooker, it was exactly the same. The difference lay in the context,
I mean, the session that prepared the plunge into divine things... »

The writer describes the catechism lesson : two records with commentary,
Grieg's *Death of Asa* and Mozart's *Petite Suite Nocturne* ; the subject
of the commentary was *human destiny*. A short talk followed this, on the
subject : we must be good to get to heaven. Then we went to the chapel
singing : « Christ, my hope, is risen again. »

That was the context.

Then the children stood round the altar. They prayed for a moment with
uplifted arms. A few ideas were suggested, praying aloud with them. Then I
suggested they could go on alone. They were very good, in spite of a few heads
turning round.

This silence and immobility could merely conceal emptiness of thought; they
at least demand an effort of will and offer homage to God. During this silence,
I saw Michel suddenly kneel down, bow his head slowly, and remain thus for
about a minute...

You see, I am repeating myself; it was just the same for Christian.

I do not know the future. But I consider that moment all-important in Michel's
destiny, whatever the upheavals of his existence. For it altered him.

How could we know this ? By very small signs.

Our catechism morning was not over. There was a recreation, with distribution
of flowers and sweets. Then a leave-taking. Is there not a difference like black
from white in a boy who pushes the others to be served first, and one who
can wait his turn, in a boy who rings your bell, watching you slyly out of the
corner of his eye, and one who leaves the bell alone ?

If he rings it again one day, the peccadillo will not interfere with his conversion. What is wonderful, is that today he is attracted towards something else,
towards the divine. If only for a moment, he has grasped the meaning of life,
and he is lit up by it. His face is serene and his manners good. In saying good-
bye to him, I thought I could venture to show I understood, by a look and a few
words. He understood too; we both stood on the same side of the abyss.

God accorded me this great joy for my last day of catechism, but I was sorry
not to follow up Michel's conversion, for he is only eight. I could only re-
commend him to the parish priest. »

In this account of a two-fold experience we notice all the traits we
have mentioned earlier :

— suddenness of an attitude contrasting with previous behaviour ;

— a moment of silence and attention in a context which permits the
belief that the child felt himself in the presence of God, and turned his
heart to God who called him ;

— certain acts and ways of acting which reveal detachment from self,
the sense of disinterestedness and gratuitousness ;

— peace and serenity visible in the countenance and in the smile ;

— a lasting change in behaviour starting from, and seemingly in conformity with, the initial experience.

This last point was only verified in the first case. But Madame FARGUES reports that some one who followed up Michel after he had left her class, asserts lasting improvement.

We point out that the traits enumerated and which mark experience are not in juxta-position, but form a coherent whole. These are the various aspects of a unique spiritual act.

7. Ambiguity of Signs.

Before concluding, we would like to speak of three frequent causes of errors in diagnosis : deceptive, superficial and parallel signs.

a) *Deceptive signs.* We mean signs of pseudo-religious behaviour. A typical case is that of child seized with devotion at sight of the Crib at Christmas or of a crucifix. The apparent piety may simply mean that the child is interested in the candles round the pretty little figure, or the painful sight of the crucifix. During adolescence and even in adult life, we find deceptive signs of this kind : emotions so-called religious but which are entirely human set up by a religious pretext or atmosphere. Resolutions taken at such moments are obviously fragile. A different emotion could overthrow everything.

b) *Superficial signs.* One of the chief pre-occupations in the discernment of spirits, is to situate the *level* of the experience in question. A young man in Retreat, for example, feels drawn towards the religious life. Does this attraction come from the depth of his soul ? Is it an expression of his most authentic self, or is it a kind of epi-phenomenon ?

A similar question arises in observing manifestations of a child's religious life. An apparently well guaranteed child behaviour can proceed from a superficial zone of his personality.

An example of this is found in the writings of Père Teilhard de Chardin. In *Le Cœur de la Matière*, he recalls his childhood :

« At that age (6 or 7 years) when I imagine other children feel their first attraction towards people, art or religion, I was affectionate, good, even pious... That is, led on by my mother... I loved the Child Jesus very much. » That is how the child appeared in the home circle. « But in reality my true self was elsewhere. To perceive this, they would have had to watch me when, secretly and silently, without even thinking there was anything to say about it to anyone, I withdrew into the contemplation, possession and appreciated existence of my own God : Iron. I mean that, iron. I can still see clearly the set of my « idols » : in the country, a plough link ... in town, the hexagonal head of a small pillar.

I feel obliged to admit that in this instinctive gesture which made me adore
a bit of metal, an intensity of gift and a host of demands were contained and
grouped together, of which my whole spiritual life has been but the development. »

The piety then of the young Pierre T. de C. devout towards the Child
Jesus, was sustained by an education which, whatever its value, passed
by the essential. The child was secretly seeking the Absolute by quite
another path. It was towards the quest of the Absolute that an interior
call was prompting him, while he was blindly seeking the way.

« As far back as I can remember, nothing seemed to me more characteristic
or more familiar in my interior behaviour than the desire or irresistible need
of « an all-sufficing and necessary One Thing. » To be quite at ease, to be perfectly happy was to know that « Some Thing essential existed, from which all
the rest is only accessory or ornamental. » [1]

Theoretically, the ideal would have been to discern this basic orientation,
and to perceive by what symbols it sought to free and express itself.
Starting from a pre-catechesis a well adapted catechesis could have been
developed. Probably, in actual fact, the boy's education in general was
excellent and his personal reactions equally healthy since, as he grew up
P. T. de C. was able to make the necessary adjustment, and discover
that it is in Jesus Christ that all realities subsist. But how many youths
would have missed the right turning ! He explains the adjustment in a
letter to the Reverend Father General in 1951.

« Ever since my childhood, my spiritual life has been completely dominated
by a sort of deep « feeling » of the organic reality of the world; at first this
feeling was fairly vague in my mind and heart, but with the years it has gradually become a precise and invading sense of the general convergence of the
universe upon itself, this convergence co-inciding and culminating at its summit
with Him « in quo omnia constant, » Whom the Society has taught me to love.
In the consciousness of this movement and synthesis of all things « in Christo
Jesu, » I have found an extra-ordinary and inexhaustible source of light and
interior strength, and an atmosphere outside which it has become impossible for
me to believe, adore and believe. » [2]

But how could anyone guess the child's deep religious personality, when
the boy exteriorized no signs of it ?

1. This and the preceding texts of Père T. are extracts from the unpublished
« Le Cœur de la Matière ». We have taken them from two transcriptions, one
from a work by P.B. GRENET (with a rather displeasing title) *Pierre Teilhard de
Chardin ou le philosophe malgré lui*. Paris, Beauchesne, 1960 (pp. 189, 190).
The author borrows his text from F.A. VIALLET, *L'univers personnel de Teilhard de Chardin*. Our other source is an article published in the *Revue diocésaine
de Tournai*, of September 1963, pp. 429-438 : Norbert GORRISSEN, a monk of
Orval, *Le Père Teilhard d'après ses lettres*.
2. Text taken from the article by Father GORRISSEN.

c) *Parallel signs.* Some signs assuredly do concern a deep religious experience. But this can co-exist along with other experiences more or less deep as well. That means a personality is in conflict with itself in the process of being born and growing. There is a remarkable illustration of this in Julian GREEN's book already quoted (*Partir avant le jour*). Besides apparently authentic religious experiences, others, of a disturbing nature, upset the child's and then the adolescent's personality. Obviously the teacher or observer, anxious to evaluate the quality and nature of a child's religious behaviour, should be able to note the diversity of the experiences of which he is either the terrain or the actor. How can he ? Possibly psychoanalytical methods adapted for children (for example, the use of puppets) or interpretation of drawings or other techniques could be enlightening in such a case. But such research could only be undertaken in particular cases. In the average number of cases, conclusions would have to be marked with a coefficient of uncertainty, and accepting a risk in deciding an educational orientation.

III. CONCLUSIONS

Amassing all the considerations set down, and concrete cases quoted here or which we have in mind, we can try to settle the limits, conditions, and perhaps some means of discerning the progress of grace in children.

Limits of Discernment.

1. There can be no question of experiment ; that is, it is useless trying to control a hypothesis, by placing artificial conditions for its coming about. We must always expect the unpredictable initiative of God's free Will and of human liberty.

2. Nor is there question of observing a child outside his normal setting. Authentic development and expression of his real personality can only exist in the network of inter-personal relations woven round the child.

3. Information obtained from children's answers to our questionnaires is but slightly significant.
— the child's ideas are not clear enough to supply accurate answers ;
— the child has only a small vocabulary, ill-adjusted to explanations ;

— the child does not always seek to state the reality, his words may give the idea of the moment, or what he thinks may please the questioner ; in a word, the child's criterion of sincerity cannot be gauged accurately.

4. Positive signs given must always be marked with a certain co-efficient of uncertainty or ambiguity ; with the small child especially, manifestations of personality are fleeting, intermittent and often ambiguous.

2. *Conditions of Discernment.*

For conclusions to be drawn with a sufficient co-efficient of pro-bability, several conditions must be fulfilled :

1. A child should be observed in his normal setting ; outside it, his re-actions may be artificial, and therefore contestable. This means that the tiny child must be observed at home, the bigger child, at school, at home, at catechism or whatever child movement or setting he usually frequents ;

2. Observation should be done in the context of friendly exchange, normally by people he knows. Indications will appear in dialogue between mother and child.

3. Since an experiment, in the strict sense, cannot be staged, as we have said above, significant events could sometimes be observed.

4. An isolated sign is ambiguous. Its significance must be con-trolled by previous and subsequent events. Prolonged observation is therefore indispensable.

5. The observer must be in « accord » with the experience he is seeking to detect. He must be in a state of spiritual progress himself, in quest of God, even if his faults deter and impede this quest.

3. *Technique of Discernment.*

It is difficult to prescribe which technique should guide experience, since the observer must be led by circumstances. We can lay down the following points :

1. The most normal mode for observation of child behaviour would be sometimes alone, sometimes guided by adults, sometimes

among other children. The aim would be to detect certain traits significant of development of a spiritual life. We have endeavoured to describe the basic characteristics of these traits in the preceding pages.

2. Dialogue should prove revealing, provided that it remains natural, not forcing the child to express more than he feels or than he wishes to disclose.

3. Drawing and picture commentary form a very interesting basis for dialogue.

4. *A Very Necessary Application.*

We need to observe a child's spiritual maturity to decide when he may approach the sacraments for the first time.

Once a child is about 7, parents, priests and teachers start preparing him for Confession and Holy Communion. A certain spiritual maturity must have been reached to do this. How can it be detected ? Three ways are put forward :

a) An objective control of *religious knowledge.*

An examination is sometimes made into the depth and extent of a child's knowledge of the catechism. Does he know the necessary truths accessible by the average child of the same age ? Does he understand enough about the Eucharist ? We think that an examination, however much simplified, often gives results contestable if not deceptive. Many children agree politely with the questioner. Their answers reveal little of their real knowledge of the things of God. Nor is it extremely rare to find children, spiritually well developed, completely at a loss because of the relative solemnity of the examination.

b) An objective control of *morality.*

This time enquiry is made into the child's conformity with the moral code; is he obedient, disciplined, devout, polite ? Here again, the enquiry must be enlightened. Generosity of heart can go hand in hand with lapses of discipline, and the absence of outbreaks is not necessarily a sign that the soul is open to God. A control of morality, to be really revealing, must fit into the context of the third point.

c) Discernment of *the child's openness to spiritual things.*

Without neglecting the modes of investigation whose limits we have just pointed out, but whose necessity we recognize — to a certain degree — the chief thing is to discern the child's spiritual

maturity. Here more than ever, it must be admitted the more worthy
the judge, the better the enquiry. More often than not, the enquiry
cannot be very successful for two reasons :

— the ordinary enquirers, that is, the parents, will not be able
to achieve this task ;

— many children keep their thought to themselves.

What can be done then ?

If the child has reached the normal age for reception of the
sacraments, and the enquiry in spiritual maturity is without proof
but not absolutely negative, judgment would normally be decided
by an examination of knowledge. This examination — which must
be made in any case — should concern the essential points in
revelation. Taking into account the training the child has been
given, the terms he is used to, and his personal dispositions, it
should seek to discover whether his reactions to the questions asked
allow us to suppose that the child is not a stranger to the Christian
mystery. Does he know that in receiving the consecrated host, he
is welcoming Jesus, the Son of God, within him ? Does he know
the all-holy God a little, Who loves us like a father ? Does he know
how we can pray to Him ? Does he know what God asks of us ?
Does he know that He loves us so much that He is always ready
to forgive ? Does he know that Christ's mother is our mother also ?

If the child stammers or gets lost in his replies, we may not conclude for certain that he is not spiritually ready. But if the enquiry
into maturity proved nothing and the knowledge test failed also,
it would seem difficult to admit the child to the sacraments. It
would be prudent, in our opinion, to delay the first Confession and
Holy Communion for a few weeks or months.

Such are the limits, but also the possibilities, of discerning
spiritual maturity, to which we think all concerned in child religious awakening are invited.

2

Technical Works

Parental Images and Divine Paternity

by André GODIN, S.J. and Monique HALLEZ

International Centre for Studies in Religious Education, Brussels.
Higher School of Assistants in Psychology, Brussels[1]

God, our Father, and the Church, our Mother ; these expressions form part of a Christian's daily vocabulary.

When a believer refers to God as a Father, he manifests a moral and religious disposition in conformity with Christian revelation. But on the level of inner attitudes, of psychic, emotionally charged images, it would be interesting to know to what reality, psychologically experienced, the expression « Father » refers. Does the interior evocation of the divinity really respond to the image of a *father* ? Or does the image of a *mother*, for example, bring in some nuances, ' although it would not be easy to determine the compatibility of a maternal image with the dogma of adoptive filiation in Jesus Christ... Would that be simply a matter of psychological preference arising from a personal background ? Are these images prevalent in evoking the divine, influenced by the sex, age, human and spiritual maturity of the believer ? Can we observe certain laws of evolution ?

The answer to these questions concerns the psychology of religion as a positive science. We can attempt to approach them statistically (not only clinically), since methods, such as the Q-technique, have been proved capable of revealing certain correlations between the psychological traits in the same personality.

It is not our purpose here to discover whether the evocation of God corresponds to certain traits which make up the concept of the FATHER, rather than to those composing the concept of the MOTHER, considered in their abstract or ideal structure, as ' archetypes ' in a given culture. To tackle this question it would suffice,

---

1. The researches forming the empirical basis of this article (except the testing for the group of contemplative religious men) were carried out by Miss HALLEZ, in order to obtain her final diploma of Assistant Psychologist (1963) under the direction of Father GODIN. Address: 184, rue Washington, Brussels 5, BELGIUM.

to prepare a long list of adjectives, nouns and verbs, corresponding to the paternal and maternal functions, and then get subjects representing the different settings in one and the same culture, to pick out the words most suitable to Father, Mother and God, by turns. This research, interesting in itself, would reveal the affinities between the three images, considered as ideals, within the limits of one culture and one acquired vocabulary. It would only approach indirectly the question we have raised : are there, among subjects taken *individually*, any relations between *their own* parental images, *whatever these may be*, and *their own* evocation of the divine ? And if these relations exist, do they reveal certain constants ?

In the study of these *intra*-individual correlations, no other method can perhaps replace the Q-method. [1] We will first summarize some results obtained by NELSON-JONES and by STRUNK with this method.

Previous Works.

In 1957, Marven O. NELSON and Edward Morris JONES first applied the Q-technique to the connection between religious concepts (God and Jesus Christ) and parental images (Father and Mother). The details of their method and the results have been published in English and French, which the reader may consult. [2]

These two writers present the answers obtained from 16 subjects (eight men between 20-24 years, eight women between 18-44 years). Three subjects were married. With the exception of the woman aged 44, all were students in a church-related college of liberal arts. All were Protestants. The most striking result was the following : with a fairly weak similitude ($r = .225$) [3] between the

---

1. The method consists in observing, on dependent variables (choices of suggestions marked on cards), the effects of independent variables (individual attitudes systematically drawn in one direction). The method is typified by the use of Q-sorting, or the Q system of classification. This letter indicates a method different from the method R, by which the object is studied through coefficients of correlation with different individuals. The R-method is fundamentally *inter*-individual; the Q-method is *intra*-individual : it seeks the correlation between different reactions in the same person solicited in different ways. The basic study is by William STEPHENSON, *Q-Technique and Its Methodology* (Chicago, Univ. Press, 1953). More recently, a work by Jack BLOCK, *The Q-sort Method in Personality Assessment* (Springfield, Ch. C. Thomas, 1961). In French, there are the critical notes by M. REUCHLIN, « Rapport sur le livre de W. Stephenson » in *L'Année Psychologique*, 1956, fasc. 1, p. 367.

2. M.O. NELSON and E.M. JONES, « An Application of the Q-Technique to the Study of Religious Concepts, » *Psychological Reports*, 1957, 3, 293-7; and « Les concepts religieux dans leur relation aux images parentales » in the volume *Adulte et enfant devant Dieu* (Bruxelles, Ed. Lumen Vitae, 1961), pp. 105-110.

3. This similitude would have been slightly higher ($r = .320$) if the authors had applied « the Fisher correction, » as they should have done, in computing the means of correlation coefficients, as we shall say later.

feelings evoked concerning father and mother, the subjects manifest a much stronger relation between *God and mother* ($r = .427$), and even between Jesus and mother ($r = .378$), than between God and father ($r = .153$), or Jesus and father ($r = .331$). This notable connection with *mother* is very significant (at .01 level), among both masculine and feminine subjects. Naturally enough, it is highest among the subjects preferring the mother ($r = .526$); it is also very strong among the subjects revealing hardly any preference between their two parental images ($r = .435$); it only tends to fade out with the 3 subjects (2 women and one man) who definitely preferred the father, while remaining positive ($r = .210$), this again being due largely to one subject (the man of 22, very unfavourable to mother). It is only in the group of subjects showing little difference in their preference for father or mother that we find a statistically significant correlation between God and father ($r = .377$), inferior in any case to the correlation already noted between God and mother ($r = .435$).

The detailed results obtained by NELSON and JONES are obviously richer than this brief sketch of their 'discovery' shows: capital discovery of a strong correlation with the *maternal image*. On examination, however, we suspect that the overall means may be dangerous for generalization, because of the variations noted within the sample which was very limited and but little homogeneous.

In 1959, Orlo STRUNK[1] made an interesting effort to select a group more homogeneous in age (10 men from 21-27 years, 10 women aged from 19-24) and especially in spiritual maturity ; this could be considered fairly good, since all the subjects attended a denominational college of liberal Arts, in preparation for pastoral ministry or religious education in the Protestant faith. His procedure was the same as NELSON-JONES.

The results obtained by STRUNK, confirmed some of the traits of the Nelson-Jones population, but with notable differences. Starting from a similitude clearly higher between feelings evoked concerning father and mother ($r = .524$)[2], the subjects again revealed a strong correlation between God and mother ($r = .505$), and between Jesus and mother ($r = .490$), this time the correlation (general mean) between God and father ($r = .453$) or between Jesus and father ($r = .513$) are not significantly inferior. It could, therefore, be asserted that Strunk's group, considering the *general mean*, projects God in *both parental lines*, of mother and father. A contrast, however, appears between the *masculine* subjects who establish a more marked relation between *God and mother* ($r = .559$) than with God and father ($r = .464$), and the *feminine* subjects with whom the relation *God-father* ($r = .442$) is more prominent than the relation God-mother ($r = .411$). As could be expected, the relation God-mother is stronger among subjects preferring the mother ($r = .672$), and the relation God-father stronger among those preferring the father ($r = .571$). With the subjects revealing no parental preference, there is found with them, as with the Nelson-Jones population, a statistically significant relation (at .05 level) between God and the mother ($r = .366$) while that between God and the father ($r = .241$) falls here below the

1. Orlo STRUNK, « Perceived Relationships Between Parental and Deity Concepts », *Psychological Newsletter* (New York University, Tresselt Editor) 1959, 10, pp. 222-6. Results briefly summarized in the same author's book, *Religion, a Psychological Interpretation*, New York and Nashville, Abingdon Press, 1962, pp. 35-6.
2. Applying « the Fisher correction, » this mean rises to $r = .620$.

level of significance. Strunk points out that the relation God and father (.453) is, as a general mean, the weakest of the four possible combinations between religious evocations (God and Jesus) and parental images.

It will be seen that these results suggest the variables presented could be fairly numerous. So Strunk was right in pointing out the necessity of repeating this research while ensuring stricter control.

For our part, we were struck by the authors' indifference over controlling the age and conjugal situation of the subjects, or whether their parents were deceased or living. We would also have wished that, in constituting homogeneous groups, which can be supposed to differ in their development of spiritual maturity, they had managed to observe a little more closely the interesting hypothesis put forward by Strunk : has the *Christian* attitude, more spiritual and cultivated, an influence over the insertion of the evocation of God into only *one* of the parental images (the image preferred ? eventually that of the father ?), or on the contrary, does it allow the evocation of God to emerge from any emotional sub-stratum, closely conditioned by the first circumstances of home life ?... [1]

Moreover, as we have pointed out in the notes, the computation of means in these two researches has neglected a point in statistical technique. The coefficients of correlation have been simply added up, and the total divided by the number of subjects in the sub-group. This is an error in the eyes of a statistician : it hides the fact that the additional correlations in the higher values of correlation have much more significance than the correlations in the lower values. Although this more correct statistical analysis would probably not have changed the general trend of the tendencies observed, it would have been better to introduce « the Fisher correction » (estimating in z-scores before totalization, with re-conversion after calculating the mean). This is the way we settled our means and our comparisons between coefficients of correlation, either global or individual.

We dropped out comparisons, Jesus-Father, Jesus-Mother, God-Jesus, on account of the length of the test. Even reduced to three variables God-Father-Mother, the 60 statements tend to make the test wearisome. Longer still, it would risk being scrambled over by some subjects.

---

1. An interesting, but limited, attempt to discover whether the concept of God emerges from parental concepts in the measure that religion corresponds more to an experienced reality has been published by A.W. SIEGMAN, « Personality and Socio-Cultural Variables Associated with Religious Behavior, » in *Archiv für Religionspsychologie*, Band VII (1962), pp. 96-104, and in French (with more details on technique and results) : « Notion de Dieu et images du père », in *Adulte et enfant devant Dieu* (Lumen Vitae Press, Bruxelles, 1963, 2), pp. 112-4.

I. THE TEST AND ITS POPULATION

The Evaluation Instrument. [1]

We translated, as faithfully as possible, the set of 60 statements arranged by NELSON-JONES, « following the pattern of the Q-technique described by Stephenson. » [2] In fact, the set includes 20 emotional responses which could be applied to interpersonal relationship.

If we try to compose a one-word list of these 20 sentiments, we get the following :

ACCEPTANCE	FAIRNESS	NEARNESS	SECURITY
ACCEPTANCE (Unconditional)	GENEROSITY	PATIENCE	SIGNIFICANT RELATION
ALLIANCE (« On my side »)	HELP	PROTECTION	SUPPORT
APPROACHABILITY	INTEREST	RESPECT	TRUST
CONFIDENCE	LOVE	RELIANCE	UNDERSTANDING

But each of these sentiments is expressed once positively (ex.: « ... *I have a sense of being protected* »), one negatively (ex.: « ... *I have a sense of not being protected* ») and once neutrally, as doubtful or conditional (ex.: « *I have a feeling of sometimes being protected, and sometimes of being left alone* »).

Each statement is so arranged that it can complete one of the phrases : « When I think of God, ... » — « When I think of father, ... » — « When I think of mother, ... » These systematic evocations appear on stimulus cards (3 $^1/_2$" × 3 $^1/_2$"), placed before the subject, three times during the test. The test always begins with selection relating to the thought of God; it continues with the evocation of father or mother alternately (according to the subjects).

The sixty statements are reproduced on smaller cards (2 $^1/_2$" × 1 $^1/_2$"), each marked on the back with an identification number (1 to 20 for the positive statements, 21-40 for the neutral or conditional ones, 41-60 for the negative statements).

---

1. The test IMAGES PARENTALES can be obtained *in French* on request, and on sending 100 Belgian francs or $ 2.00 (postage paid) to *Lumen Vitae — Psychologie religieuse* (184, rue Washington, Brussels 5, Belgium). This includes : a copy (special issue) of this article, two sets of the 60 statements and 5 loose cards, printed on stiff paper (to cut in the size mentioned), ten (mimeographed) work sheets for records and computations, with full instructions on how to draw up the statistical analyses without wearisome calculation. — For 100 copies of record and correlation work sheets : 100 Belgian francs or $ 2.00. — Two trays of light wood, easy to make (cardboard can be used as well), can be sent (with a month's delay) : 300 Belgian francs, or $ 6.00 (postage extra). — *In English*, a separate copy of this article (with 10 work sheets for records and computations) can be obtained from the same address : 50 Belgian francs or $ 1.00. But *the English texts of the statements and instructions* for statistical analysis can only be obtained from : Marven O. NELSON, 8, Valley View Terrace, Suffern, N.Y., U.S.A.

2. *O. c.*, p. 106 (French), p. 293 (English text).

Trays of light wood, fairly long (25 ^{1}/$_2$") were divided into 9 compartments (2 ^{3}/$_4$" $\times$ 2 ^{1}/$_2$") to receive the 60 cards. Each compartment is marked with a value from 0 to 8. The values are marked vertically on each compartment in red figures. At the 0 end was placed a movable card (3 ^{1}/$_4$" $\times$ 2") bearing the words: « Least like I feel. » At the 8 end another card bore: « Most like I feel. »[1] Finally, on each compartment, black figures (placed on the lower edge) so as to be always visible, mark the number of cards which the compartment must finally contain. In a word, it is a « forced choice » dividing 60 cards according to a settled number (normal distribution). The whole therefore, appeared like this:

	Least like I feel.						Most like I feel.		
Scale (Value)	0	1	2	3	4	5	6	7	8
No. of cards	1	2	6	12	18	12	6	2	1

Recording and statistical analysis are very simple. After each division of the 60 cards to evoke God, father and mother, the position of the cards is noted on a *record sheet* (specially prepared for this purpose) by inscribing its order number in the category where it is placed on the tray (which is thus free to be used again).

The *Feeling* or *Favour-Index* is calculated by the algebraic sum of the scores obtained by the positive (1-20) and the negative (41-60) cards. It is easy to see that if the 20 *positive* statements were found at the end of the scale of categories corresponding to the subject's feeling (« Most like I feel »), these 20 cards would give a total of 113 points. Vice versa, if the 20 negatives were at the other end (« Least like I feel »), they would entail a total of 47 points (to be substracted). Therefore, by finding the algebraic sum of these two groups of cards, we can obtain the *F*(avour)-*Index* for each subject: a score, positive or negative, which can never go beyond 66 points (the extreme case supposed above).

This *F-Index* served to settle the sub-groups of those preferring father or mother, according to whether the positive emotion for one parent made a difference of *ten points or more* in their favour (F or M). Lesser differences have been counted as from neutral subjects (N) without a marked preference.

Lastly, a *correlation sheet* compares the scores obtained by each of the 60 statements in the three associations FATHER/MOTHER, GOD/FATHER, and GOD/MOTHER, and serves to compute (by a simple formula, given on this sheet) the correlations of *each* subject. We can then obtain the *means* of these correlations by using the Fisher correction, of which we have spoken (conversion into standardized scores or z-scores), for the total group, and for the subjects grouped once more into categories according to age, sex, or the fact that they expressed a preference for father or mother.

---

1. We slightly modified the arrangement of the NELSON-JONES material here. For them the value 0 represented the idea: « Most like I feel, » and vice versa. This arrangement, besides demanding inversion of the totals obtained, seemed but little in conformity with the natural inclination of the subjects: to give 8 points shows a maximum of approbation, to give 0 expresses disapproval.

Population.

We intended to study a population as homogeneous as possible on the religious plane, and to neutralize certain variables which could be important in the problem under study.

In each category the subjects are practising, even fervent Catholics ; the young people, boys and girls, were studying or had studied, in good Catholic establishments; the married adults belonged to « Catholic Homestead » groups; the unmarried laity were teachers or members of Catholic Action, and the two groups of contemplative religious men and nuns can be considered a priori as an elite on the plane of Christian maturity.

We did our best to increase this homogeneous character of the categories by the following procedures: sampling the subjects according to proximity in age (17 to 19 years for the young men — 20 to 28 years for the young girls); excluding unmarried subjects in the groups of lay adults (men aged from 30-44, women aged from 30-39); keeping apart a group of older women (aged from 40-50), and the groups of religious both men and women.

Besides this, some subjects were removed from the statistical analyses after passing the test : those subjects who had lost one parent before reaching the age of 5; a few others who declared during the test that they either did not practise or were unbelievers. A few of these, however, will appear in our qualitative analysis, by way of comparison.

All together, fifteen subjects were thus put aside, because they did not fulfil some of the above mentioned conditions favourable to the homogeneity of the sample in our sub-groups.

The seventy subjects retained for statistical analysis of results were grouped as follows :

30 MEN	*Age*	*Code*	
10 young men (unmarried students)	17-19 years	HJ	1 to 10
10 married men (with families)	30-44 years	HA	1 to 10
10 contemplative religious	23-57 years	HR	1 to 10
40 WOMEN			
10 young girls (students, teachers)	20-28 years	FJ	1 to 10
13 married women (with families)	30-39 years	FA	1 to 13
7 older women (2 were married)	40-50 years	FA+	1 to 7
10 nuns (teachers)	24-52 years	FR	1 to 10

No time limit was fixed for the passing of the test. Some subjects finished the three divisions of the cards in 45 minutes. Others took as long as 1 hour 20 minutes. Each one was allowed to work at his own pace. The average for our population was about an hour.

II. SOME RESULTS

Now let us examine the results, beginning by the more general (global means and group means) to get to the more specific (individual correlations classed by sex and age), and conclude with some particular observations or comments by some subjects.

1. *Global Means and Group Means.*

1) *For the total 70 subjects* the correlations as a whole offer these figures [1] :

Father/Mother	God/Father	God/Mother
.553*	.518*	.531*

The evocation of God is projected almost equally in the two lines of feelings evoked concerning father and mother. These statistically high correlations (significant at 1 %) show that, in general, over the feelings roused by the evocation of God, the father and mother lead to a globally fairly convergent choice. Thus our population proved to be, on the whole, nearer to that of Strunk (whose three figures are .524*, .453*, and .505*) than to that of Nelson-Jones (.225, .153 and .427*). One is tempted to find there confirmation of the hypothesis that a certain spiritual development (presumed among Christians chosen from an elite for all the sub-groups) protects or frees the evocation of God from a too close connection with the maternal image (prevalent in the more mixed population of Nelson-Jones). Nevertheless, it must not be forgotten that this global mean in reality covers and conceals considerable variations. As such, therefore, it can teach us nothing except perhaps the fact, that the 60 statements of Nelson-Jones, which we translated into French, constitute a sufficiently valuable and indifferentiated verbal universe to be applied (in a fairly large Catholic population) eventually to God, to the father and the mother.

---

1. * These correlations, above .330, reach the 1 % level of significance *.
   (*) These correlations, above .255, reach the 5 % level of significance (*).

2) Separating the correlations of *masculine and feminine subjects* we obtain these global tendencies :

	Father/ Mother	God/Father	God/Mother
Total of 30 masculine subjects	.566*	.470*	.582*
Total of 40 feminine subjects	.542*	.561*	.476*

Although these correlations are all still very high, we can perceive a vague tendency emerging among the *masculine subjects* to connect the evocation of God with the image of the *mother*, and a tendency among the *feminine subjects* to turn towards the image of the *father*. It is hardly necessary to add that there is no significant difference between these two means, which still remain general, and continue to conceal real variations.

3) Let us now distinguish between *the subjects expressing a marked preference* (at least ten points of difference on the Favour-Index) for the father, or for the mother, or not expressing any difference of this kind. Sorted out this way, we obtained the following means :

	Father/ Mother	God/ Father	God/ Mother	Degree of difference[1]
22 subjects preferring the father	.373*	.539*	.259(*)	(°)
18 subjects preferring the mother	.384*	.262(*)	.581*	(°)
30 subjects without marked preference	.727*	.637*	.642*	

---

1. Using the « Table des valeurs significatives de la différence entre 2 r » (R. PIRET, *Notions de statistique élémentaire*, Liège, Candidature en Sc. Pédagogiques, 1957), we find (after averaging z-scores) :

°°° Difference above .474 : significant at 1 % level °°°

°° Difference above .360 : significant at 5 % level °°

° Difference above .301 : significant at 10 % level °. Besides that, we have marked (°) as 'notable,' the difference above .17, which seemed a well placed threshold, when examining the data, to serve in organizing the results.

As could be expected, the evocation of God borrows the traits (qualities *or* defects, be it remembered) evoked by the image of the parent preferred. The correlation also becomes clearly significant between the choice of feelings towards God and the choice of feelings towards the parent preferred ; this correlation ceases to be significant (at 1 % level) when the non-preferred parent is in question. Besides, as can be seen in the first two groups, the *difference* (°) between the coefficients of correlation becomes 'notable' and approaches statistical significance.

Let us stress the fact again that these correlations are established between two sets of choice made by *each* subject, *whatever the statements chosen* to express their feelings. A statement selected by one to express preference for the mother, could be equally well selected by another to express preference for the father ; what counts, in establishing the correlation with a series of statements chosen in the evocation of God (which evocation was at the beginning of the test for all the subjects), is not the content of each statement, but simply the fact that, selected for either father *or* mother, it was *also* selected when the subject was thinking of God. If we may so express it, the *pure* relation (statistically speaking) comes into play here. This relation remains unknown to the subject, in the sense that he or she had not got to choose, for God, the statements chosen for their father « because God is called a Father » ; these indeed can contradict current usage culturally admitted ; [1] traits usually selected as maternal, for example, will be sometimes chosen both for the father and for God — and vice versa.

The results show, then, that the fact of evoking traits which are associated with the parent preferred, runs parallel with evocation of the same traits when thinking of God. This declaration confirms the results obtained by Strunk more clearly than it was with the Nelson-Jones population.

4) Again using a difference of 10 points, or more, on the Favour-Index, we can finally examine differential correlations between the choices, distinguishing *also* between the masculine and feminine subjects. This gives us the following :

---

1. On the traits of the paternal and maternal images, as currently accepted in our culture, there is an interesting page quoted by Professor François Duyckaerts in the preface to his translation of *Psychologie sexuelle* by O. Schwarz (Paris, Presses Un. de France, 1952). In it, the mother is seen as the source of all security, as a reliable power of protection; and the father is the person representing values, and a stimulant for action (p. XXII).

	Father/ Mother	God/ Father	God/ Mother	Degree of Difference
Masculine Subjects preferring the Father (5 subjects, or 17%)	.445*	.404*	.210	(⁰)
Masculine Subjects preferring the Mother (10 subjects, or 33%)	.314*	.212[1]	.623*[1]	ooo
Masculine Subjects without marked preference (15 subjects, or 50%)	.720*	.627*	.650*	
Feminine Subjects preferring the Father (16 subjects, or 42,5%)	.352*	.576*	.273(*)	o
Feminine Subjects preferring the Mother (8 subjects, or 20%)	.457*	.323(*)	.530*	(⁰)
Feminine Subjects without marked preference (15 subjects, or 37,5%)	.734*	.649*	.634*	

1. The means of standard (Z) scores are .215 and .730*.

It can be seen that the tendency to attribute the preferred parent's traits to God stands out more clearly still when the subjects are re-grouped according to sex. This time, the correlations are more and more in contrast ; *only* the Mother-preferences become significant among the masculine subjects ; among the feminine subjects, the Father-preferences dominate the other by *a higher level* of significance (1 %* instead of 5 % (*)); but more than that : *all the differences* between the means of the coefficients of correlation, in each of the 4 groups expressing preference for one parent, become notable (°), significant °, or even very significant °°° (at 1 % level, in the case of masculine subjects projecting towards God the traits belonging to their mother).

It can therefore be considered as a well-proved fact that, *where there is a marked preference for the parent of the other sex, the evocation of God is strongly drawn in that direction.* It emerges with a heavy stress on the evocation of the traits attributed to the favourite parent (whatever the defects or qualities attributed to him or her).

As we shall see when we have examined the individual answers classified according to age and sex, it is not the mere preference for one parent which will lead to a propensity to use their traits to designate the divine ; it is also the fact that the two parents are perceived or evoked with a more marked *differentiation* (weak positive correlations between *Father/Mother*, or even negative correlations) which, combining with a marked preference, ends by forming an evocation of God which rests on very ' conditioned ' feelings. We will come back on this aspect which probably yields an important key to decipher the elements of the problem we are studying.

2. *Individual Correlations Classed according to Age and Sex.*

A. Masculine Population : Students

TABLE A

Code	Age	Parental Preference[1]	COEFFICIENTS OF CORRELATION [2]			Degree of Diff.[3]	Favour-Index		
			Father/ Mother	God/ Father	God/ Mother		God	Father	Mother
HJ 1	17	M	.42*	.26(*)	.33*		4	-34	3
HJ 2	17	N	.82*	.68*	.73*		45	52	48
HJ 3	17	M	.47*	.40*	.86*	oo	57	16	51
HJ 4	17	N	.54*	.37*	.57*	(o)	63	35	42
HJ 5	17	N	.82*	.82*	.80*		48	53	58
HJ 6	17	N	.83*	.75*	.61*		41	47	52
HJ 7	18	F	.21	.03	-.04		8	23	10
HJ 8	18	M	.21	.26(*)	.47*	(o)	43	7	35
HJ 9	19	M	.41*	.29*	.54*	(o)	50	11	26
HJ 10	19	N	.76*	.33*	.35*		28	46	41
Means of correlations (r) :			.599*	.461*	.569*				

1. There is parental preference when the Favour-Index shows a difference of ten points or more.

2. * Correlation above .330, reaching the 1 % level of significance (df = 58)*. (*) Correlation above .255, reaching the 5 % level of significance (df = .58)(*). In the case of means, these significances have been calculated with the application of « the Fisher correction » (z-scores).

3. The signs ooo, oo, o, have been used to indicate differences statistically significant at levels 1 %, 5 % and 10 % respectively for differences above .47, .36 and .30, when the coefficients of correlation are small or medium (lower than .70), and for differences above .49, .37, and .31 for coefficients above .70. When a difference was over .17, it has been retained as 'notable' and marked (o).

The tendencies of this group of ten students (aged from 17-19) are as follows :

— the correlations Father/Mother are in general very high, as if the young men perceived the same parental qualities with *slight difference* in both parents ; only two cases fall below the level of significance ; [1]

— when parental preference appears, it usually favours the *mother* (4 cases), rarely the father (1 case);

— when the difference is notable (3 cases) or significant (1 case) between the correlations God/Father and God/Mother, it *always* favours the *mother*.

B. *Masculine Population : Married Men.*

TABLE B

Code	Age	Parental Preference	COEFFICIENTS OF CORRELATION			Degree of Diff.	Favour-Index		
			Father/ Mother	God/ Father	God/ Mother		God	Father	Mother
HA 1	30	M	.30(*)	-.11	.44*	ooo	53	-12	27
HA 2	32	N	.70*	.35*	.43*		24	53	57
HA 3	32	M	-.29*	-.40*	.57*	ooo	46	-36	43
HA 4	36	M	-.50*	-.46*	.48*	ooo	44	-46	47
HA 5	38	M	.78*	.63*	.81*	(o)	60	41	61
HA 6	38	N	.72*	.75*	.78*		58	51	56
HA 7	39	N	.76*	.58*	.60*		41	55	59
HA 8	39	F	.72*	.53*	.28(*)	(o)	34	55	43
HA 9	39	N	.49*	.38*	.51*		41	45	47
HA 10	44	N	.93*	.81*	.83*		47	58	60
Means of correlations (r) :			.564*	.365*	.605*	oo			

The tendencies noted in this group of 10 married men (aged 30-44) are these :

— Father/Mother correlations can be very high here also (.93, .78, .76 etc.) but they can be extremely low : there are two cases of negative

---

1. *HJ7* is probably a problem-case in the religious sphere : on the Favour-Index, God has the lowest figure of the whole population retained for our statistical analyses (Index : 8), with parents also marked very low (23 and 10); his correlations God/Father and God/Mother are practically nil. *HJ8* corrects a very low Index for Father (7) by a very marked maternal preference (35), and a fairly strong correlation God/Mother (.47).

correlation (*HA3* has —.29 and *HA4* has —.50), that is, with very strong *differentiation* evoked in sentiments towards father and mother,[1] stronger than in any other sub-group ;

— as for the young men, when there is parental preference, it favours the *mother* (4 cases), rarely the father (1 case) ;

— when there is a significant difference between God/Father and God/Mother (3 cases at 1 % level), it always favours the *mother* ; when there is a notable difference (2 cases), one connects with the mother, the other with the father (*HA8*, aged 39).

C. Masculine Population : Contemplative Religious.

TABLE C

Code	Age	Parental Preference	COEFFICIENTS OF CORRELATION			Degree of Diff.	Favour-Index		
			Father/ Mother	God/ Father	God/ Mother		God	Father	Mother
HR 1	23	F	.44*	.61*	.47*		25	42	30
HR 2	24	F	.52*	.38*	.26*		50	34	21
HR 3	30	M	.50*	.70*	.64*		53	34	48
HR 4	30	N	.74*	.68*	.74*		41	46	51
HR 5	33	N	.68*	.66*	.63*		55	59	50
HR 6	35	F	.22	.39*	.04	o	52	30	4
HR 7	35	M	.53*	.31(*)	.77*	oo	48	25	55
HR 8	42	N	.30(*)	.59*	.37*	(o)	48	35	36
HR 9	43	N	.46*	.53*	.62*		47	41	43
HR 10	57	N	.75*	.73*	.81*		58	54	57
Means of correlations (r) :			.535*	.574*	.574*				

Tendencies noted in this group of 10 religious aged between 23 and 57 (seven are between 30 and 43 years) are these :

— the *nondifferentiation* of parental images is strong; only one correlation was not significant (*HR6* whose r = .22), and not one negative correlation between Father/Mother ;

---

1. Very marked differentiation for *HA3* (Father/Mother = —.29), whose father is an unbeliever, and who idealises a mother he has never known on account of a separation.

— parental preferences tend *to fade* (5 cases with none) or *to become equal* (3 cases preferring the father, 2 cases the mother);

— evocation of God connects sometimes with the *paternal* image (2 cases of ' notable ' or significant difference), sometimes with the *maternal* (1 case of significant difference).

On the whole, this group gives the impression of evoking God with attributes very free from conditionings of early parental situations.

This fact strengthens the hypothesis already mentioned according to which a certain degree of spiritual maturity liberates the attitude towards God, and purifies it from the old influences of childhood's parental images. We cannot however disregard the fact that with these contemplative religious, unmarried, living away from their families for a long time, parental images tend to become blurred, losing their differential vivacity, or — as a few conversations confirmed — to be idealised, becoming themselves mixed with the evocation of the divine.

D. *Feminine Population : Young Girls (Unmarried).*

TABLE D

Code	Age	Parental Preference	COEFFICIENTS OF CORRELATION			Degree of Diff.	Favour-Index		
			Father/ Mother	God/ Father	God/ Mother		God	Father	Mother
FJ 1	20	F	-.03	.49*	-.11	ooo	35	34	-6
FJ 2	21	F	.57*	.65*	.52*		50	50	27
FJ 3	21	F	.63*	.69*	.67*		30	52	23
FJ 4	22	F	.38*	.59*	.24		54	50	18
FJ 5	23	N	.72*	.60*	.58*		45	51	51
FJ 6	23	F	.13	.29(*)	.07	(o)	52	26	9
FJ 7	24	N	.55*	.58*	.55*		51	46	42
FJ 8	25	M	.67*	.41*	.49*	(o)	27	42	56
FJ 9	28	F	.45*	.41*	.19		36	43	30
FJ 10	28	F	.53*	.80*	.34*	oo	43	52	39
Means of correlations (r) :			.485*	.569*	.377*	(o)			

In this group of ten young girls from 20-28 years, unmarried, we observe the following tendencies :

— Correlations Father/Mother are weaker than for the group of young men (who are also younger); but parental images are but slightly differentiated, except in 2 cases with whom correlation falls below the level of significance ; [1]

— very frequent preference appears *in favour of the father* (7 cases), rarely in favour of the mother (1 case);

— in the evocation of God, when there is a ' notable' difference (twice), a significant (2 cases), or very significant (1 case), it is *always* in correlation with *the father*.

E. *Feminine Population : Married Women.*

TABLE E

Code	Age	Parental Preference	COEFFICIENTS OF CORRELATION			Degree of Diff.	Favour-Index		
			Father/Mother	God/Father	God/Mother		God	Father	Mother
FA 1	30	F	.63*	.73*	.46*	(°)	43	55	44
FA 2	31	M	.73*	.62*	.63*		55	35	48
FA 3	31	F	.24	.58*	.36*	(°)	48	41	19
FA 4	32	N	.77*	.63*	.58*		42	49	54
FA 5	32	F	.42*	.39*	.41*		12	19	6
FA 6	32	N	.78*	.75*	.74*		47	48	53
FA 7	34	M	.65*	.41*	.61*	(°)	39	27	46
FA 8	34	M	.36*	.33(*)	.30(*)		14	-12	16
FA 9	37	M	-.29(*)	-.48*	.48*	°°°	58	-41	41
FA 10	38	N	.71*	.74*	.67*		57	50	54
FA 11	38	M	.40*	.43*	.56*		45	32	59
FA 12	39	M	.16	.16	.45*	(°)	53	- 5	38
FA 13	39	N	.88*	.73*	.71*		50	60	62
Means of correlations (r) :			.555*	.503*	.549*				

This group of 13 women aged from 30-39, all married, and most of them with children, shows the following tendencies :

— in this group, correlations Father/Mother reveal maxima (.88, .78, .77 etc.) and minima (—.29) which appear nowhere else in the feminine group. Here again, for women as for men, in the group of married adults,

---

1. These young girls (*FJ1* and *FJ6*) are not acute problems on the religious plane; both have a fairly high F-index for God, on which show very clearly the traits of the paternal image, itself greatly favoured in comparison with the maternal image : .49°°° and .29(°).

we find *the strongest differentiation* between the paternal and the maternal images. Comparison with older women, often unmarried, and with nuns, will show that it is the conjugal and parental situation which seems to be the factor responsible for this differentiation. The reality of maternity (as of paternity in the masculine sub-group) comes to enrich and radically renew the 'maternal' image ; it becomes, if we may so express it, an actively orientated evocation, instead of corresponding, as before marriage and in general during childhood, to a need of 'being mothered,' rather passively and egocentrically, by parental personages more or less idealised and but slightly differentiated ;

— the F-Index for the *mother* is very much higher (6 cases of preference) than in the preceding group. The *father* is also represented (by 3 cases of preference);

— correlation with the evocation of God connects sometimes with the *father* (2 cases of 'notable' difference, at the ages of 30 and 31), sometimes with the *mother* (2 cases of 'notable' difference, and another of very significant difference, aged 37 and 39). [1]

F. *Feminine Population : Older Women.*

TABLE F

Code	Age	Parental Preference	COEFFICIENTS OF CORRELATION			Degree of Diff.	Favour-Index		
			Father/ Mother	God/ Father	God/ Mother		God	Father	Mother
FA + 1	40	F	-.16	.51*	-.23	ooo	46	53	-30
FA + 2	40	N	.66*	.67*	.75*		56	49	52
FA + 3	43	N	.81*	.68*	.77*		58	42	46
FA + 4	43	F	.08	.23	.08	(o)	46	14	-24
FA + 5	47	F	.29(*)	.27(*)	.03	(o)	55	32	- 8
FA + 6	50	F	.18	.58*	.18	oo	36	46	-10
FA + 7	50	N	.59*	.53*	.37*		40	57	56
Means of correlations (r) :			.404*	.512*	.335*	(o)			

In the group containing 7 older women (ranging from 40 to 50 years of age), two of whom are married, and the majority have either lost both

---

1. The very significant difference for *FA9* (aged 37) whose father was an unbeliever, converted before his death which occurred recently, corresponds to a very unfavourable image (— 41 on the Favour-Index). As regards God, the problem seemed to be avoided by investing thought of Him with most of the traits belonging to the maternal image (.48ᵒᵒᵒ).

parents (3 cases), or their father only (3 other cases), the following tendencies are noted [1] :

— *variable differentiation*, but with a fairly high mean (from .81 to —.16) between the two parental figures, with 4 cases below significant correlation ;

— 4 cases of *paternal* preference (not one case of preference for the mother);

— all the cases of 'notable' difference (2) or of significant difference (2) place evocation of God in positive correlation with the *father*.

G. *Feminine Population : Nuns.*

TABLE G

Code	Age	Parental Preference	COEFFICIENTS OF CORRELATION			Degree of Diff.	Favour-Index		
			Father/ Mother	God/ Father	God/ Mother		God	Father	Mother
FR 1	24	N	.91*	.64*	.62*		39	57	61
FR 2	26	F	.30(*)	.63*	.25	oo	42	50	21
FR 3	27	N	.70*	.66*	.61*		43	47	46
FR 4	39	F	.21	.61*	.19	oo	46	57	15
FR 5	39	F	.77*	.73*	.63*		49	49	37
FR 6	41	N	.78*	.66*	.73*		52	56	60
FR 7	44	F	.04	.58*	.14	oo	44	45	-10
FR 8	44	N	.82*	.81*	.78*		55	57	55
FR 9	50	M	.65*	.56*	.66*		54	26	45
FR 10	52	N	.72*	.57*	.65*		62	55	54
Means of correlations (r) :			.656*	.652*	.559*				

In the group composed of ten (teaching) nuns, whose ages range from 24-52 years, the following tendencies are noted :

— *strong nondifferentiation* concerning Father/Mother (maximum: .91 ; 6 cases above .70 ; 3 cases not reaching the level of significance, but no negative correlation);

— 4 cases of *paternal* preference and one case of preference for the mother ;

1. This last sub-group is obviously thinly represented. We only isolated it to bring out the difference, very marked, between it and the preceding sub-group, and to raise the question of a variable, which we consider important and requiring to be better studied : the fact of one or both the parents being no longer living.

— all the differences of correlation to the evocation of God (three of them are significant) are connected with the *father*, although the Favour-Index is often high for the mother (with about one exception, which was ' unfavourable ' towards the mother).

Setting aside the last observation (Index favouring mother), one is at first struck by the resemblance between the tendencies in this group of nuns and those noted in the group of young girls (group D). But perhaps more remarkable still is that this group of nuns is like that of the young girls (nondifferentiation over Father/Mother — and strong connection God/Father), whilst their Favour-Index, fairly high for the mother, brings them close to the group of married women.

This brings up again, in fashion parallel to the sub-group of contemplative religious (men), the hypothesis of a spiritual maturity inclining to free the image of God — at least with many subjects — from its too close connections with the images of the parent preferred. Obviously, this purification is brought about in the contrary sense (that is, as regards the maternal image) for the contemplative religious (men), and for them will be a more laborious process than for the nuns, since these (if one may venture to say this) have *only* to turn towards « God the Father, » starting from their own father, *but* without fixation at the aggressive opposition towards the maternal image, so often found in the case of young girls.

As for the group of contemplative religious, the question of psychological *factors* at work in this spiritual maturity (at least on the level of the replies obtained in our test) naturally remains open : idealisation through separation from the family ? parental evocations drawn closer and closer to the ' sphere of the divine ' ? emotional guilt (unconsciously) preventing the choice of statements unfavourable to the image of father or mother ? etc. All these explanations or hypotheses are probably valid in some cases and various proportions.

3. *Special Comments and Observations from Certain Subjects.*

The limits, but also the meaning and certain possible developments, of our method of research into *parental images*, were revealed by some reflections made on the spot by some of our subjects, and by some special observations (qualitative aspect of the research) concerning certain protocols.

Immediate Comments.

a) Spontaneous comments, during or after the test, often referred to the greater or lesser *difficulty* of choosing statements, sometimes in the evocation of God, sometimes concerning the parents.

Subjects finding more difficulty in choosing their feelings for God usually say that « things are less clearly felt concerning God than over concrete people » (*HJ4*, aged 17).

Alluding to a greater difficulty in choosing feelings towards parents, they usually find it painful to evoke negative attitudes towards the less favoured parent. Examples : « For my father, I was much less whole-hearted » (*HJ3*, aged 17, whose Favour Index gave 16 to the father, 51 to the mother). « For mother, it will be more difficult ! » (*FR4*, aged 39, whose Index gave 57 to the father, 18 to the mother).

b) For the less favoured parent, there was sometimes *hesitation* over the appreciation *once* (always ' more aggressive ') and the appreciation *now* (always ' more favourable '). We made a point of verifying how subjects overcame this kind of hesitation, whenever they mentioned it ; it was always by adopting (spontaneously) their *present* attitude : « I used to be very indignant against my father, but that is over now ; I have answered as I feel now » (*FR7*, aged 44, whose Index gave : God 44, father 45, mother —10). This uncertainty, as it concerns the method, does not seem to be greatly important.

c) In general, subjects are *largely unaware* of the global significance of their choice, especially as regards God. This was surprisingly expressed by some. *HR10*, aged 57, whose mother died when he was 25, states that he « regained feelings of sympathy for his mother, after her death, finding her once more in God. » He said that he had « answered according to his present feelings evoked for his mother as he had known her. » In practice, this conscious effort, expressed by this rather complicated phrase, merely produces the *idealisation nondifferentiation*, the importance of which we have noted. The results for this subject are :

F/M	G/F	G/M	Index
.750	.729	.807	G : 58 ; F : 54 ; M : 57

In the opposite sense, *FR13*, aged 42 (who took the test too late to figure in our statistical analysis), believing she had grasped the exact meaning of the selections to make, told us : « In my case, the fact of having elderly parents, *therefore* (?) with much greater balance, means that for me they had much more of God's qualities. » Yet her results contradicts her statement completely :

F/M	G/F	G/M	Index
.607	—.007	.007	G : 46 ; F : —11 ; M : 3

d) A fair number of subjects did not find, in the 60 statements offered, *certain shades of feelings* which they would have chosen. As a matter of fact, those whom we questioned on this point rarely put forward positive suggestions which would improve the test. We mention the three following opinions which seem to us to carry real weight :

ML (Nun) wrote : « This test has enlightened me. I would have liked to have passed it in an atmosphere of absolute silence... For the first part, it was difficult to give accurate answers to questions always based on impressions or feelings, whereas the whole life of Faith tends to surpass this level... As a whole, I would have liked to have come accross a few statements on *gratuity, disinterestedness*, in relation to love. »

FM (Monk) wrote : « Kindly thank your assistant for allowing a monk to marvel at all God gave him of Himself in his parents. May I venture on a suggestion : to love, is to become centred on another. Each test-card seemed to say : « When I think of so-and-so I find advantages... (I feel respected, understood, etc.). » Could there not be expressions like : I *marvel*, I am filled with *admiration*, I cannot get over the fact that I am His child (etc.). The complementary cards would have expressions such as : I feel *indifferent to...*, *embarrassed by...*, *unworthy of...* his love (etc.). »

MF (Teacher) wrote : « Why not control the suggestion of God-father making the laws, by some statements expressing the sentiment of *obligation, revolt*, etc. ? »

We think these three suggestions deserve special attention in the event of revising the test in order to improve it. In any case, they apply to the three relations whose mutual incidence we are studying : towards God, mother, and father

Individual Analyses.

It may be asked whether certain aspects of the personality of each subject are reflected in the test, either as regards their individual history, or the very structure of their attitudes combined towards their parents and towards God. The small number of subjects, questioned by a method inevitably long, if not tedious, limits us to mention only three points :

1. A certain *idealisation of a deceased parent* tends to appear in the Favour-Index, and *to raise the relation between God and the parent dead*. It will be remembered that we eliminated from our quantitative analyses the subjects who had lost one parent before reaching the age of 5. But within our analysed population, we found :

FJ5 (aged 23) lost her mother at the age of 10 ; her *Favour Index* gave God 45, father 51, mother 51 (very rare in our feminine population of that age).

FJ10 (aged 28) lost her father at the age of 6 : her *Index* gave God 43, father 52, mother 39 ; her correlation *God/Father* reached .80, a record figure for her age group, and which was only reached by one another in our feminine population (by a nun aged 44).

FA13 (aged 39) lost her mother about 20 years ago ; her *Index* gave God 50, father 60, mother 62 (a record score in all 70 subjects of our population). This idealisation nearly always leads to a very high figure of correlation (indifferentiation) between Father/Mother : .88 in the present case, another record score among our feminine population (40 subjects).

Traces of this idealisation are much weaker when parents were lost later in life (for example, in the group of seven older women between the ages of 40 and 50), where it affects attitudes in evoking God very little.

2. *The transfer to God* of the traits selected for the 'less favoured' parent leads to a fairly general lowering of the Favour Index for God. That may sound like a truism, and yet let us note that, while the Favour-Index for God is the result of very conscious choices, made when evoking the attitude before God, it is not the same for the *correlation between traits* chosen as suitable for the relation with God *and* with the less favoured parent. One escapes with difficulty from the idea, that there is here, at least genetically, a question not only of concomitance but of causality between these two types of relation.

FA5 (aged 32) and *FA8* (aged 34) had an *extremely low F-Index* for God, 12 and 14 respectively, that is the lowest of our whole feminine population (believers and practising) in the test. It is noteworthy that these two people have a *stronger* relation between God and the *less favoured* parent than between God and the parent favoured (respectively : .41 with the mother obtaining 6 in the Index, and .33 with the father obtaining —12 in the Index).

HJ1 (aged 17) and *HJ7* (aged 18) had an *extremely low F-Index* for God (4 and 8 respectively, the lowest of all our masculine population (practising believers) in the test. It is noteworthy that these two offer correlations .33 and .03 between God and, respectively, a mother given 3 in the Index (father : —34) and a father with only 23 in the Index (mother : 10).

If we have drawn attention to these 2 last cases, obviously unusual in our population of practising believers, it is in order to compare them with the four unbelievers (excluded from our statistical analyses) whom we must mention in conclusion.

3. *Four subjects were found to be unbelievers* during the test and contrary to our expectation. A glance at their figures shows how deeply disturbed is the relation *God/Parents* (in the first two cases) and *Parents/ Children* (in the two last cases).

Non-practising Subjects	Preference	Father/ Mother	God/ Father	God/ Mother	F-Index		
					God	Father	Mother
H NP 1 aged 16	N	.66	-.39	-.26	-33	49	57
H NP 2 aged 18	N	.70	-.06	-.04	-13	56	51
F NP 1 aged 30	N	.68	.31	.50(°)	-22	-46	-41
H NP 3 aged 33	N	.31	.17	.26	-14	29	-31

These four subjects declaring themselves non-practising, naturally chose very negative cards for God, as their F-Index, all minus scores, reveals. But it is very remarkable that for the two youngest, relations with their parents appear, at least, to be psychologically good, while for the two older cases relations with parents are deeply disturbed.

From a conversation *H. NP.2* (aged 18) kindly afforded us, it was clear that God is only an abstract and remote principle for him, more of a philosophical idea than a Christian image. God could not be considered as a helper in any way. And yet feelings for parents, as chosen by the test cards showed : love, nearness, easy access, etc. Historically, this young man lost his father very early, and his mother, being obliged to work, had entrusted him to a grandmother, rather imperious and unsympathetic. She had trained her grandson in religion, but in a way which bred utter boredom, and later, exasperation. We may, therefore, wonder whether his Favour-Index, high for his parents, does not reflect a strong idealisation for parents he hardly knew, and whether his grandmother's personality does not largely influence the re-action he seems to feel towards the image of God he has received from her, and his idea of God being remote... Our test has proved inadequate here, since it does not include the image of a grandmother !

With *F. NP.1* (aged 30) and *H. NP.3* (aged 33), conversation only confirmed what the selection of statements showed in the results of the test. The religious crisis is clearly connected with former relations lived with the parents. The feelings chosen with regard to God express : doubt, want of security, confidence. Historically, for *F. NP.1*, relation with her father, a drink addict, had been marked by insecurity, while relation with her mother was cold and conventional. Moreover, it is in actually living her own experience as a *mother*, that she is going through a religious crisis, while at the same time she is re-living and revising all that she once thought about her own parents. In the history of *H. NP.3*, the mother's preference for her son was very protective, while the father, kept at a distance by the mother, remained distant and cold. Sentiments expressed for God show doubt, remoteness, difficulty of access. Now also, it is in actual life, by bringing up into question what he once saw of the relations between his father and mother (especially in his present relations with his wife) that this subject is undergoing a religious conflict.

Thus it would seem that the test of « parental images » applied to a more varied public as to religious convictions and practice, could reveal certain incidences of relations experienced with parents, explaining religious attitudes or crises. It would be very interesting to discover to what extent or with what frequency certain mechanisms are influential, such as *idealisation*, compensating for parents one has not known, or *accusation* of an imaginary God, the dumping-ground for resentment accumulated in parental relations. And above all, it would interest psychologists and educators to know in which psychological structures these mechanisms end by undermining the religious attitude itself.

We shall end with a quotation from one of our correspondents : « In consultation, I often come across young men and women who, even at the age of 20 or 25, are so little free from parental images, that they do not reach the minimum of independence which would permit them to develop their own religious personality. I am struck and even dismayed at this : will one never break away from the father... ? »

Should the tall tree, rising heavenwards, feel « dismayed » to discover the real nature of its roots, buried and twisted in the soil ? We keep this question in mind as we conclude our research with a few comments.

III. SUMMARY AND COMMENTS

In spite of the still limited number of subjects that our research adds to those of Nelson-Jones and Strunk, we can assert, without too much fear of future contradiction, that certain psychological *trends* come to light in a Christian population (of Western culture like our own) :

a) Parental images play a variable but important part in the psychic conditions from which the evocation of God is built up, and in consequence, from which the psychological attitude to God develops.

b) The conditioned-link (correlations) appears stronger and more frequent with the maternal image among men, and the paternal image among women.

c) This structuration of the evocation of God connected with parental images tends to fade out with age, without possibility of discerning whether this ' purification ' of the psychological disposition towards God is due to an increased spiritual maturity or culture (for example, living among contemplatives, nuns, a life of prayer, theological training, etc.), or to a growng nondifferentiation of both parental images (idealisation of former home conditions through distance from parents or their decease), to both these series of influences combined, or to yet other factors, but little controllable up to now (for example, guilt feelings, hardly noticed but active, at the moment of choosing statements which reflect unfavourably against one parent).

d) Conditioning based on the two parental images is all the stronger when there is a more marked rejection or preference for one of the parents. In this case, the evocation of God can be vigorously drawn towards the characteristics of the parent *preferred*, or seriously compromised by close relation with the *unfavoured* parent (this seems to last a long time with some people). This last situation can practically cause a religious crisis, as the examination of some individual cases, rare enough in our privileged population, led us to suspect.

These were the tendencies observed.

They call for plenty of comment. Here we can only outline them in three directions.

1. *Psychological Reflections.*

The interest of the method we have just applied, in French, is that it allows a much wider approach to a problem which had hardly been mentioned till now except in a clinical, notably psycho-analytical, perspective.

In a book which we review elsewhere in this volume, Margaretta K. BOWERS writes : « How our Semitic ancestors changed from the worship of a Mother-God to that of a Father-God I do not know ; but if we look into the personal unconscious religious life of our patients, we find that their personal God is intrinsically Mother or Father according to their personal life experience and their psycho-sexual development... » [1] This psychotherapist criticizes Freud for analysing the bases of religiosity too exclusively in terms of aggression against the father, neglecting the deep and nostalgic desire to incorporate the mother. She illustrates her views with clinical extracts which she compares with certain observations brought out by contemporary anthropology.

Unlike the authors we have already quoted (Nelson-Jones and Strunk) we do not think that from the data collected, conclusions can be drawn for or against a certain Freudian interpretation of the origins of religiosity. Although the ' chiasmus ', or *cross development* of paternal and maternal images in the feelings of men and women towards God, is one of the most striking statements from this research, we do not see how, from these data, an interpretation for or against the mechanisms at work in the œdipal situation would

---

1. Margaretta K. BOWERS, *Conflicts of the Clergy.* New York, Thomas Nelson, 1963, p. 58.

be justified. To be frank, we do not even see the usefulness of such interpretations *in this context* ; they seem to us too distant to be enlightening, or even to organize better the statistical correlations collected. These, be it remembered, rest on the reactions after reading sixty statements (Nelson-Jones, translated) ; and the selection of these statements might appear rather arbitrary. We have seen how some of our subjects, especially in the groups of nuns and religious men, complained of not finding in the statements the expression of some feelings or attitudes which they deemed more appropriate to their relation with God, without being necessarily excluded from the evocation of parents. The test seems open to improvement on this point.

On the other hand, even within the limits of the 60 statements, the question of the relative *nondifferentiation* towards the two parental images assuredly deserves the attention of research-workers and of psychotherapists.

Personally, we would hesitate to think that the most favourable psychological situation to sustain the development of Christian maturity would be one in which the parental images fuse or melt into an impoverishing idealisation, accompanied with an F-index for God always very high and unruffled. On the contrary, the few conversations we managed outside the application of our test, prompt us to think that clearly differentiated images for both parents, eventually accompanied with a certain aggressiveness or less favour for one of them, correspond in some cases to the awakening of an attitude, *ambivalent* but full of promise, towards the sacred. This slightly ill-at-ease attraction, when it comes to evoke the divine, expresses itself by a choice of statements which are not too exclusively 'favourable.' All said and done, in this state of ambivalent psychic dispositions (reflected in some of the results in our test [1]), the divine mystery seems more susceptible of being approached as a *reality*, [2] as something truly other (is not a certain emotional 'am-

---

1. As examples of subjects in whom psychic dispositions seemed to favour an attitude of Christian maturity towards God, we mention : HA8, aged 39 (whose wife is an unbeliever), paternal preference: Index: God 34, father 55, mother 43. — FA7, aged 34 (father not practising), maternal preference: Index: God 39, father 27, mother 46. — HR8, aged 42; Index: God 48, father 35, mother 36. — FR9, aged 50; Index: God 54, father 26, mother 45.

2. Using Freud's categories, we would say that religious reality should be approached in maturity under the primacy of reality-principle. As Freud says : « The supremacy of the pleasure-principle can end in actuality only with the complete mental detachment from the parents » (*Collected Papers*, Hogarth Press, London, Vol. IV, p. 15, n. 3, « Two Principles in Mental Functioning », 1911). Among the psychoanalists who have not fully discerned the role of the

bivalence' quite normal in face of 'the other' as such?), better protected against the danger of only signifying the imaginary evocation of a beautiful dream, a return to childhood, to a lost paradise, or the hope of a fulfilment of personal integrity, ego-centrically recovered.

Perhaps this perspective opens upon a « spiritual » interpretation of the text in which Saint Matthew speaks of Our Lord who « came to set a man at variance against his father, and the daughter against her mother, and the daughter-in-law against her mother-in-law » (X, 35); a hard but beneficial reality, different enough from the euphoric myth of parental images reconciled at last...

2. Theological and Phenomenological Comments.

To theologians, the results of research such as this, place an old question on a new basis, very delicate to solve : when we confess as Christians, that « God is our Father, » when we hope to see penetrate, and strive to make sink, even into our psychology, the reality, lived in faith, of our « adoptive filiation, » are we not committing ourselves only to a kind of pure relation to the Father (that is, to a begetting-begotten relation), beyond all representation connected with the phenomenal diversity (father-mother) ? Or may we think that masculinity and femininity, theologically assumed and lived in the divine adoption, are each in their own way, orientated towards a divine term, bearing in some way, certain paternal attributes, distinct from maternal attributes ? [1]

Father in the genesis of religious feeling, and who tend to bring it to the maternal relation, we may mention E. FROMM, Psycho-analysis and Religion (New Haven, Yale Un. Press, 1950, pp. 79-84) and H. ELKIN, « On the Origin of the Self », Psychoanalysis (New York), Vol. 45, No. 4, Winter 1958-59, pp. 57-76. Many psychologists and phenomenologists study religion by analysing the relation to parents without differentiating parental images; for example, the study, interesting however, by H. DIEM, « Was sagt die theologische Anthropologie dem Erzieher über das Kind ? » in Untersuchungen zur Anthropologie des Kindes (Heidelberg, Quelle und Meyer, 1960). More detailed suggestions are to be found in the volume Vorträge über das Vaterproblem (Dr. W. BITTER, editor, Stuttgart, Hippokrates Vg., 1954), especially in the pages by D.A. KÖBERLE, « Vatergott, Väterlichkeit und Vaterkomplex im Christlichen Glauben », and D.O. HAENDLER, « Unbewusste Projektionen auf das Christliche Gottvaterbild und ihre seelsorgerliche Behandlung. »

1. We point out that, put in this way, the question refers rather to certain attributes which would be « paternal » or « maternal » objectively, if one may say so, that is, within a particular culture. Our research, on the contrary, gives series of correlations issuing from individual reactions to family situations, the

Concerning the « Masculinity in the Church, » Father Karl RAHNER wrote in a book recently translated into French :

« We should ask why the Christian message gives God the name of Father (and not Mother). We should ponder over the meaning and limits of such a way of speaking ; this would help to understand, as far as we are able, the weight of the assertion that all paternity (and therefore all virility) is named, that is, receives its very essence from this Heavenly Father (*Eph.*, III, 15). On this point, we need nothing less than a treatise on ontology, hardly sketched so far, on the sound basis and course of the intellectual process by which we use the experience of a world ontologically inferior (here the biological world) as a mass of comparisons and outlines to express realities of a higher order, even if the concepts borrowed from the former can only be *applied* to the latter. We could also ask why the Father's Eternal Word became man rather than woman. » [1]

In answer to this, Father Rahner merely says that for the moment the question is « so difficult that it is impossible to even sketch the solution... » [2]

We have, however, asked the opinion of two professors of theology whose answers proved to be the same over this point [3] : the profession « God is our Father » is connected in some way with the profession « the second Person of the Blessed Trinity is the Son of God » ; in other terms, our adoptive affiliation is thought of in

---

history of which does not necessarily coincide with the images culturally accepted of the father and mother. Nevertheless, since it is through the slant of the family as lived in practice, that cultural determinations (and theological instruction) reach every man and every woman, the two questions, though separate, are so closely connected, that it is legitimate to pass from one to the other, as we do in these last two sections of comments. On cultural variations in conceiving the role of Father, see « Civilisation et paternité » by J. GOETZ, S.J. in *Paternité et Virilité* (Paris, Spes, 1963).

1. Karl RAHNER, S.J., *Serviteurs du peuple de Dieu.* Paris, Mame, 1963, chapter X : L'homme dans l'Eglise, p. 265.

2. *Ib.*, p. 266. It is to be feared that, to obtain « the modification of the image of the threatening father, which was so important in Freud's attack on religion, » some theologians may advise, in pastoral, a return « to God on his self-giving nearness..., by elements of the embracing and supporting mother. » This is the proposal, to our thinking too easy, and even regressive, expressed by the Rev. Paul J. TILLICH, from whom we quote these few words (« Speech on Religion and Psychotherapy, » Academy Reporter, New York, V, 3, March 1960). How much more valuable, even in pastoral, is the dialectic of the *father* and of *death*, of which Père L. BEIRNAERT gives the chief articulations in « Freud, la religion et la civilisation », *Problèmes de psychanalyse* (Paris, Fayard, 1957).

3. While thanking these two professors for their kind reply, we think it best not to publish their names concerning an opinion inevitably simplified, since we are obliged to set it down here so briefly.

relation and in analogy with the Sonship of Christ. The latter
has its *full* meaning independently of *all* connotation of the diversity
father-mother.

This opinion is clear. It speaks in favour of the independence,
by right, of the evocation « God our Father » with regard to any
parental image, even if, *in fact*, there is question of an independence
to be won psychologically (a victory as delicate for men as for
women, as we have seen).

Is it so sure, however, that the filiation of the Word *incarnate*
has its full meaning independently from *all* reference to the father
mother diversity ?...

On this point of theological exegesis, the substratum of Hebrew
mentality would have to be taken into account. Père Xavier Léon-
Dufour points out on this subject :

« It looks as if the guides of Israel wished to purify the idea of paternity
current among their neighbours [for whom the Baals make earthly beings
fruitful] from all sexual associations, in order to retain the one aspect
of transferring to God the social terminology regarding the heads of
families [of a clan : *sheik*] and ancestors. » [1]

Père Philippe remarks, and describes with references to the Old
Testament, [2] how imperfect and vague is the analogy of « generation, » as is testified by the Latinized expression « *in sinu Patris* »
(which we would translate « in the lap of the Father » — for can
one speak of the « bosom of the Father, » except by a bold transposition ?) This expression deserves an attentive (not only philo-
logical) study !

Père L. Beirnaert, on his side, when commenting on a text
from St. Augustine for whom the role of Mother-Church is to lead

---

1. *Vocabulaire de Théologie Biblique.* Ed. du Cerf, 1961, p. 804. We have
added, from the context, the words within brackets.
2. M.D. Philippe, O.P., « Saint Thomas et le mystère de la Sainte Trinité »,
in *Lumière et Vie* (Saint-Alban-Leysse, Savoie, France), No. 30, Nov. 1956,
pp. 73-88. For St. Thomas, what we carry *in sinu*, we carry in secret. There
is something hidden in the Father..., the most secret in the Father's nature and
essence, surpassing all power of the created, is His Only Son, and that is why
He is consubstantial with the Father » (*Com. S. Jean*, Prol., less. XI, no. 218).
In No. 29, of *Lumière et Vie* also (Sept. 1956), A. George recalls the Hebrew
significance of Father, as authority, lord, king, head, leader of a people or
tribe (« Le père et le fils dans les évangiles synoptiques », p. 31). This shows
how the community dimension of Paternity completes, but also corrects, an
instruction, or prayer, based on an individual relation, slightly tinged with
sentimentality, with « the very kind father. »

to Father-God (« *Interposita matris auctoritate, de patre creditur,* » De utilitate credendi, XII, 26), insisted on « the dependence of man as regards the paternal function, without the father being able to be an object of evidence. » He mentioned with Freud « the victory of the spiritual over the senses, which the passing from matriarchate to patriarchate shows ; maternity is revealed through the senses, whilst paternity is a conjecture demanding that man, at the heart of his reality, may recognize a mystery (an absence) which gives him to himself, and to which he has never finished replying. » [1]

There would therefore be in the strictly paternal relation, psychologically tested and phenomenologically analysed, a trait of ' distance ' eventually overcome by the ' Word, ' which admirably suits the relation with God, as it stands out in the Judaeo-Christian tradition. This trait would have less direct basis in the primitive child-mother relationship, or would be deeply different in some matrilineal societies.

Describing the (œdipal) stage when the small boy discovers that the object of his initial love (his mother) is subject to the law of « the other » (his father), Dr. J. LACAN has this striking phrase : « He discovers the mother's relation to *the word* of the father. » And Dr. Serge LECLAIRE comments on this sentence, hoping that « the mother who should be the mediatrix and the way, may no longer impose herself as end and object. » [2]

If this phenomenological analysis must be held as theologically valid, we could see in it the basis of a cleavage between the religiosity to be found fixed and instituted in some primitive religions (often linked to forms of matriarchate), and the evolution of this religiosity in cultures of different structure among which the Jewish religion developed. The conclusion would be to suggest that *if the Mother-image inspires the primordial religiosity of man, and as it were, his pre-history, it is certainly to the Father-image to which it is called to accede (as adopted son), which constitutes his religious and Christian history.*

That there was question not of conscious data, even spiritually acute, but of a work to be accomplished in and by Faith, can easily

---

1. L. BEIRNAERT, « Psychanalyse et mystère de l'homme », dans *Expérience chrétienne et psychologie.* Paris, Ed. de l'Epi, 1964, p. 285.

2. Text from Lacan, quoted by S. LECLAIRE in « L'obsessionel et son désir », *L'Evolution psychiatrique,* 1959, 3, 401, to be put near many texts or stories from the Old and New Testaments where God enters in contact with men by his only WORD. For St. John of the Cross also : « Dios es Voz infinita » (*Cant.* XIII, 10).

be seen by the laborious journeying of the men among whom the maternal image remained too long prevalent. One could understand also that women should be more ' spontaneously ' drawn, and more easily faithful to a ' religion of the Father. ' But these emotional bases of masculine or feminine religiosity evidently have no right to get the last word in the discovery of the mystery of God.

3. *Psycho-educational (Catechetical) Advice.*

The fore-going reflection settles already the limits and uncertainty of all catechetical gloss concerning parental images, the feelings they arouse, and their use in the education of a Christian sense.

Perhaps someone may be tempted to conclude : since theology, when speaking of our adoptive filiation in Christ, does not take up position on its « *phenomenally* paternal » character (that is, different from ' maternal ') or « *purely* paternal » (that is, beyond all connotation of the father-mother diversity), no orientation is imposed in practical catechesis...

This declaration of uncertainty, or assertion of liberty, would not correspond accurately to the terms of the question.

Whatever the theological opinion on the full sense of the term employed, when we profess the divine « Paternity, » it is quite certain that the attitude of the spiritually adult Christian conforms to a quite different model than that which he found in his human father, however perfect this earthly fatherhood may have been. Perhaps it is true that early relation towards the father (or an archetype of father) had some exclusive right to put forward ; perhaps it is true that the child-father relationship possessed some traits which predisposed him to signify the mystery of adoptive filiation (notably that of « word-from-a-distance »), to symbolize a call through which the human being becomes, in God, more fully himself. But even so, the conditionings of the old relation to the father would have to undergo a change and be surpassed, for the Christian attitude of sonship to reach maturity and plenitude of expression.

This can be seen if we compare some of the feelings chosen with enthusiasm, by some of our subjects, to evoke God or their father : *help, support, confidence, protection, proximity, security,* etc. All these feelings, suggested by the statements of our test (which should be applicable with some appropriateness to father, mother or God), are not counter-indicated, indeed, any more than that of *love* (so ambiguous any way) when connected with our attitude before God the Father. Dare we assert that they correspond *by themselves* to those of the man (or woman) whom maturity in spiritual experience is leading to discover existentially (*pati divina*) their encounter with the true God ?... Even without appealing to mystical experience and its vocabulary (*wound, flame, death, night*) is not God-Love revealed as : *friend of poor sinners, servant, humiliated, food, the Saviour accepting death, risen again*, etc. These features in the Gospel, all but slightly conforming to parental images, should therefore come to complete, if not disturb, the ' catechetical reper-tory, ' and mark out the way for adolescents and adults (if not of children) to recognize the living God, as He freely reveals Himself in the word He speaks to us.

A Father both near and distant, longed for but awe-inspiring, fascinating and disturbing, strong yet humiliated : if Christian cate-chesis hopes to prepare the full development of Christian attitudes, it should signify the divine Paternity in some other way than by parental images (either paternal or maternal), evoke other attitudes, other feelings than those aroused by the happiness of a tender home atmosphere, make it understood that the final reality is more than a heaven with a father and mother found again and for ever. Christianity is not simply a religion of happiness in which one is spiritually at ease ; it is not belief and commitment to wonderful persons in the Gospel for commonplace emotional reasons and easy rewards. Christianity means peace, a gift of peace, but a peace to be built up. It is to discover, beyond the needs of a too human religiosity (always threatened by the progress of critical reflection) God as He is, where He says He is, in Jesus Christ, God at work in the world, operating through His Spirit in the sacramental Church.

To recognize this divine Paternity, any parental image is bound to fall short (the maternal image as much, if not more, than the paternal one). A catechesis which, under pretext of winning hearts, encourages these outlines, is in danger of strengthening, unwittingly and in spite of good intentions, these basic conditionings, in danger of delaying spiritual maturity, especially with those who had a more pronounced preference for one parental image. More en-lightened will be the catechesis which seeks to find, beyond parental traits conditioned by culture or personal experience, the paths which help most to draw near to the Father « in spirit and in truth. »

The Idea of God :
Its Emergence Between 7 and 16 years

A *Semantic Approach Using Free Associations*

by Reverend Jean-Pierre DECONCHY
Professor at the Diocesan College of Roubaix[1]

The child hears the word « God » in catechism. He would never discover it alone, even if he starts with an immanent exigence of the sacred (besides the information he receives). This word sinks into the child's panorama of ideas ; it becomes connected with other information, plays the part of a new epicentrum like all the other notions he is taught, enters into a whole network of linguistic and psychological consequences. The idea of God, brought by the word, is fed by all these connections ; it focuses an entire mass of linguistic data, as well as the psychological components, and more strictly intellectual ones which these data take for granted. To get near the child's idea of God, we have tried to disengage the harmonics which the word « God » rouses in the child's mind, thus seeking to reveal a whole series of connections in his psychological and his linguistic field.

I. STAGES AND TECHNIQUE OF THE RESEARCH

Method.

To carry this out we applied a very simple test to a fairly large population ; each subject had to evoke or induce in writing and

1. Reverend Jean-Pierre DECONCHY was born on March 13, 1934, at Tourcoing (Nord). A student at the Faculty of Letters at Lille and Lyons, he obtained a Licenciate in Philosophy. After teaching for several years in Lebanon, he won a Diploma for Higher Studies with a Dissertation on *La lecture du Français et la tendance à l'orientation Droite-Gauche chez l'enfant de langue arabe* (Beyrouth, 1958, 152 p.) at the Ecole Supérieure des Lettres, Beyrouth (Lyons mission university). In 1962, he presented a Memoir at the Faculty of Catholic Theology of Lille to obtain his 'Licence en Théologie' : *Recherches expérimentales sur l'idée de Dieu chez l'enfant: aspects méthodologiques* (Lille, 1962, 202 p.). He received his Doctorate in Theology from the same faculty for his thesis : « *Contribution à l'étude expérimentale des idées religieuses: l'idée de Dieu chez le garçon de 7 à 16 ans* » (Lille, 1963, 575 + 156 p., mimeographed copy $ 10.00 at the address below). At present, Professor at the College of Roubaix (for Philosophy), he continues research into the semantic bases of religious vocabulary and its psychological vibration. — Address : 10, rue Notre-Dame des Victoires, Roubaix, FRANCE (Editor's note).

under uniform testing conditions, five associations with the word
« God. » This stimulus word — the only one submitted up to now
to our analyses — was in fact buried in a list of six stimulus
words of religious or secular connotation. This list was definitely
fixed after the text had been tried out previously in groups widely
differing in culture (Secondary and Primary Grades, youth groups,
delinquents, mental defectives) and according to provisional techniques (paper-and-pencil tests, interviews, oral replies, work in
groups).

Population.

The experimental basis for interpretation was so restricted that
we had to apply it to a fairly large population. The overall population included 8,062 children from 7-16 years (4,163 boys and
3,899 girls) divided into 266 groups tested by 147 examiners under
rigorously identical testing conditions. [1]

We considered that only a study of children effectively taught could
be enlightening ; we did not aim at disengaging a priori structures
of the religious attitude previous to organized catechesis. For practical
reasons we chose denominational schools only, all situated in and
around Lille and Dunkerque (Diocese of Lille). This homogeneous
geographical origin of our subjects was naturally the first guarantee
which our samping work should have, a work of much importance. The
population in the denominational schools naturally does not present the
same socio-cultural characteristics as that on which we wish to base our
study : all the children from 7-16 taught in the diocese of Lille. As
criteria of this sampling we first took the ' Catégories Socio-Profession-
nelles ' used in the census of 1954 reduced to the figures of tens, the
differential fecundity of each *C.S.P.* (information supplied by the ' Institut
National des Statistiques et des Études Économiques '), and the indication
of instruction of the children from each *C.S.P.* The Diocesan Centre for
Socio-Religious Studies had undertaken an analysis of this last criterion
(the interest of which is obvious), but it was not yet available. This led
us to use the co-efficient of the Sunday religious practice of the father
in each *C.S.P.*, doubtless an imperfect criterion, but probably fairly representative of the father's interest in the religious instruction of his
children. The 10 partial samples constructed for each sex and corresponding
to an age-year, thus retained 2,389 boys (or 57.38 % of the overall population, and 64.04 % of the population effectively used) and 2,344 girls
(58.31 % and 67.73 %). These 4,733 subjects were taken from the population according to the rules of Random-sampling.

---

1. We regret that the importance of these groups was not more homogeneous.
For an average of 30.30 individuals by testing group, the standard-deviation
is 14.90 — which is obviously rather high.

Organization of the Induced Words.

It was from a sub-sample, also taken at random that we sought to organize the semantic material thus obtained from the stimulus word GOD.

Obviously we could not discover *patterns* of connection between linguistic elements at the very level of the mass of 23,665 induced words presented by the 4,733 sets retained for analysis from the sample ; their number and diversity (2,398 different elements) makes such a task unthinkable without electrical computers.

The 876 real induced words (the others were 'white' answers), using 307 different linguistic elements, have been re-grouped according to their probable resemblance of content. Such re-grouping in « *themes* » destined to organize all the induced words in the experimental sample clearly presents a big problem in method.

In fact, one may wonder whether in doing so, we are not already presuming as known the connections these themes should reveal ; will not these connections be, at the same time, of measured and of measuring ? In reality, we do not think that this re-grouping in themes at the level of the more easily managed sub-sample, argues knowledge of the connections before classification. We think we have made re-groupings recognized as such at the cultural and institutional level. It remains for us to realize, as a self-evident definition, that this ambiguity of measuring and measured is inevitable, and all we can do is to restrict and weaken it.

The simplest example of this is the dictionary, in which any linguistic element is « *defined* » by other linguistic elements, themselves needing to be *defined*, sometimes (with or without intermediary) by the very elements they have helped to define.

We have then to find language to translate the enormous linguistic matter (organized into sets of five elements at the most) at our disposal, language with the *themes* as elements. These *themes* must be both numerous enough to create a sufficient power of separation (one might say, their quantity of information) and few enough for economy in operative use. After some hesitation, we settled upon 27 themes, a 28th. to receive nondescript induced words and a 29th. to reckon the white answers. By current statistical means we verified that this distribution in *29 themes* could not be put down to random reckoning. The reader will find these 29 themes listed in TABLE I (p. 289).

To appreciate the mass of induced words in the sample by these themes, it cannot be determined once and for all by what theme such a linguistic element is to be mechanically understood whatever its real meaning. For example, the word « *love* » has a notably different connotation depending on whether it designates *descending* love (from God to us) or *ascending* love (from us to God); the word « *heaven* » has a special status depending on accompanying induced words describing *created nature*, or the « *situs* » of God, or an *eschatological* idea. Each individual series, therefore, had to be examined separately.

The 29 themes taken from the sub-sample, and which served to organize the induced words of the whole sample (23,665 elements) proved very satisfactory (from the formal standpoint, of course); in fact, the distribution in 29 themes of the induced words of the sub-sample (from which they were taken) and the distribution of induced words from the experimental sample show a correlation of .931 for the boys, .955 for the girls, and of .958 for the whole population (Bravais-Pearson coefficient).

Quadruple Statistical Elaboration.

To treat the data statistically, we worked at the level of each partial sample, confined to an age-year (separating the sexes, of course). We can only give a brief survey of this work here.

a) From the *quantitative and statistical* angle, we chiefly tried to give the typical answer for each age (or TYPICAL FORMULA), indicating the distribution of 5 theoretical induced words in the 29 themes of examination, and to note exactly the formal status of this distribution. Speaking structurally, this *Typical Formula* differs notably from the individual series by the use it makes or can make of the 29 themes.

Thus a set like John's (aged 8) (« *Powerful*, » « *Strong*, » « *Good*, » « *To pray*, » « *Mass* ») uses successively the *themes* of « Power » (twice), « Goodness, » « Prayer, » and « Worship and Sacraments. » As example, we give the histogrammic representation of the Typical Formula for boys of 7, and in contrast, that for boys of 14 (TABLE I).

It was during this first stage that we measured the tendency of a theme to appear grouped, which we called COAGULATION. One frequency can characterize quite different situations for two themes within the same sample. For instance, at 16 the themes Spirituality of God and Sovereignty have the same frequence (.19), which corresponds to an effective number of induced words equal to 18. But this score of 18 has been obtained by very different ways : 14 subjects gave in the theme spirituality with only one induced word, while 2 others gave groups of 2 induced words ; in contrast, Sovereignty was given singly by 9 subjects, in groups of 2 induced words by 3 subjects, and in a group of 3 induced words by one subject. Therefore, the theme Spirituality is less « redundant, » so to speak, than Sovereignty ; simple calculation can mark very usefully this difference of status. That is what our COEFFICIENT OF COAGULATION means.

b) From the *quantitative and dynamic* angle, besides the study of the evolution of dispersion parameters for the coefficients of the 29 themes in the Typical Formulas, we tried to *compare these distributions* (in 29 themes) of the 5 induced words by calculation of the COEFFICIENTS OF CORRELATION (Bravais-Pearson); it was the only way to find out *stages* in development. This led us to divide that of the boys (the only sample finished so far) into 5 phases : 7 years, 8-9-10 years, 11-12-13 years, 14-15 years and 16 years. The stage between the 3rd. and 4th. period was

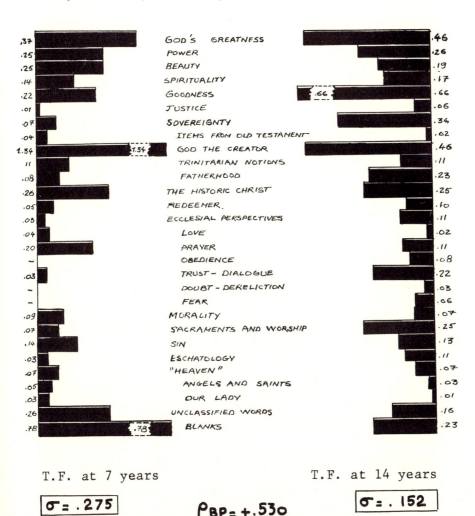

	T.F. at 7 years		T.F. at 14 years

$$\boxed{\sigma = .275} \qquad \rho_{BP} = +.530 \qquad \boxed{\sigma = .152}$$

TABLE 1

TYPICAL FORMULAS FOR BOYS OF 7 AND 14

particularly hard to determine (As example, we have reported the Bravais-Pearson coefficient of correlation (BP = +.530) in TABLE I).

c) From a *qualitative and statistical* angle, we have tried to reconstruct the connections found in each of the individual series on the general level. For each theme we established a COEFFICIENT OF CO-PRESENCE (for each age-year). We thought this analysis important since it allows us to perceive the repulsion or attraction that each theme shows in regard to the others, and this at differential level.

This calculation is particularly suggestive. Let us take for example the *Typical Formula* for 7 year-olds. Three themes being absent (Obedience, Doubt, Fear), this Typical Formula collects 26 frequencies (out of 5 theoretical induced words) which it presents univocally placing them side by side. Among these 26 frequencies, let us take « God's Greatness » (0.37) and « Prayer » (0.20); these are two fairly marked frequencies which the Typical Formula places opposite one another. Now, if we refer to the protocols of the boys aged 7, we discover that *not one* of the individual series contains *both* the themes « God's Greatness » and « Prayer. » It is obvious that it is very important to know this repulsion, as will be the knowledge of the degree of attraction each theme reveals for the others. The coefficient of co-presence is therefore extremely useful.

d) From a *qualitative and dynamic* angle, we tried to calculate the active part taken by each of the 29 themes in development strictly envisaged from the angle of the evolution of the Typical-formula considered as a structure. Taking each of the series of ten frequencies marking the evolution between 7-16 years, from each of the 29 themes as distribution of a variable, we went on to a FACTOR ANALYSIS of this development, all the correlations being taken as positives, since the total of these frequencies is also a constant. It was thus possible to calculate for the *evolution* of each theme its saturation in a *« Factor Delta »* or Organizer of Development. This factorial strength does not depend on the massive presentation of a theme. A theme such as « Goodness of God » which is quantitatively the strongest theme of the whole evolution is only saturated at .71 in *Factor Delta* (14,5th. rank), while « Justice of God, » very rarely sent in, is saturated at .84 (2,5th. rank), which can probably be attributed to its re-actional power, which links it to the movement of growth, adolescence especially.

II. SOME RESULTS

We cannot examine here in detail an interpretation which no doubt allows us to disengage some very clear connections between different elements of vocabulary, certain semantic harmonics aroused by the inducing word GOD, and the psychological vibration it seems to have for children. Each of the 5 phases sketched above had been subjected to careful study based on statistical analysis enlightened, when necessary, by reference to the individual series.

This enabled us to study for each phase : the idea of God the Creator, the transcendence of God and His essential attributes. Christ, the idea of God as a person, the emotional effect of the idea of God, parental relations and their influence on the idea of God, God and action.

We would like to give some idea of the whole of this interpretation by noting what seems to us the organization of development as such, and then describing very briefly some of the operations the child performs to aim at the being of God.

1. *Three Stages of Development.*

Development between the ages of 7-16 seems to be organized in three stages.

a) A first phase could be called ATTRIBUTIVITY, with its peak at about 9 or 10 years. The child would be led to think of God chiefly (not exclusively) through means of attributive data recently learnt at school. Among the attributes learnt and revealed in the test of associations, we seem to discover three attributive levels of very different status and very specific factorial tenor. A first attributive cluster would form round the attributes Greatness, Omniscience, Omnipresence, Spirituality... we would call these *objective-attributives*. A second cluster would group « qualities » of God like Goodness and Justice, easily made interior ; there would be *subjective-attributives*. A third attributive cluster would form round the attributes of Strength and of Beauty (*affective-attributives*) the plasticity of which is far the most remarkable of the whole. These three layers, with very specific factorial activities, seem to converge towards a unification, the principal agents of which may be the attributes of Strength and Beauty. We think (many differential indices seem to confirm our views) that this unification (specially made apparent by the co-presences more and more frequent which the attributive themes sustain among themselves) reveals a whole effort at aiming towards God's Transcendence. Once this unification is reached, and the attributive edifice is coherently set up, the attributive vogue fades. All the effort tending to establish God in Transcendence is no longer made in a strictly attributive perspective. The attributive phase then gives way to another, in virtue even of the dynamism of the themes called *affective-attributives* (Strength and Beauty).

b) This second phase, which could be called PERSONALIZATION, is probably rooted into the attributive level by these two latter themes. During this phase, with its peak at 12-13 years, stress is found on three themes, whose developments are closely parallel between 7-

16 years, and whose respective saturations in Factor Delta are similar ; these themes are Sovereignty, Redeemer, and Fatherhood. Of very specific content, they tend to converge, however, towards more and more marked co-presences, at the risk of losing their specificity. Rather like the previous phase, the personalization phase gives way before another one.

c) The third phase, with its peak at 15-16, could be called the phase of INTERIORIZATION. From the quantitative angle, it is marked by a great rise in the themes called subjective : Love, Prayer, Obedience, Trust-Dialogue, Doubt-Dereliction, and Fear. The themes, Trust-Dialogue, and Fear are the most active, but their respective factorial tenors are very specific. Both organize development of the subjective attitude as a whole, as a factorial analysis limited to the development of subjective themes shows. The theme Trust-Dialogue, massively saturated in the *Factor Delta* (general development), probably assures an equalizing role in the insertion of subjective development into global development ; the themes of Trust and of Dialogue with God would then give a guarantee of harmony in development. In contrast, the themes of Fear and Doubt, which bring with them indisputable reactional links, play only a very small role in the whole of development. Thus, Fear and Doubt, powerful organizers of emotional development, would be disturbers of development. We regret not being able to presume the future of this phase of interiorization, since our sample stops at the age of 16.

Even at the 14-16 stage, the study of Typical Formulas and the connections of the themes *among themselves* has a certain interest. Perhaps we find there (this time transversally) the three phases of *attributivity - personalization - interiorization* which we seemed to detect in the chronological axis (longitudinally). In the adolescent we hardly ever find attributive themes given at the same time as subjective ones. And yet, attributive themes appear in very frequent connection with personalist themes, which are just as closely connected with themes of interiorization. Just as, chronologically speaking, the personalization phase was a transition between attributivity and interiorization, with the young adolescent, the interior God (Whom he likes to contemplate in intimate sweetness) may only have attributive roots through the intermediary of personalist themes. If these disappear for one reason or another, there will be the gap between the God *of his thoughts* (attributivity) and the God *of his life* (interiority) ; either he will have an abstract idea of God without living contact, or he will live in contact, or think so, without wishing to know Who He is. Many statistical signs suggest that personalist themes are threatened, partly for their integration in pure attributivity (saying that God is Ruler, Saviour and Father, becomes a mere idea), partly for their immersion in the immanence of interiority (saying that God is Ruler, Saviour and Father to stir a heart that yearns for the ineffable).

We can see : an analysis of development on the purely statistical level, even if a bit rugged in some aspects, can lead to very concrete and discriminating psychological data in the end. We can perceive, in the 14-16 year olds, *the three extreme* (and excessive) *types of the religious attitude we find in adolescents* ; either making God a *problem*, all the more *metaphysical* that He may serve as instinct of defence against the difficulties of more concrete life ; or else making God into a *person*, but seeing Him chiefly as a *danger* to budding personality, turning the instincts of defence into fear, aggressiveness and doubt ; or lastly, *dreaming* of God, losing Him in the *softness* of a shadowy intimacy.

2. *Some Psycho-semantic Operations.*

Each period of development has been studied in detail ; here, we only wish to indicate a few points of general interest.

a) If, from the very first phase, a delicate work of co-adaptation of the attributes among themselves, tends to see God as truly transcendent, it goes without saying that this transcendence is not caught at once, and the being of God is tinged with *anthropomorphism* for a very long time. Yet prudence is needed here, we should not think too easily that this anthropomorphism is just flatly physical. Of a bearded, muscular, marble statue God, we found practically no trace. But a moral anthropomorphism remains in the child's mind for a long time. This makes God « *obliging,* » « *devoted,* » « *kindly,* » « *fair,* » « *sincere* » : transposing to God, moral imperatives which have weight in the child's axiology. We have also found a kind of empathic anthropomorphism, fairly akin to the preceding kind ; this leads the child to say that God is « *cheerful,* » « *glad,* » « *happy* » and « *joyful,* » probably because the child has been told that by serving God or in seeing Him (later on) he will be glad, happy and joyful.

These entertaining and very « human » induced words applied to God (not only about Our Lord) lead us to think that some exteriorly very sound induced words (« *great,* » « *strong,* » « *good* ») are also undermined by anthropomorphism. Nevertheless, we think that this anthropomorphism is not quite so coarse as is generally supposed, and is a particularly primitive form of analogical thought, already not entirely flat and inert. Analysis of the series given on GOD, FATHER, MOTHER, reveals a real anaphatic[1] activity between the qualities attributed or denied to parents and the attributes assigned to God. This activity rejoices in comparatives, superlatives and absolute superlatives. It is not without interest also to notice that at the peak-moment of attributivity, deprivative or negative types of words abound.

b) We should give in detail the evolution of the idea of *God the Creator*. The theme is massively present, with all the marks of an *easy* theme. Its evolution of frequency (cf. TABLE 2) follows closely that of the blanks, obviously the easiest of all. Inflation of this theme is partly caused by a tendency to join this idea with series descriptive of nature : a nature from which God does not seem disengaged, especially not in the axis of a causal relation.

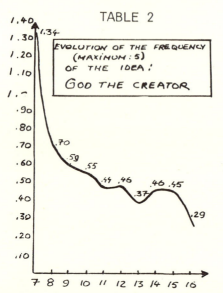

TABLE 2

Between the ages of 7-13 the theme slowly declines from a quantitative angle. The idea of creation instead of extending in a description (enthusiastic, be it said) of nature, focuses more and more upon something beyond nature. This is particularly noticeable by the fall in co-agulations. The word *creator*, practically absent at 7 when the theme is at its height, becomes more and more frequent. Besides, the theme of creation which, at 7 and 8, seems unwilling to join attributive themes, links stronger and stronger co-presences with them, at least, as long as the phase of attributivity lasts.

When sorting out, at a statistical level, this attributive tonality of the theme Creation, we are bound to pass over the originality of some series which, quite exceptionally, reveal that a certain child has got beyond the attributive magma, and can perhaps already penetrate the essential of God's plan for man. Thus YVON (aged 8) gives in five induced words nearly all narrative in style : « *Creates*

---

1. By this word 'anaphatic' we transpose the concept of 'analogy' to the semantic sphere.

the earth, » « *has created us,* » « *does not forsake us,* » « *forgives us,* » « *good.* » The series is exceptional, but mentioning it humanizes the rigidity of statistical analysis...

As long as transcendence is not arrived at, the causal link cannot be established. A causal link supposes two coherent and distinct beings, although susceptible of union by one existential aim. The principle of causality is only the onto-dynamic aspect of a metaphysics of participation. As long as the being of God is even slightly immersed in nature, there is no real causal link. It is only with the 12 year-olds that we begin to find the word CREATOR and a description of nature in the same series. Until then, no child succeeds in placing the two words simultaneously.

Incapable of establishing in a causal link the relation God-World, the child slips between the two still insufficiently separated terms of activities of substitute. First, he will think of the creative activity as an artisan type : comparisons of the series of induced words from FATHER are enlightening, like the statistical status of the notion of creation given on GOD, and that of the idea of work given on FATHER. Then — and we think transcendence gains here — the notion *miracle* will come in between God the Creator and the created world ; this is probably the last stage before the true aim at a real causality.

The decline of the quantitative importance of the theme God the Creator betrays less a diminution of interest in the idea of creator than a slow labour of tearing away God the Creator from the created world. We think it is less the idea of God the Creator that helps to situate the Transcendence of God, than the latter which is indispensable to really establish God as Creator. Since the Transcendence of God will not be truly placed until He is truly placed as a Person during the phase of personalization (during which the co-presences of this theme with those of Sovereignty, Fatherhood and Saviour are very marked) we can see that things are not easy.

It will have been noticed that at 14-15 years, the frequency of the theme ceases to diminish and even increases significantly. This urge seems to be caused by a certain sexualization of the idea of God the Creator. Study of the words induced from that of MOTHER shows that till now the activity of God had been essentially considered as paternal, but gradually it becomes maternal in tone. MOTHER by itself is more and more presented as « *creating,* » and in series with clearly sexual connotations.

c) It seems that many ideas in catechism get lost through « *anecdotality,* » without much psychological striking of roots. This appears through a whole net-work of converging connections among a mass of details about the life of Christ, hagiography and ritual activity. In one series, an induced word like « *cross* » serves as a hinge between description of the Gospel Christ and words referring to religious objects or furniture : altar, chair, holy water stoup. The « apostles » and other figures that surround the historic Christ are placed beside more recent saints (Saints Bruno, Vincent, Remy), more unexpected (« Patron » Saint) or less... admissible (Santa Claus). Ritual activity, especially, calls forth a massive list of induced words, but does not seem to have much influence at the aim of the being of God. It seems to exhaust itself in anecdotality.

d) A function, which might be termed « *pantheon*, » unites a disorder of ideas, Christological, Trinitarian, Old Testament, hagiographical and mythological. Connections between mythological and biblical material, especially in Grade VI, are exceptionally frequent and rather alarming. Most of the children of this age gave a series like this : « *Athene*, » « *Jesus-Christ*, » « *Pharaoh*, » « *Julius Caesar*, » « *Moses*. »

e) It is interesting to observe how the *transcendence* of God tends to establish itself also as regards a group of spiritual subjects : angels, saints and even devils. Notions of the Trinity, however, are almost entirely of logomachical type. Even up to 13 or nearly, the series quoting or suggesting the three Persons of the Blessed Trinity stop thereafter and are hardly ever completed ; the child is caught by a kind of verbal rhythm he cannot get out of. A series on the Trinity, starting from any Person but the Father, is never complete, or else off into sheer fantasy. Daniel (aged 11) gave in : « *Holy Spirit*, » « *the Father*, » « *the Mother*, » « *the Son*, » (*Blank*).

*

*   *

We cannot go into the details of the analyses of which these pages can only be a brief summary. Nor can we stay satisfied with our first results, which have already demanded more than five years work. The method has seemed to us efficient and we intend to make use of it again, without being so lacking in common sense — or humour — as to think it is the only one, or even think that it is the best, and realizing above all that it raises delicate epistemological problems.

We intend to attempt the same study on the sample with Girls, as soon as possible. We have already undertaken the study of the parallel development of semantic sub-foundations and the psychological associations of stimulus words with *secular* tonality, with the aim of settling the eventual specificity of the stimulus word GOD.

Petitionary Prayer :
Belief in its Appropriateness
and Causal Efficacy
among Adolescent Girls

R.H. Thouless, *University of Cambridge,*
and L.B. Brown, *University of Adelaide* [1]

Two Meanings of ' Prayer '.

The popular use of the word 'prayer' is often restricted to an individual or communal utterance directed to God or some supernatural being, in the form of a request or petition that some desired change shall take place in the physical world, in the petitioner himself, or in other people. The efficacy of prayer in this sense is commonly judged to be the extent to which the results asked for are supposed to have been attained as a result of the utterance of the prayer.

The religious writer, on the other hand, uses the word ' prayer ' in a much more extended sense for utterances or certain other kinds of behaviour which have as their aim the bringing of the person praying into relationship with a postulated supernatural world. Prayer then covers a large class of « acts » including praise,

1. R.H. Thouless was born in Norwich (England) in 1894. After a degree in Natural Science at Cambridge and service in the first world war, he took a Ph.D. degree at Cambridge with a dissertation on the psychology of religion (published in 1923 as *An Introduction to the Psychology of Religion*). He has taught in the Psychology Departments of Manchester and Glasgow Universities and in the Education Department of Cambridge University. He retired from his teaching post at Cambridge in 1961 and spent a year lecturing in various Universities in Australia. — Address: 2 Leys Road, Cambridge, Great Britain.

L.B. Brown was born in Wellington, New Zealand, in 1927 and studied at Victoria University of Wellington until he went to London for post-graduate study in psychology. He completed a Ph.D. at the University of London in 1954 and since 1957 has been a faculty member of the Psychology Department in the University of Adelaide, South Australia. He has recently been working on a series of studies concerned with the correlates of religious belief, as well as a study of anxiety and illness. — Address: Department of Psychology, University of Adelaide, Adelaide, South Australia. (Editor's note).

offering, acts of faith, thanksgiving, penitence, and submission, as well as making petitions. The efficacy of prayer becomes its success in achieving a relationship with the supernatural order. Prayer which embodies requests is a sub-class and the extent to which objects of petitionary prayer are observably attained becomes only a part of what is meant by ' the efficacy of prayer. ' This part may conveniently be called the ' causal efficacy of petitionary prayer. '

The second wider use of prayer is the one here assumed although it is with the narrower problems of petitionary prayer that our enquiry was primarily concerned. We asked our subjects questions about their use of prayer in seeking benefits for themselves and for others, and we enquired into their belief in its causal efficacy as a means of controlling the course of events. Suggestions have sometimes been made as to how the causal efficacy of petitionary prayer could be scientifically tested ; with such tests the psychologist is not directly concerned. He is, however, concerned with such questions as that of how far causal efficacy is believed in by the person praying, of how far belief in causal efficacy is regarded as a necessary justification for the practice of petitionary prayer, and of how far and in what situations people believe it to be right to use petitionary prayer.

Two Uses of Speech.

When petitionary prayer is regarded as an effective means of controlling or modifying outside events, it belongs to the class of verbal sequences having the purpose of environmental control. Other examples are charms and spells. In all of these cases a sequence of words is used with the purpose not of *communication* but of *direct environmental control.* [1] For this class, which includes petitionary prayer so far as its object is its causal efficacy, we may use the term Environment Controlling Verbal Sequence (ECVS). ECVSs are part of a larger class of magical or quasi-magical methods of getting results, which includes the use of lucky objects (such as a rabbit's foot) or of environment controlling gestures (such as that of crossing the fingers to avert ill-luck).

---

1. Italics are ours. The difficulty of categorisation, both of prayer and of the behaviour patterns called ' magical, ' comes from the fact that both of these can be treated as ways of communicating, or achieving unity, with a supernatural Being or a transcendental reality, at the same time as one hopes for certain modifications in things or persons in this world. Nevertheless, one cannot overlook the usefulness of the psychological categories of ' modification ' and ' communication, ' as ways of evaluating the attitudes of people praying. Otherwise it

Main Goal of this Investigation.

The present investigation is concerned with only a limited aspect of the psychological problems of petitionary prayer, since such prayer may be valued for reasons other than a belief in its causal efficacy. We had originally planned a wider enquiry into the relation of belief in the causal efficacy of petitionary prayer to belief in the effectiveness of other ECVSs, but it became clear that this would spread a single enquiry too widely. We have however retained from the original plan two items of magical or quasi-magical practices : crossing the fingers and carrying a St. Christopher medallion. The primary purpose of our enquiry was to examine beliefs about the propriety of petitionary prayer and about its causal efficacy in certain situations. These situations can be regarded as varying in three main dimensions :

a) as to the moral value of the action or object prayed about,

b) as to the type of end prayed for, whether a change in the outside world, in the behaviour of other people, or for a spiritual end, and

c) the direction of the petition, whether to the ends of the person praying, to those of a social group to which he belongs, or to those of some other person or group (these may be briefly referred to as ' me-directed, ' ' us-directed ' or ' them-directed ').

Another respect in which the situations varied was as to whether the person prayed for knew, or did not know that prayers were being offered for him.

The question as to the appropriateness of prayer was whether it was ' *right* ' to pray in the stated situation. No explanation was given as to what was here meant by ' *right,* ' since the problem was how the subject would think she ought to behave in the imagined situation. To find opinions about causal efficacy, subjects were asked whether the use of prayer would affect what happened. Obviously there are many difficulties in such a question, but we found that our subjects generally gave a simple ' yes ' or ' no ' answer.

---

would be difficult to distinguish between the magical and the religious components in mental life, sometimes too much confounded, sometimes too much separated, according to the philosophical or religious presuppositions of the person writing. The aim of *modification* and the aim of *unifying communication* are two fundamental purposes behind speech, *even in dialogue between two human beings,* and the interaction of these two aims in prayer requires more exact knowledge and more careful attention than has often been given to them by the religious educators of our time. — *Editor's note.*

The experimental material.

Following a method originally employed by Piaget (1932) and also used by Godin and Van Roey (1959) to explore ' magical mentality ' in young children's use of prayer, the subjects were given a series of problem-stories. The stories embodying these problems were each on a separate sheet of paper with questions below them and spaces for the subject's replies. To reproduce all this material would take too much space, so only one of them will be presented in full and the others briefly described. [1] The third item (c) may be taken as typical.

C. « Miss Smith kept the accounts of a small firm. Once she took £ 5 from the cash box to buy a new hat to wear to a wedding, with the intention of paying it back when she received her wages at the end of the month. She prayed earnestly that the loss would not be discovered before she had paid back the £. »

Questions. Was she right to pray that the loss would not be discovered ?
Why do you think this ?
Would her prayer have made it less likely that she would be found out ?
Why do you think this ?
Was there anything else that Miss Smith should have done ?
What do you think is important in this story ?

There were thirteen items in all, which we may distinguish by the letters A to N. The first two dealt not with petitionary prayer, but with magical control of the environment. They were,

A. A story of a boy who committed a theft, crossed his fingers and wished he would not be found out. (Crossing the fingers is an act commonly reputed in Great Britain and in Australia to avert ill-luck, particularly when making a wish.) Questions were asked about the effectiveness both of the wish to escape detection and of crossing the fingers.

B. A story of a young man who placed a St. Christopher medallion on his sports car, hoping that this would make him safer. The questions concerned the effectiveness of this use of the medallion.

The next six items (c to h) all concerned petitionary prayer in different types of situation and the questions were similar to those already given for item c. These items were :

D. A boy who accidentally broke a window prayed that he should not be found out.

---

1. Copies of the questionnaire may be obtained from the Australian author of the study: Dr. L.B. Brown, Department of Psychology, University of Adelaide, Adelaide, South Australia.

E. A man invested some money in oil shares, hoping that they would rise in value so that he could afford a better car than his neighbour. He prayed that his shares would increase in value.

F. Another man wanted money to pay his household bills and so put £ 5 as a bet on a horse and prayed that the horse would win. The horse did win and Mr Jones could pay his bills.

G. A Minister said, « We are having our Church Fete next Saturday. You must all pray for fine weather. »

H. A girl used to pray every morning that she might be kept safe during the day. One day she forgot to pray and was knocked down by a car that afternoon. (No question was asked here about the rightness of prayer.)

The next item (I) related not to the causal efficacy of petitionary prayer, but to Mr Giles, a farmer, who sowed his pumpkin seed at the time of the New Moon and sent his biggest pumpkins to an orphanage as a thanksgiving for his harvest. One year he sold all his pumpkins, and sent none to the orphanage and in the following year he did not bother about the time of sowing. Now his pumpkins did very badly. The questions concerned the relative causal efficacy of the gift to the orphanage, the time of sowing, and the weather. As this item raised many issues not closely related to the main purpose of the study, we have not made any direct reference to the results. Belief in the efficacy of such sacrificial behaviour as sending gifts to an orphanage is peripheral to the question of petitionary prayer.

The item J concerned a prayer for escape. The situation involved a boy who had fallen into the sea from a yacht. While swimming towards a rescuing dinghy he saw the fin of a shark between him and the boat. The usual questions were asked, with the additional question, « Would he be more likely to escape the shark if the man in the boat prayed, too ? » The purpose of this question was to see if the expected causal efficacy would be different for a prayer for oneself from a prayer for another, but it was apparent that the question was interpreted as asking whether the prayer of the man in the boat would produce additional causal efficacy to that of the prayers of the person in the water. This grammatical ambiguity makes the replies uninterpretable.

Items K and L were of a different character. In K the situation was a school cricket match for which the senior boys discussed a suitable form of prayer. Five suggestions were presented, ranging from simple petition for victory to total submission to the will of God. Item L suggested the same forms of prayer but with reference to an impending battle as a situation of greater seriousness. In both of these items subjects were asked whether they would have voted for any of the suggested forms, which they would prefer, and the reason for their choice. These two items promise interesting results but their interpretation is complex and will not be undertaken here since they represent attempts to go beyond the simple problem of belief in the rightness and in the causal efficacy of petitionary prayer.

The two final items, **M** and **N**, were concerned with petitionary prayer for other people. **M** concerned a person, John, who had the habit of praying each evening for members of his family, mentioning each by name. He forgot to do this one evening and heard next day that his

brother, Jim, had been injured in a car accident. No question was asked
about the rightness or propriety of such praying and the question was
whether the accident to Jim would have been less likely if John had
not forgotten to pray for him. The last item, **N**, was about Jill who
prayed for her old grandmother who had been taken to hospital, seriously
ill. The question here was whether Jill's prayers would make any difference to her grandmother if her grandmother had known she was being
prayed for and if she had *not* known she was being prayed for.

In presenting the results, only those answers giving an unqualified
positive response will be considered systematically, although some
analyses of qualitative material will be mentioned.

The subjects.

The subjects for this study were 181 girls from two secondary
schools in Adelaide. One was a Roman Catholic School and the other
a State Technical High School. In both schools second and fourth
year classes were tested, as well as a first year class in the Technical
School. The ages of the subjects ranged from 12 to 17 years. Each
child was asked to state the Church which she attended. On the
basis of these answers the sample has been divided into denominational groups, distinguishing Roman Catholic, Church of England,
the Free or Non-conformist Churches (the main ones being Metho-
dist, Presbyterian, Congregational and Baptist) and those who
attended no Church ('None'). Table I shows the ages and denominational affiliation of the subjects.

TABLE I

Age and denominational affiliation of the sample

	Roman Catholic	*Church of England*	*Free*	*None*
Number	57	24	69	31
Mean age (yrs.)	14.5	14.4	14.6	14.5

The test was administered to the school classes by one of us
(L.B.B.) during school time, without special reference to the fact
that it was concerned with prayer. Each class was told that they
were to be given a series of stories or incidents, after each of which
there were a few questions that they were to answer. They were
encouraged to work quickly, and although no one refused to
cooperate, there were a few who did not attempt some of the
items. As it is not known whether the refusals were due simply

to lack of time, or whether it was thought that some of the items were too difficult or meaningless, the unanswered items have been disregarded, and the percentages reported have been calculated over the subjects who answered.

Pupils at a third State school completed five of the items. These results are not reported here since they do not differ significantly in any response category from those in the State Technical High School. The very close similarity between these two quite different samples may be seen as giving some evidence of reliability.

Results and discussion :
1. Superstitious practices compared with prayer.

Two of the items referred to behaviour of a semi-magical nature, and it is interesting to notice whether opinions as to the effectiveness of the practices of crossing the fingers and carrying a St. Christopher medallion show age and denominational trends similar to those observed for the prayer items. The medallion item is not ideally chosen to contrast with prayer since the Roman Catholics were found to interpret the situation differently from the Protestants. This is shown by answers to the question about how the medallion might be effective. Almost all of the Church of England and Free Church children who gave a reason thought the effectiveness wou'd depend on ' having faith. ' The Roman Catholics on the other hand gave a variety of answers, including ' Christ protects ' (without elaboration) or ' He protects if you have enough faith ' and ' He protects if you obey the law of the road, ' each of these being given with the same frequency. A few said ' The medallion would make him remember. ' These answers are too inexplicit to interpret certainly, but they do point to the importance of considering both background factors and the kind of formal instruction that has been given, in interpreting results from this study.

The answers expressing an unqualified belief that the medallion would be effective can be compared with unqualified belief in crossing the fingers as an effective means of avoiding detection in a theft, and with the mean responses to questions of the efficacy of prayer in the situations C, D, E, F, G, J, and N (omitting answers to the question about the effect of the friend praying in item J) as shown in Table II.

The results must be accepted with some caution because of the relatively small sample of activities tested, but they point to some conclusions. Beliefs concerning the causal efficacy of petitionary prayer seem, within the age range tested, to fall off from 35.2 per cent in the youngest group to 19.4 per cent in the oldest group.

There are no significant differences in this belief between the Roman Catholic group with 32.6 per cent, and the Free Church group with 28.6 per cent and the Church of England with 24.4 per cent. It is rather surprising to find that those with no religious affiliation show 18.4 per cent believing in the causal efficacy of petitionary prayer.

TABLE II

The causal efficacy of prayer and superstitious practices (unqualified positive answers)

	DENOMINATIONAL AFFILIATION				TOTAL	AGE GROUPS		
	R.C.	C. of E.	Free	None		12-13	14-15	16-17
Efficacy of prayer	177 33 %	47 24 %	167 29 %	46 18 %	437 28 %	112 35 %	251 29 %	74 19 %
Finger-crossing (A)	12 21 %	9 38 %	17 25 %	6 19 %	44 24 %	9 26 %	30 29 %	5 11 %
Medallion (B)	28 50 %	4 17 %	8 12 %	4 13 %	44 24 %	11 31 %	25 25 %	8 18 %

Belief in the efficacy of the magical practice of finger-crossing is highest in the Church of England group and lowest in the Roman Catholic group, in which the percentage is only slightly higher than for those with no religious affiliation. It has already been noted that the use of a St. Christopher medallion may not be a purely magical practice for all subjects, and it is therefore not surprising that 50 per cent of the Roman Catholics and 16.7 per cent of the Church of England group stated belief in this question. In all but the Roman Catholic group the percentage expressing belief is lower for the medallion than for the finger-crossing. The age trend for belief in the medallion is similar to that for the effectiveness of prayer.

A declining tendency to believe in the efficacy of petitionary prayer as a means of achieving results in the outside world, or in influencing other people does not, of course, imply declining belief in the value of prayer. The age trend may mean that older children are adopting a more mature attitude towards prayer, and are not regarding it as a means of gearing supernatural powers to personal ends. It was particularly to clarify how far prayer changes from a purely petitionary form, that the cricket match (K) and battle (L) items were included. (The results from these items are to be reported in a later article).

2. *The approval or non-approval of prayer.*

Although there were nine situations in which questions about the effectiveness of prayer were asked, in only six of them was a cognate question about the rightness of prayer also included. In the answers to *only one of these questions* was there a *consistent age trend*. This item concerned the effect of prayer on a horse race to provide money to pay household bills, with 68 per cent of those aged 12-13 and 46 per cent of those 16-17 believing it right to pray for the horse to win. In each of the other situations there is a close similarity between the age groups in their answers to the question about the rightness of prayer.

Differences between the items suggest that there are differences in the approval shown for various objects of prayer. *The least approved prayer* is that of the schoolboy asking not to be found out after breaking a window, in which 23 per cent over-all said that he was right to pray. Only a few more (28 per cent) believed it right to pray that a theft would be undiscovered before the money was repaid, and 31 per cent believed prayer appropriate for a man wanting his shares to increase in value so that he could buy a

TABLE III

Approval of prayer, showing the numbers and percentages of those expressing belief through unqualified positive answers

Item	DENOMINATIONAL AFFILIATION				TOTAL	AGE GROUPS		
	R.C.	*C. of E.*	*Free*	*None*		*12-13*	*14-15*	*16-17*
D Broken window	14 25 %	3 13 %	17 25 %	7 23 %	**41** **23 %**	7 20 %	19 19 %	15 34 %
C Unauthorized borrowing	16 29 %	8 33 %	20 29 %	7 23 %	**51** **28 %**	12 34 %	28 28 %	11 26 %
E Oil shares for new car	20 36 %	6 25 %	20 30 %	7 25 %	**53** **31 %**	10 30 %	31 32 %	12 28 %
F Bet for household bills	46 82 %	12 50 %	28 41 %	18 58 %	**104** **58 %**	23 68 %	61 60 %	20 46 %
G Church Fete	50 89 %	14 61 %	44 67 %	14 48 %	**122** **70 %**	22 67 %	73 74 %	27 64 %
J Shark escape	54 100 %	19 91 %	56 90 %	24 92 %	**153** **94 %**	30 88 %	85 98 %	38 91 %

bigger car. There were 58 per cent who approved of prayer for the horse to win, although it may have been the unpaid household bills in this situation that influenced the answers of some. Prayer for fine weather for a Church Fete was approved by 70 per cent, and prayer to be rescued from an approaching shark by 94 per cent.

The least approved situation involved escape from deserved punishment, while the other two infrequently approved situations involved social aggrandisement. Table III shows that there are *no great differences in frequency between the denominations*, apart from an apparently random drop in the percentage of those in the Church of England approving of prayer to escape punishment. However, for the two non-personal situations — for the horse to win and for the Church Fete — there are significantly more Roman Catholics than subjects in other groups approving of the use of petitionary prayer. The first of these situations can be explained with reference to the teaching of the Free Churches about the immorality of betting and gambling. The minority among the Church of England and the Free Church groups who thought that the boy should not have prayed when seeing the shark, appeared from their comments to believe that he should have conserved his energies for swimming.

It may be concluded from these answers that *the moral evaluation of the situation in which prayer is offered is an important variable in attitudes to prayer*, and one which reflects specific training rather than reliable age trends. This conclusion is reinforced by the spontaneous comments of the subjects to the question « Why ?, » in which many stated that one should only pray in those situations in which there are moral sanctions for success.

3. *Causal efficacy of petitionary prayer.*

Although there is a close correspondence between the rank orderings for approval and efficacy of the items discussed in the previous section, there are *low correlations between the beliefs about approval and efficacy for each item separately*. The highest correlation between these is 0.31 in the item concerning the horse-race. For each item, however, there are consistently fewer people who believe that the prayer will be effective than approve of prayer.

Thus 94 per cent thought that the boy should pray to escape the shark, but 56 per cent believed him more likely to escape if he prayed, and 38 per cent thought that the chance of escape would be even better if the man in the boat ' prayed too. ' This is the item with the greatest percentage expressing belief in the efficacy of prayer. The prayers believed to be least effective were those concerning social aggrandisement and escape from deserved punishment.

TABLE IV

Causal efficacy of prayer, showing the number and percentages of those expressing belief through unqualified positive answers

Item	DENOMINATIONAL AFFILIATION				TOTAL	AGE GROUPS		
	R.C.	C. of E.	Free	None		12-13	14-15	16-17
D Broken window	6 11 %	1 4 %	9 13 %	5 16 %	21 12 %	7 20 %	12 12 %	2 5 %
C Unauthorized borrowing	6 11 %	3 13 %	8 12 %	3 10 %	20 11 %	5 14 %	13 13 %	2 5 %
E Oil shares for new car	1 2 %	0 0 %	5 8 %	1 4 %	7 4 %	2 6 %	5 5 %	0 0 %
F Bet for household bills	31 55 %	2 8 %	13 19 %	5 16 %	51 29 %	13 38 %	29 29 %	9 21 %
G Church Fete	40 71 %	9 39 %	30 46 %	9 31 %	88 51 %	25 76 %	49 50 %	14 33 %
J Shark escape	34 63 %	13 62 %	33 53 %	11 42 %	91 56 %	21 62 %	53 61 %	17 41 %
H Accident to oneself	10 18 %	5 22 %	18 28 %	5 18 %	38 22 %	7 21 %	24 25 %	7 17 %
M Accident to another	7 14 %	3 30 %	15 38 %	3 18 %	28 24 %	8 30 %	16 26 %	4 14 %
N' Jill's grandmother (not known prayed)	21 41 %	4 40 %	16 40 %	3 20 %	44 38 %	10 37 %	23 37 %	11 41 %
N" Jill's grandmother (if knew she was prayed for)	21 41 %	7 70 %	20 50 %	1 7 %	49 42 %	14 52 %	27 44 %	8 30 %

In the answers to questions about causal efficacy there are *clear age trends* for the situations concerning the avoidance of deserved punishment, the success of the horse race bet and the Church Fete's weather. In each of these, increasing age shows a decrease in the percentage believing that petitionary prayer will be effective. There is a similar age trend for two of the items involving prayer for another person ; these are the sick grandmother when she *knew* she was being prayed for, and avoiding an accident to one's brother.

Among the denominational groups the Roman Catholics have the greatest percentage believing in the effectiveness of prayer, which

for the horse race, Church Fete and shark escape items differ significantly from the other groups. In the items involving personal
prayers these differences do not occur. Thus it appears to be *the
circumstances of prayer rather than its object that is believed to be
important in determining causal efficacy.* A rational analysis might
suggest that the rain would be less likely to be influenced by prayer
than would a shark, although of course it is true that rain has been
a traditional object of prayer.

To summarize these answers : the most effective of our situations
for petitionary prayer was believed to be escape from the shark, in
which 56 per cent over-all expressed unqualified belief. Not surprisingly those expressing no religious affiliation have the lowest
percentage and the Roman Catholics have the highest percentage
of subjects believing that prayer would be effective, although the
three items involving prayers for another person have similar over-
all percentages. The horse race item is atypical because it involves
a moral judgment. The two remaining items concern avoidance of
accidents, and fewer Roman Catholics than people in the other
groups believe in the causal efficacy of these prayers. [1] The least
causal efficacy is attributed to the prayer to increase the value of
oil shares (4 per cent) while only 12 per cent believe in the efficacy
of prayer to avoid deserved punishment. There are the expected age
trends but no denominational differences in these items.

Belief in the causal efficacy of prayer thus appears to be age
related, and varies with the moral circumstances of the prayer ;
the least effective prayers are believed to be those for objects which
are morally disapproved.

Some educational implications.

The differences that have been observed between the frequencies
of positive answers to questions of approval and effectiveness may
be due to the different teaching that the subjects have received
about prayer. In the absence of firm evidence about the manner
in which the practice of prayer is taught to children it can only be
conjectured that children are probably given specific advice about
what may be prayed for while they are told much less definitely

---

1. It may be noted, however, that in both of these items the accident followed
the forgetting of an accustomed prayer. Those who accepted a causal link between
the accident and the forgotten prayer may not be expressing belief in the causal
efficacy of the daily prayers but may be producing an interpretation of the accident
based on the projection of a guilt feeling. Whatever the reason, educators should
note that there are still girls of 16-17 who react in this manner to the situations
described in N and M. — *Editor's note.*

about the causal efficacy of petitionary prayer. Children are therefore left to formulate their own beliefs ; this may account for the age trends since these depend upon the children's cognitive development. *In response to questions about causal efficacy, older children show a consistent movement away from responses asserting high causal efficacy, but no such change with age is found in responses to questions as to the rightness of petitionary prayer.* Godin and Van Roey (1959) make a similar point from their data on much younger Roman Catholic children in Belgium.

It may well be that the child's discovery that petitionary prayer may not be of direct causal efficacy, and the development of a more mature conception about it, threaten religious beliefs during development through adolescence if an immature conception of petitionary prayer has been taught. It may be suggested that it is a task of educators by appropriate instruction to convey mature conceptions about prayer in which the hope that petitionary prayer will change the course of events is no longer of central importance. [1]

Before accepting the postulated continuum from magical mentality to sacramental mentality (Godin, 1960) it is necessary to collect more information about the manner in which prayer is believed to have causal efficacy and the kinds of prayers that are thought to be appropriate in various situations. It is only by enlarging the information that is available, that all of the variables in the development of these beliefs may be described. There is little known in detail of the beliefs about prayer, and less is known about the manner in which children develop these beliefs.

---

1. Some hold, not without reason, and basing themselves on the witness of the saints, that mature Christian prayer may include very precise requests, not only for spiritual benefits but also for temporal favours ('everything for the body and the soul'). Familiarity with God, in a mystical sense, allows us to expect His assistance, which we seek in complete subordination to His will. The present psychological study tends in no way to exclude or to devalue these prayers. The study however calls our attention to the ambiguous psychological attitudes which may lie behind certain prayers, especially during the transition from childhood through to the end of adolescence. To determine the forms of prayer which are suited to a Christian maturity it is necessary to turn to theological sources. Among the most recent Roman Catholic writings on this subject we may note a profound treatise on the language of prayer by Mgr. M. Nédoncelle (*Prière humaine, prière divine*, Bruges et Paris, Desclée De Br., 1962), a psychological analysis by L. Beirnaert (« La prière de demande dans nos vies d'homme », in *Expérience chrétienne et psychologie*. Paris, Ed. de l'Epi, 1964, pp. 333-51) and a theological meditation on petitionary prayer by Fr. Karl Rahner (*Von der Not und dem Segen des Gebetes*, Freiburg, Herder Vg., 1958) Some basic considerations for a pedagogy of prayer are in a special number of *Lumen Vitae* (1963) *18*, 2 (English edition), where very little place indeed is given to requests for temporal favours. — *Editor's note.*

New lines of enquiry.

In the course of evaluating our results many imperfections in our earlier plans were apparent. It is our intention to carry the research further with new material. The range of the enquiry has been too great, and it became clear that many problems we approached could be readily subdivided. The use of such environment controlling practices as finger-crossing is an important problem by itself, and is too complex to be made a minor item in a research into the causal efficacy of petitionary prayer. The number of items was too large, and often the content was not stated in such a way that girls could readily identify with them. We have prepared a new form of the material which is shorter and we hope more informative.

We had hoped to clarify the extent to which the use of simple petitions is replaced by other kinds of prayer, such as submission, with increasing age and the other conditions that must be satisfied before petitionary prayer is believed to be effective. These problems are too complex for our present data, and further work is required on them.

Conclusions.

The main conclusions that may be drawn from the present enquiry are :

a) age trends occur in belief in the causal efficacy of petitionary prayer but not in beliefs about the appropriateness of such prayer.

b) the age trends that have been observed appear to be independent of denomination.

c) belief in the appropriateness of petitionary prayer appears to depend upon specific instruction which varies from one denomination to another, and is largely independent of belief in the causal efficacy of such prayer.

d) belief in both the appropriateness and the causal efficacy of petitionary prayer appears to depend upon the type of situation in which the prayer is offered and the moral object of the prayer.

REFERENCES

GODIN, A. and VAN ROEY, Bernadette. Immanent justice and divine protection. *Lumen Vitae* (1959), 14, 129-148.

GODIN, A. and Sister MARTHE. Magical mentality and sacramental life in children of 8 to 14 years. *Lumen Vitae* (1960), 15, 277-296.

PIAGET, Jean. *The Moral Judgment of the Child.* London, Routledge and Kegan Paul, 1932.

Religious Knowledge Among Pupils of Secular and Religious Catechists : a Comparative Study

by Jean-Jacques Larivière, C.S.V.

Professor at Montreal University [1]

Aim of the Research.

This research sets out to compare, by a scientific method, the catechetical *knowledge* acquired by pupils taught by religious and by secular catechists. We wish to stress that the comparison, we intend, bears purely on catechetical matter, and not on a child's life of faith or moral training.

Nor is it useless to emphasize the spirit that prompts this study. It will be easily understood that there is no question of discriminating between different groups of catechists. Such an intention would be unfair. All true religious teachers, be they men or women, seculars or religious, have the same ambition : to give a thorough religious education to the children entrusted to them. If the school results of one catechist are less good than those of another, it is permissible to compare their methods objectively with the intention

---

1. Father Jean-Jacques Larivière was born at Montreal in 1921. Ordained priest in the Congregation of the Clerics of Saint Viator, he has obtained a doctorate's degree in Education from Louvain University. He has also graduated in theology at the Angelicum of Rome, in guidance at the University of Montreal and in religious teaching at the Catholic Institute of Paris. After being for many years a teacher in High Schools and Colleges, Father Larivière became Principal at the Normal School, Rigaud, Province of Quebec. Presently, he is Superior of Champagneur College, Rawdon, P.Q. Meanwhile, he teaches Religious Psychology at the University of Montreal. Besides writing in different reviews. Father Larivière published : *Connaissances catéchistiques et contrôle objectif* (Editions Robert, Lyon, 1961), and *Test objectif de connaissances catéchistiques* (Centre de Psychologie et de Pédagogie, Montreal, 1962). He will publish in 1964 : *Enquête sur la foi religieuse des collégiens au Canada français.* — Address : Champagneur College, Rawdon, Canada. (Editor's note).

of improvement, but it would be objectively unscientific to conclude a priori one teacher's superiority over another.

This objective attitude is all the more necessary here, since we are comparing only the results in catechetical knowledge, without examining moral training. Now, if one of the aims of religious instruction certainly is to transmit knowledge, it is neither unique nor complete by itself, nor is it the most important. The catechist who can assert that his pupils merely « know » their religion, may be far from having fulfilled his task, that is, the mission confided to him by the Church. From knowing the truths of their religion, the children have yet to develop a living faith, and train themselves to an integral Christian life. Who will argue that these last two objectives of religious instruction yield to the first in order of importance ?

Locality of the Research.

We carried out this research in Montreal. The name implies, not only the city, but also the surrounding municipalities — what we usually call « greater Montreal. » This area includes a population of about one and a half million. Naturally the districts vary a great deal. Some quarters are peopled almost exclusively by workers and families of lesser economic resources. Or, as the other extreme, some quarters contain almost exclusively professional or wealthy families. Some districts again, have a majority of what we call « white collars. »

If we re-consider this variety as parish groups, we again find all categories. The populations of these parishes vary between 1,000 and 15,000 souls. There are further differences in the organization of parish activities, Catholic Action movements, youth's leisure hours, etc.

In a word, we think that the subjects chosen among the thousands of Montreal school-children, form a representative sample of a town population in the Province of Quebec.

Choice of Subjects.

Now, we will consider the school point of view. For this, Montreal is divided into eight districts. For our definitive sample we chose 4 schools in each district, 32 schools in all. Of these, 16 were girls' schools, 16 were boys' schools. In order to represent as many different settings as possible in our research, we took only one school from each parish, which means that the 880 pupils used for the enquiry belonged to 32 different parishes.

All these pupils were in Year VII, therefore, finishing their primary education.

As regards School direction, we chose 16 schools under secular teachers, 8 under masters and 8 under mistresses ; and then 16 schools kept by religious congregations, 8 by teaching Brothers and 8 by nuns.

TABLE I

Religious Congregations that contributed to the research

A. Congregations of Women	B. Congregations of Men
Congregation of Notre-Dame	Brothers of the Christian Schools
Sisters of the Holy Names of Jesus and Mary	Clerics of Saint Viator
	Congregation of the Holy Cross
Sisters of the Holy Cross	Brothers of the Sacred Heart
Sisters of Saint Anne	Marist Brothers
Sisters of the Assumption	Brothers of Christian Instruction
Daughters of Wisdom	Brothers of Saint Gabriel
Sisters of Saint Francis of Assisi	
Little Franciscans of Mary	

Besides this, we wanted as many religious Congregations as possible to take part in this research. Therefore, the 8 schools directed by nuns, are of 8 different Congregations ; 7 Congregations of men participated, that is, all who devote themselves to public primary education in Montreal.

Table I gives the list of these Congregations of men and women. Table II shows the division of the 880 subjects concerned in the enquiry. Of these, 452 boys came from 16 schools and 428 girls also came from 16 different schools. Examining the direction of the schools, it will be noticed that the 16 schools kept by different congregations have supplied 452 subjects (232 boys and 220 girls), while the schools under secular teachers supplied 428 candidates (220 boys, 208 girls).

TABLE II

Division of the 880 subjects in the enquiry

Schools		Subjects		Direction of School
Boys	Girls	Boys	Girls	
8		232		Religious masters
8		220		Secular masters
	8		220	Religious mistresses
	8		208	Secular mistresses
16	16	452	428	

Age of the Subjects.

On the whole, the boys were slightly older than the girls : an average age of 13 years 1 month against 12 years 11 months. The average age of the 880 subjects is 13 years with a sigma of 3 months. [1] This means that 95 % of the pupils examined ranged between 12 ^{1}/$_2$ and 13 ^{1}/$_2$ years. This age can be considered normal for children in 7th. Year primary, since most of them begin school at the age of about 6 years.

Intelligence Quotient of the Subjects.

In order to compare Catechism results with intellectual aptitude, we gave an intelligence test to the pupils of the 32 schools. The test chosen was the « Mental Ability Test » of the St. George's Educational Institute of Montreal University. The intermediate series of this test is for children of the 6th., 7th., 8th., and 9th. school years. It comprises 75 questions to be answered in 30 minutes; preliminary explanation needs about 9 minutes.

TABLE III

Combined results of the mental ability test

	Pupils	*Av.*	*-69*	*70-9*	*80-9*	*90-9*	*100-9*	*110-9*	*120-9*	*130-*
Boys	452	100.2	7	26	65	115	116	90	28	5
Girls	428	99.5	3	20	69	132	103	72	27	2
Totals	880	99.8	10	46	134	247	219	162	55	7
Per cent			1.1	5.2	15.2	28.	25.	18.4	6.3	.8

Even according to the authors, this test « does not necessarily measure innate intelligence, which is difficult to estimate when schooling has already influenced the children's mental development. It measures more the way in which a subject uses his faculties, his aptitude to profit by school instruction. » [2]

---

1. The sigma (standard deviation) is a statistical value indicating the dispersion or scattering of scores aroud an average. Thus if the average of the scores of all pupils taking an examination is 80 with a sigma of 4, it means that the scores of 68 % of the total group will be found between 76 and 84 (the average 80 plus or minus 1 sigma), while the scores of 95 % will range from 72 to 88 (80 plus or minus 2 sigma). The values 68 % and 95 % are constants, based on the supposition that the distribution of scores conforms to the Gauss curve or normal curve of probability.

2. Institut pédagogique St.-Georges, « Epreuve d'habileté mentale », Manuel de directives, p. 1.

TABLE IV

Intelligence Quotients of our subjects compared to the ideal division of a non-selected population

Intelligence Quotients	Ideal Population	Subjects of the Enquiry
130 and over	1 %	0.8 %
120 to 129	5 %	6.3 %
110 to 119	14 %	18.4 %
100 to 109	30 %	25.0 %
90 to 99	30 %	28.0 %
80 to 89	14 %	15.2 %
70 — 79	5 %	5.2 %
Less than 69	1 %	1.1 %
	100 %	100.0 %

We chose this intelligence test rather than another, chiefly because it was gauged on the school population of Montreal and its district. Table 3 shows the results obtained in it by the girls and boys.

It should be pointed out that the average intelligence quotient of the boys and girls is about the same : 100 · 2 and 99 · 5. The average intelligence quotient of boys and girls together, 880 subjects, is 99 · 8.

For the boys, the sigma of distribution is 14, while for the girls it is 13 · 08. The average sigma of combined distribution is 13 · 57.

If we compare the average intelligence quotients of each of the 32 schools, we notice considerable differences. Beside classes intellectually brilliant, there are others in which the majority are slightly favoured intellectually. Thus, among the boys, we find a school in which more than 60 % of the pupils have an intelligence quotient above 110, while in another, nearly 80 % are below 100. It is the same for the girls; where one class has more than half its members with intelligence quotients over 110, another contains 75 % with quotients below 100. This shows that *comparison between these different classes would be impossible, concerning the results in catechetical knowledge, without taking into consideration these very different degrees of intellectual aptitude.*

These results allow us to declare already that our group of 880 subjects formed a representative sample of the school population in general. In fact, psychologists think that in a non-selected population, the intelligence quotient is according to the normal curve of probability. Since the average intelligence quotient of our subjects was 99 · 8 with a sigma of 13 · 57, our data approximate the normal curve.

Table IV shows this more clearly. It compares the distribution of the intelligence quotients of our subjects, with that of a large non-selected population, a distribution now recognized by several authors.

Objective Control of Catechetical Knowledge.

To evaluate objectively the catechetical knowledge of our subjects, we used our « Objective Test of catechetical knowledge. »[1] This test, constructed for

---

1. J.-J. Larivière, C.S.V., Test objectif de connaissances catéchistiques, Centre de Psychologie et de Pédagogie, Montreal, 1962.

scholars of Standard VII Primary, of the Montreal district, comprises 100 questions and bears on the whole content of religious knowledge in the Catholic Catechism, Canadian edition. It was administered to the pupils of the 32 schools already chosen for the enquiry. We visited these 32 schools in person during the month of May, so as to be certain of identical conditions of its administration. Of the 880 subjects who underwent the mental ability test in December, only 857 took our test of catechetical knowledge. This difference of 23 is explained either by illness or change of residence among the pupils at the time of our second visit.

TABLE V

Time of the Catechism Test

Time	1st. day	2nd. day	3rd. day	4th. day	5th. day	6th. day	7th. day	8th. day
9 a.m.	A	B	C	D	A	B	C	D
10.30 a.m.	A	B	C	D	A	B	C	D
1.30 p.m.	A	B	C	D	A	B	C	D
3 p.m.	A	B	C	D	A	B	C	D

A : Group of schools under secular masters
B : Group of schools under religious masters
C : Group of schools under secular mistresses
D : Group of schools under religious mistresses

To be able to compare the boys' results with the girls', as well as those between the Congregations' schools and secular schools, each of these four groups of children had to be treated exactly the same way. We were able to visit four schools each day, two in the morning (9 and 10.30 a.m.) and two in the afternoon (1.30 and 3 p.m.). We did it this way. In the 8 schools under secular masters, two were examined during the first lesson in the morning, at 9 o'clock, and 2 others in the second part of the morning at 10.30. Again, 2 classes in the first part of the afternoon, at 1.30, and 2 more during the last period at 3 o'clock. We did the same for the classes in the other three categories: religious men, nuns, secular mistresses. Table 5 demonstrates this. In this way, none of the four categories had any advantage over the other.

Choice of a Method of Research.

The aim of our study is clearly defined : to compare the catechetical knowledge acquired by pupils of nuns and religious, and those taught by secular masters and mistresses. To this end, we had to choose a method of investigation which allowed objective comparison.

At first sight, there would seem to be a simple and quick way of doing this : calculate the average result obtained in an objective examination on catechism by the 441 boys and 416 girls, and draw conclusions. But it is obvious that such a procedure could only give a very summary and but slightly objective result. We cannot fairly compare the success of two children without counting many factors which can condition this success to a greater or lesser degree.

We must, then, find a method of comparison which considers the different influences in the acquisition of religious knowledge. In other words, *we can only really compare two groups of pupils, when the children are equal from all points of view other than that of catechetical knowledge.*

We have said « from all points of view. » As an ideal, it should be so. The demands of experimental method go as far as that. In practice, however, it is not always easy to control all the factors that influence a situation, an order of measures. Besides, the objective value of the use of the method we employ will precisely depend on the number of variants, more or less considerable, which we can hold as constant. Even if in practice, we cannot attain the ideal perfection in the use of the experimental method, we think we can sufficiently control variant factors, so as to reach valid results at the end of our study. It is here we must bear in mind the reply always given to objectors against measures in education: a little is better than none.

The method we chose lies in finding equal pairs of pupils, one taught by a religious, the other by a secular, and to compare their catechetical knowledge. The scheme is very simple. The whole difficulty lies in finding groups of pupils, two and two alike. Here arises the problem of controling variant factors.

Factors that Influence the Acquisition
of Catechetical Knowledge.

When setting out to study the cause, or rather causes, of pupils' success in acquiring religious knowledge, there are many factors to consider. Some concern the pupil personally, others depend on the teacher, some even on the family. Among those concerning the pupil are : age, sex, mental ability, application to study, general school achievement. Among those concerning the teacher are : intellectual preparation, method of instruction, duration of lessons, personal qualities. Lastly, among factors depending on the family, we could mention : help or encouragement given by the parents with school work, intellectual atmosphere of the home, economic level, more or less Christian mentality, etc.

Not all these factors have the same importance for our present study. To give only one example, we mention the last, the more or less Christian mentality of the home. Obviously, in an enquiry into the children's religious training, and not their mere acquiring of religious knowledge, which is our present subject, this factor would be much more important, and its effects would need to be controlled.

Whatever may be the relative importance of these different factors, for our present need, we can divide them into three categories : first, those of secondary and negligible importance ; then, those which the limits of our present study force us to omit; lastly, those whose control we can establish.

a) In the first category, we put *age*. We have said that the average age of our pupils was 13 years with a sigma of 3 months. That means that 95 % of the subjects in the enquiry ranged between 12 $1/2$ and 13 $1/2$ years. This slight difference seems to us insignificant.

b) Then there is the factor of the *frequency of and length of lessons*. According to the official division of the daily time-table, which all teachers depending from the Catholic Schools Commission of Montreal are obliged to follow, the religious lesson for Year VII is given every day. The teachers were kind enough to answer a questionnaire of information which we sent them. Their replies indicated the following facts.

Length of the Catechism lesson from secular masters, 30-45 minutes, average length, 35 minutes. From Religious masters, 30-45 minutes, average length, 40 minutes. Secular mistresses: 45-55 minutes, average length, 52 minutes. Nuns: from 45-50 minutes, average length, 47 minutes. 30 out of 32 teachers declare that they give their lesson of Catechism at the beginning of the morning; the two others, a secular and a Religious master, give theirs in the first hour of the afternoon. For the work done by the pupils outside the Catechism lesson, the facts are : secular masters demand from 15-35 minutes study, with an average of 23 minutes ; Religious masters demand from 15-30 minutes study, with an average of 22 minutes ; secular mistresses ask 20-30 minutes, average 25 minutes ; and nuns demand 20-30 minutes, with an average of 22 minutes. These figures are set out in Table VI.

TABLE VI

Length of Religion Lessons and Study according to each group of teachers

	Length of lesson	Average	Study time	Average
Secular masters	30-45 min.	35 min.	15-35 min.	23 min.
Religious masters	30-45 min.	40 min.	15-30 min.	22 min.
Secular mistresses	45-55 min.	52 min.	20-30 min.	25 min.
Nuns	45-50 min.	47 min.	20-30 min.	22 min.

Examining the averages, it will be noticed that the amount of study demanded by the different groups of teachers is about the same. The difference is more marked for the average length of the daily lesson : 35 minutes from secular masters and 52 minutes from secular mistresses. Such a difference cannot be a negligible factor. Nevertheless, since in this research we compare the girls among themselves and the boys among themselves, and since between the groups of children of the same sex the difference is much less (5 minutes only), we think the factor, length of lesson, can be ignored.

c) For the *method of exposition* in religious instruction, the official programme's directives are also very explicit. All the religious doctrine in the « Catholic Catechism » for the province of Quebec is classified under 5 general ideas, forming a « frame-synthesis » : a) there is one God, I am His child, He speaks to me through the Church ; b) I must know about my Father in heaven ; c) I must love Him and serve Him ; d) I need His help to know, love and serve Him ; e) after death, I will be happy with Him, or unhappy without Him, for all eternity.[1] As to the general trend of the lesson, the « Programme d'Enseignement religieux » indicates these phases : a) observation from concrete data ; b) thought-conversation ; c) transposition ; d) expression.[2] Besides that, as special directives for Year VII, the « Programme » declares that, while keeping to the frame-synthesis and the same basic truths, these will be represented round 13 centres of interest.[3] The content of each is clearly settled. Given these precise orders, we think that the differences that can exist between catechists, would arise more from the personal qualities and preparation of the teacher than from the programme and its method of exposition.

d) In the category of factors that our research could not control, undoubtedly the most important is *the teacher's personal equation.* Here we would mention the qualities that make a good teacher : general culture, immediate preparation for teaching, ascendancy over the pupils, moral personality, motivation, personal convictions, etc. There is no doubt that this factor is very important in the school success of the pupils. The limits of our enquiry did not permit us to go into this element. Nevertheless, *if our enquiry shows that there are real differences between the pupils of different groups of teachers, it is probable that they can be largely attributed to this factor.*

e) Another element our research could not control is what could be called the *Christian climate of the family.* This factor can influence the children's acquisition of religious knowledge, but it is less vital here than over their moral training. In any case, this is another factor which the frame and limits of our study did not allow us to consider.

Then we come to the third category of factors, those we have striven to control. These are : mental ability, general school achievement, help and encouragement from parents with school work, the father's profession, and the family's economic level. We will explain briefly how we controlled these factors.

---

1. Programme d'enseignement religieux des écoles primaires élémentaires, Quebec, 1952, p. 10.
2. *Id.* p. 14.
3. *Id.* p. 32.

Questionnaire of Information.

To be able to assess these factors we needed some information on each child's family setting. There were two ways of obtaining this: interviewing the parents, or a questionnaire for the children. The interview would have been the best method theoretically. Its use however, came up against a great difficulty: it would have taken us a very long time to visit each family of our 857 subjects. Therefore we chose the questionnaire.

The validity of the use of a questionnaire depends on the knowledge and sincerity of those who answer it. We had to be sure that the children knew enough about the things involved, and were giving candid answers. On one side, we took care to ask questions which the children could answer objectively by a word or a figure; the questions only concerned facts the children knew, and not judgment or situations to be appreciated.

On the other side, we took some precautions regarding the sincerity of answers. First, we visited all the classes in person. Before giving out the questionnaire, we carefully explained our aim to the children, which was, to help the teachers who were working for their good, and it was in this spirit that we were asking for their collaboration. Moreover, we assured them that their answers would be considered strictly private, that we alone would read them, not even their teacher. In conclusion, we invited individual questions if they needed any explanation before recording their answers.

To verify the objectivity of the answers, the teachers kindly showed us their class registers, which contained information on the children and their parents. In a subsequent visit to each of the 32 schools, we made a fresh sounding, this time oral and individual, among some of the children, to see if the answers corresponded with those given a few months earlier. These various precautions allowed us to conclude that we had sufficient reasons to accept the questionnaire answers as sincere.

We have now to relate how, with the information obtained, we managed to control the 5 factors mentioned above: mental ability, general school record, help and encouragement from parents, the father's profession, the family's economic level.

Factors Controlled by Our Research.

1) *Mental ability.* We had previously submitted each pupil to the « Mental Ability Test » of the Institut St.-Georges of Montreal University. According to its results, we grouped our subjects in 5 categories: I) those whose intelligence quotient was below 90 ; II) those whose I.Q. varied between 90 and 99 ; III) between 100 and 109 ; IV) between 110 and 119 ; and V) those with an I.Q. above 120.

2) *General school record.* We took into consideration each pupil's combined result in the official examinations at the end of Primary Instruction (Year VII). As these exams are the same throughout Quebec, and are corrected by central committees using the same reckoning, we could compare the results of pupils from different schools. According to these successes, we again divided the pupils into 5 categories : I) those with results lower than 60 ; II) those that varied between 60 and 69 ; III) between 70 and 79 ; IV) between 80 and 89 ; V) those with 90 or over.

3) *Help and encouragement from parents.* The questionnaire given to the children asked whether their parents helped or encouraged them at home with their studies, sometimes, often or never. To measure these answers we assigned the following values: the reply « never » received 0; « often » received 2 points, and the answer « sometimes » got 1 point. The same scale was used to assess encouragement, the answers being able to gain 4 points. We then divided our subjects into 4 categories, according to the 1, 2, 3 or 4 points they obtained for the factor help and encouragement from parents.

4) *The father's profession.* It is obvious that the intellectual atmosphere at home influences for good or evil the children's general record. It is not easy to control this factor, since it depends much on circumstances. We thought it possible, at least partially, by noting the father's profession. On account of the different levels of intellectual training which condition it, this is often a valuable index, without being perfectly adequate, of the level of intellectual interests in the family circle. We used the « Minnesota Scale » which divides a list of 350 occupations into 7 classes. As one of these concerned land-workers, we divided our subjects into 6 groups, according to the father's occupation. These classes were : I) workmen ; II) unskilled workers ; III) skilled workers ; IV) clerks ; V) managers ; VI) professional men.

5. *Economic Level of the home.* This factor can also influence general school results. There are homes in which several children are all together in a few small rooms, where it is practically impossible to have the silence and quiet necessary for real study. Other homes are much more favoured in this respect, and children can find the material conditions favourable to intellectual pursuits. It is clear, however, that a family's economic level is also a factor hard to assess quantitively, because of the complexity of influences over it. After consulting a specialist in economic statistics at the Montreal University, we decided to gauge the family's economic level, for the purposes of our research, by the presence or absence in the home, of a certain number of objects which indicate material comfort, and which families can procure and enjoy according to their economic position. These objects are : a radio set, television, an electric refrigerator, a car ; we added the fact of house ownership. To estimate each of these elements we used the « Recensement décennal du Canada. » The figure attributed was in inverse proportion to the frequency of the object in question in Canadian homes. Thus, the radio set, now found in almost every home, was marked as one point ;   a television set, 2 points ; a refrigerator scored 3 points ; a car, 8 points, and lastly, the fact of owning the house lived in counted for 10 points in our scale. The whole added up to a possible total of 24 points. For the family's economic level, we divided our subjects into three categories : first category : those who obtained less than 7 points ; second category : those who scored between 7 and 16 points ; and then the third category : those whose score ranged from 17 to 24 points. Table VII shows the building up of the categories for each of the five factors we set out to control.

TABLE VII

Constitution of Categories for each of the 5 factors controlled

1. Intelligence Quotient : 5 groups	{	... — 89 90 — 99 100 — 109 110 — 119 120 — ...
2. General school record : 5 groups	{	... — 59 60 — 69 70 — 79 80 — 89 90 — 99
3. Help and encouragement from parents : 4 groups	1 p. 2 p. 3 p. 4 p.	occasional help gains 1 point frequent help, 2 points occasional encouragement, 1 pt. frequent encouragement, 2 pts.
4. Father's occupation : 6 groups	{	Workmen Unskilled workers Skilled workers Clerks Managers Professional men
5. Economic level : 3 groups	{	... — 6 pts (radio, 1 pt.) 7 — 16 pts. (television, 2 pts.) 17 — 24 pts. (refrigerator, 3 pts.) (car, 8 pts.) (house ownership, 10 pts.)

Table VIII shows the number of subjects belonging to each of the 4 groups of teachers, masters secular and Religious, secular mistresses and nuns. Here we must point out a difference, from the beginning of our enquiry, in the boy's section. We had chosen 8 schools under secular and 8 under Religious direction. Then we found that in two of the latter

TABLE VIII

Number of pupils taught by the 4 groups of instructors

10	Secular masters :	272	boys
6	Religious masters :	169	boys
8	Secular mistresses :	209	girls
8	Nuns	207	girls
32		857	

schools, Year VII was taught by a secular master, which obliged us to add them to the secular school group. That gave us 10 classes with secular, and 6 with Religious, masters.

Formation of Experimental Groups.

The information gained by the questionnaire having helped us to control a certain number of factors, we still had to form experimental groups of boys and girls. For this we formed « individual pairs. » This means choosing, among the boys and the girls, *pairs of subjects alike in all the factors controlled, differing only in the factor under experiment.* Thus each pair of boys or girls must belong to the same category for mental ability, general school record, help and encouragement from parents in school work, father's profession and home economic level, but one taught by a secular master or mistress, and the other by a Religious master or mistress. With pupils paired off in this way, their results in Catechism can be validly compared. By this process, we found *80 pairs among the boys and 76 among the girls.*

TABLE IX

Percentage of pupils supplied by each class to make up the 80 pairs of boys and 76 pairs of girls

10 classes with secular masters	6 classes with Religious masters	8 classes with secular mistresses	8 classes with nuns as mistresses
33.3 %	48.0 %	51.5 %	53.3 %
30.3 %	50.0 %	33.3 %	57.1 %
29.6 %	53.1 %	48.3 %	36.3 %
24.1 %	28.0 %	38.4 %	33.3 %
39.1 %	56.5 %	36.0 %	31.8 %
34.7 %	47.0 %	29.6 %	5.0 %
17.8 %		18.5 %	37.5 %
29.6 %		31.0 %	31.5 %
37.5 %			
20.6 %			

Table IX shows the proportion in which each of the 32 classes in our research supplied subjects for our experimental groups. Except for one of the nuns' classes which is represented by only 5 % of her pupils, it will be noticed that all the other schools supplied more or less important contingents, varying from 18 to 57 % of the pupils in the class. It will be noticed also that the percentage of scholars supplied is explained by the fact that there were only 6 Religious masters and 10 secular ones.

At first sight, it may seem that the number of subjects in each experimental group (80 pairs of boys, 76 pairs of girls) is very few to made valid comparisons between the groups. No doubt, a greater number of subjects would give our results greater certainty. Nevertheless, we must remember, that with the method of paired subjects, more valuable results can be obtained from fewer subjects rigorously controlled in several factors, than from more subjects divided into 2 groups, and merely making their averages equal. This was statistically proved by Chapin in a research made in the United States a few years ago. [1]

Analysis of Results.

Before comparing the Catechism successes of the 80 pairs of boys and 76 pairs of girls, we will do that for all the 857 pupils who took the test, without considering the different factors we tried to control. These will give us a preliminary result, which a closer analysis can confirm or modify. Table X gives the results obtained in our test by the 4 groups of pupils ; the average result of the boys taught by seculars is compared with the average result of those taught by Religious. Then the average result of girls taught by secular mistresses is compared with that of girls taught by nuns. It will be seen that the Religious masters' classes lead by a margin of $5 \cdot 8 \%$ and the classes taught by nuns lead by $2 \cdot 7 \%$. It remains to be seen whether the comparison of results in more rigorously controlled conditions will confirm this.

TABLE X

Results of the 4 groups of pupils in the Catechism test

Boys			*Girls*		
	Pupils	*Average*		*Pupils*	*Average*
Classes taught by secular masters	272	68.6 %	Classes taught by secular mistresses	209	72.5 %
Classes taught by Religious	169	74.4 %	Classes taught by nuns	207	75.2 %
Difference		5.8 %	Difference		2.7 %

Boys in Similar Pairs.

Table XI sets out the results in our Catechism test when the 80 boys taught by secular masters are compared with the 80 boys taught by Religious. Results obtained in the examination for the Year VII certificate, as well as for the Catechism test, are compared.

---

1. F.S. Chapin, Experimental Designs in Sociological Research, Harper Bros. New York, 1955, p. 123.

Table XI requires a word of explanation which holds good for Table XII which shows the girls' results. The second comparison, that of the Year VII certificate verifies the result of the Catechism test. After comparing the religious knowledge, it was interesting to know whether one of the two groups was also superior in general school achievement, as the certificate awards reveal. We were able to compare the two groups from the angle of general school average because, when we had controlled this factor in our enquiry, we had only done so within the limits of our 5 selected groups presented in Table VII, fairly wide limits of 10 points for each group. Thus, for example, the second group includes all pupils whose general school marks range between 60 and 69 %. Now from the very extent of these limits, it was possible that 2 pupils, one taught by a secular master and the other by a Religious, could belong to the same schooling *group*, and yet have a wide difference as to the *marks* obtained in the Year VII certificate; one, for example, could get 61 % and the other 69 %, and yet both belong to the same group according to our categories. So it was interesting to know whether an eventual difference in catechetical knowledge was confirmed or weakened by a difference in the general school result. To this end we compared the scores of the two groups of pupils in the Year VII certificate, this time considering not only the *category*, as with the controlled factors, but the individual *marks* obtained for the Year VII certificate.

Analysis of Table XI shows several things. It shows first that for both religion and scholastic achievement the members of Group B ; that is, the pupils of Religious masters, have an average that is higher by 3.8 % and 1.9 % respectively.

Then the experimental co-efficient for the two sets of results present considerable differences. Thus, for the Catechism test, the experimental co-efficient being 0·70, we have 38 chances to 1 that there is a real difference between the results of group A and of group B. Contrarily, the experimental co-efficient for the Year VII certificate being 0·50, we have only 11 chances to 1 that the difference between the averages of groups A and B is not due to measuring errors. This difference is therefore too small to be significant from the statistical standpoint.

TABLE XI

Compared results of the boys taught by secular masters (group A) and by Religious masters (group B)

	Group A			Group B			Superiority Group B	Experimental co-efficient	Approximate Chances
	No.	Av.	P.E.*	No.	Av.	P.E.*			
Catechism Test	80	69.6	8.71	80	73.4	7.97	3.8	0.70	38 to 1
Year VII Certificate	80	69.8	6.56	80	71.7	4.10	1.9	0.50	11 to 1

* P.E. : probable error.

Speaking statistically, the superiority of the boys taught by Religious masters is negligible in the Year VII certificate, but well marked in the religious knowledge test.

Girls in Similar Pairs.

Table XII gives the results when girls from group C (secular mistresses) and group D (taught by nuns) are composed. As for the boys, we observe that the average results of the schools taught by nuns are better than those taught by secular mistresses ; the average is 4 % higher in the Catechism test and 5·3 % higher for the Year VII certificate.

TABLE XII

Compared results of the girls taught by secular mistresses (group C) and by nuns (group D)

	Group C			Group D			Superiority Group D	Experi-mental co-efficient	Approx-imate Chances
	No.	Av.	P.E.*	No.	Av.	P.E.*			
Catechism Test	76	71.8	8.77	76	75.8	7.83	4.0	0.70	38 to 1
Year VII Certificate	76	69.8	6.50	76	75.1	5.59	5.3	1.30	67C0 to 1

Moreover, if we consider the experimental co-efficient for each of these differences, we see it is above 0.70. That means we have 38 chances to 1, that there is a real difference between groups C and D for the catechism test, and 6700 chances to 1 for the Year VII certificate.

Speaking statistically, the superiortiy in religious knowledge for the girl group taught by nuns is just as marked as it was for the boys. Besides, the superiority of this group in Year VII examination is ever so much higher.

Summary.

We sum up briefly the results of our enquiry.

1) To avoid any danger of misinterpretation of these results, we repeat once more that the comparisons we have made between the different groups of pupils, bear exclusively on catechetical *knowledge*, at the end of primary education. We have in no way touched the domains of the children's life of faith or their religious practice.

2) Comparing the results obtained in our Catechism test by the pupils of secular masters or mistresses (481 subjects) with those of the pupils with Religious masters or mistresses (376 subjects), we see that the latter lead by a difference of 4·2 %.

---

* P.E. : probable error.

3) As a first verification of this rough result, we compared the results of 80 pairs of boys, differing only in the factor of their secular or religious master. We did the same for 76 pairs of girls, differing only in their secular or religious mistress. These results confirm our first statement : the pupils taught by religious of either sex obtained the highest marks : superiority of $3 \cdot 8 \%$ among the boys, and of 4 % among the girls.

4) A second verification is possible by comparing the results in the official examination at the end of primary studies for these 80 pairs of boys and 76 pairs of girls. The average score of the boys taught by religious masters was $1 \cdot 9 \%$ higher, and the girls taught by nuns had a superiority of $5 \cdot 3 \%$. It must be noted, however, that in schools kept by religious masters the margin is too small to be significant from a statistical standpoint.

5) Even if this enquiry seems to indicate significant differences between these groups of scholars for their acquisition of catechetical knowledge, it does not indicate the cause of such difference. To take stock objectively of these, a supplementary and closer study would be needed with a suitable method of enquiry. The field is open to research.

Conclusion.

Before finishing, we would like to add a few words about the role of seculars in religious instruction. Some of them think at times that they are only catechists to avoid a greater evil, and that being neither priests nor religious, they cannot give really profitable instruction. Let them banish this idea. Provided they have the necessary training, doctrinal, pastoral and spiritual, it is positively certain that they can give the children an authentic religious training.

We would even venture to say that in some respects they are better equipped than religious, nuns or priests. Facing the problems of family life daily, they know the dangers that threaten Christian life in the home, and can prepare children to meet them. Having experienced the need for a solid religious training in the modern world so full of snares for the young, they can convince them of the need of a preparation adapted to confront such perils.

In the Church, the religious instruction of children belongs by divine natural right to the parents, and by divine positive right, to the Pope and the bishops. But those to whom God confided this care are often incapable of fulfilling this function completely. They appeal to helpers and delegate some of their responsibility to them. It is thus that priests, religious, nuns and seculars are called upon to collaborate in this primordial task.

The law of the Church officially recognizes the place of seculars in religious instruction of the young. Canon 1333 foresees that priests can be helped, and if necessary replaced, for catechetical teaching, by devout seculars, preferably those who belong to the Confraternity of Christian Doctrine.

In his many addresses, Pope Pius XII often referred to the need for secular collaboration in teaching religion. At the International Catechetical Congress in Rome, 1950, he stated clearly : « If the number of priests is insufficient, let them obtain secular helpers of both sexes. » [1] The previous year, in his Letter to the Italian Week of Catechetical Studies, he had also recalled the need of securing secular help, « especially for the catechetical instruction of little children. » [2]

But, if lay catechists need to be convinced that in the Church a place awaits them in the religious instruction of youth, they must be equally convinced of the necessity of a very careful preparation for this mission. We can rejoice that in the last twenty years, considerable progress has been realized. Among French-speaking universities alone, we can mention the fine work done by the Institut Catéchétique of the Institut Catholique, Paris, as well as by the Institut de Sciences religieuses of the Universities of Louvain and Montreal. The Lumen Vitae International Centre, Brussels, deserves special mention. Even if it is a recent foundation, this splendid institution has a world-wide reputation already. It is consoling to notice that in these Institutes for catechetical specialization, not only seculars are welcomed, but their numbers are steadily increasing.

Besides, it sometimes happens now, that the public authorities, realizing their higher interests better, encourage secular masters and mistresses to acquire specialized training in religious instruction. Thus, for example, the Schools Commission for the city of Montreal, allows study-leave with full pay to secular masters wishing to devote a few years to full-time university studies, to acquire a solid training in religious teaching. We can but congratulate these authorities who prove their keen appreciation of their responsibilities. We would also encourage in this direction all secular masters and mistresses who wish to devote themselves to the magnificent apostolate of religious instruction. Let them not regret these few years that they dedicate to acquiring a better preparation ; this will increase the efficiency of their devotedness in the cause of youth, to which generosity and affection prompt them to consecrate their lives.

---

1. Pius XII, To the International Catechetical Congress at Rome, 14 Oct. 1950.
2. Pius XII, Letter to the Italian Week of Catechetical Studies, 2 July, 1949.

3

Psychological
Problems in
Religious Education

Religious Expression and Mental Deficiency

by Reverend Henri BISSONNIER

Professor at the 'Institut Supérieur Catéchétique' Paris[1]

Mental Deficiency.

After many years of regular contact with subjects suffering from mental retardation, feeblemindedness, oligophrenia, mental deficiency, we are more and more inclined to say that we know less and less what it really is. We admire those who, after some slight contact with medico-pedagogical consultations, or a few periods of experience, calmly state their « certain » opinions on the character and prognostics of « feeblemindedness. » We admire their serenity, but we pity the children, adolescents or adults, classified as « feeble-minded, » who are in danger of falling into their hands.

What we see, after all, is a school backwardness, with a complete backwardness in the development of personality as well. In diagnosing a case of real mental deficiency, the psychiatrist supposes that this backwardness is irreversible, that it is at least partly of

---

1. We print here a few pages from a book soon to be published, entitled: *L'expression, valeur chrétienne* (Series « Pédagogie psycho-sociale », Fleurus publishers, 31, rue de Fleurus, Paris VI). Starting from approximation of the idea of expression in its widest sense, and placing this idea within the context of revelation and the Christian life, the author considers different conditionings and different forms and applications, dwelling particularly on religious education, and especially on religious orthopedagogy. In other words, the work treats expression in general and its function in every life and all Christian education, but the writer is chiefly concerned with the pathological states and their specialized religious education, following his own personal line of research. This is probably the first work of its kind. On the whole, it will interest all Christian teachers and catechists, not specialists alone. We thank Father BISSONNIER for allowing our readers immediate access to Chapter 23 of his next book. Other publications by Father BISSONNIER: *Introduction à la Psychopathologie Pastorale* (Paris, Fleurus, 1960); *Catechetical Pedagogy of the Mentally Deficient Children* (Brussels, Lumen Vitae Press, 1962); *Pédagogie de Résurrection* (Paris, Fleurus, 1961). — Address: 53, rue de Babylone, Paris VII, FRANCE (Editor's note).

organic, endogenous, origin. The best definitions speak of « agenesia » of the personality. [1]

The more serious studies, like those in the United States by Seymour B. SARRASON, [2] are more critical, detailed and reserved than many of the theories actually current. They stress the difficulty of reaching a satisfactory conception on this subject. SARRASON has the merit of having reviewed a good number of researches and approaches. These exist, in fact, within the frame of references from nearly all the great schools : experimental by REY, [3] psycho-pedagogical by A. DESCŒUDRES, [4] genetic by INHELDER, [5] psycho-analytical by CLARK, [6] gestaltist by BOSCH, [7] dynamic by LEWIN, [8] medico-psychological by TRETGOLD, [9] KOHLER, [10] socio-psychological with DOLL... [11] not forgetting the intuitions, of genius sometimes, of pioneers like SÉGUIN [12] or BINET [13]. In the United States very fine research work is being done, the results of which are published in the *American Journal of Mental Deficiency.*

In some countries, it looks as if the subject is closed and no longer open to study. At the most, they seek to teach the mentally deficient to work — which is already something — so as to spare him or her a mere asylum existence. However, study of their psychology or pathology is considered useless. Students of psychology

---

1. Cf. Henri EY and Charles BRISSET : *Manuel de Psychiatrie.* Paris, Masson, 1960. The chapter on oligophrenia is rather disappointing.

2. *Psychological problems in mental deficiency.* Harper and Brothers, New York, 1949-53.

3. André REY, *Etude des insuffisances psychologiques.* Paris-Neuchâtel, Delachaux et Niestlé, 1947; *Arriération mentale et premiers exercices éducatifs.* same publisher, 1953.

4. Alice DESCŒUDRES, *L'éducation des enfants arriérés,* same publisher, 1932.

5. Barbel INHELDER, *Le diagnostic du raisonnement chez les débiles mentaux,* same publisher, 1943.

6. L. PIERCE CLARK, *The nature and treatment of amentia.* London, Baillière, 1933.

7. Gerhard BOSCH, « Zur Psychopathologie des Schwachsinns im Kindesalter », *Der Nervenartz,* 1955, p. 416, Berlin, Springer Vg.

8. Kurt LEWIN, *A dynamic theory of personality* (Chapter V : « A dynamic theory of feebleminded »), New York and London, Mc Graw-Hill, 1935.

9. A.F. TRETGOLD, *A text-book of mental deficiency,* London, Baillière, 1908.

10. Claude KOHLER, *Les déficiences intellectuelles chez l'enfant,* Paris, Presses Univ. de France, 1954.

11. E.A. DOLL, *The Vineland social maturity scale (Manual of Directions).* *The Training School.* Vineland N.J., 1935.

12. Edouard SÉGUIN, *Traitement moral, hygiène et éducation des idiots et des autres enfants arriérés,* Librairie de l'Académie Royale de médecine, Paris, 1846.

13. BINET et SIMONS, especially in : « L'intelligence des imbéciles », *Année psychologique* 1909, et « L'arriération », *Année psychologique* 1910.

or special education who would like to undertake a thesis or diploma subject in this domain are even dissuaded from doing so. « It is not interesting, » they are told, « you have too good a brain for a subject like that. » It is almost scandalous, but we have known such a thing to happen, when a brilliant scholar wanted to take up this section of research or of re-education. Objections are made. They are encouraged to study emotional disturbances and delinquency.

And yet, how far is the problem, called « mental retardation » from being solved ! Is there even in fact only one mental retardation ? Or rather, are not backwardness, deficiency of mental development, agenesia of personality, all in the order of symptoms or syndromes, behind which hide the most various etiologies... and by this very fact nosological entities ?

Once we get past the stereotypes and what is called the « primary » mentality, we discover in what is called *mental deficiency* or *mental retardation*, an amazing « garden variety »... [1] But this « garden variety » is also one of the most beautiful flower-beds if only we would take the trouble to look at it more closely.

It is precisely through a study of their outward *expression*, particularly their religious expressions, that we discover these riches.

Opinions on the ' Expressive ' Work Done by the Mentally Disturbed.

The opinion put forward by VINCHON sums up fairly well the current mentality described above. It is contained in four lines : « ... As to exceptional works produced by the feeble-minded, distant relations to popular art, they are the results of conditions now rare, like the traditions of an exceptionally well-preserved peasant setting... » [2] Need we say that this opinion seems to us neither very felicitous nor very accurate, either concerning peasants or sufferers from oligophrenia ?

We do not think works done by the feeble-minded are rare. Personally, we have spent a whole afternoon looking at drawings and paintings in a recently founded educational centre, which cares for only twenty girls from 6 to 14 years old, all suffering from serious deficiency. We also have a cupboard full of these productions of « religious » expression from catechism classes with mentally defective children and adolescents, and have made use of various drawings and paintings done during four years by this type of boys and girls to illustrate talks to a study group on « the use of drawing when teaching catechism to the mentally deficient. »

---

1. To repeat the expression used by Sarrason.
2. Jean VINCHON, *L'art et la folie*. Paris, Stock, 1950, p. 205.

Fortunately VOLMAT [1] is more generous. « The mentally deficient, » he writes, « draw clumsily and with difficulty, but they are
sometimes capable of delightful works, akin to the popular arts,
in striking contrast with their weak mental level, and their lack
of other means of expression. Thus the case presented in No. 45
shows a striking contrast between the deep mental backwardness
and the plastic quality of the paintings. We have published (1952)
three observations of mentally defective artists. Two of these were
original works: harmony and play of colours, sense of constructing
a scene, and of the marvellous, richness of ornamentation », (p. 150).

The case mentioned by Volmat is by no means rare. In our
personal experience, it is more the rule than the exception. The
book by Isabel DIAZ ARNAL [2] goes further in the analysis of works
by mental defectives, and their richness; it is full of original and
pertinent remarks. Unfortunately, she refers to a very poor bibliography on oligophrenia, which affords her a rather rudimentary
psychopathological basis, but her documentation on children's
drawing, is, on the contrary, much more developed. Isabel Diaz
Arnal purposely limits her study to slight and medium mental
deficiency. We regret that she is not interested in lower levels. It
is because, she says, the drawing of movement does not exist in
the works executed by those afflicted with acute mental deficiency.
It would be easy to contest this opinion with many proofs to the
contrary.

To start with, research should not be confined to the making
of pictures only. Modelling by these subjects, their musical expression
(on which only a few rather fragmentary studies exist), their bodily
expression above all, merit much deeper study. It is obviously
more difficult to collect productions of this sort into files. Photo-
graphy, tape-recording and films should help here.

May the few lines that follow urge others besides ourselves, or
with us, to carry out such research. Is it presumptuous to say —
though sceptical readers will probably burst out laughing — that
such work would enrich « humanity's patrimony » ?

Expressive Works and Their Conditionings.

When we try to summarize in a few lines the results of our
personal research and our group discussions, we reach the following
declarations of fact :

1. R. VOLMAT, *L'art psychopathologique.* Paris, Presses Universitaires de
France, 1956.
2. I. DIAZ ARNAL, *El Lenguaje grafico del niño deficiente.* Thesis, Consejo
Superior de Investigaciones Cientificas, Madrid, 1959.

1. *Psycho-physiological Conditionings.* It seems to us incontestable that with the mental deficient, the bodily schema is but little organized ; psycho-motility often disturbed, is one of the greatest handicaps though fairly frequent.

In contrast, their physical suppleness is often amazing, even to the hyperlaxity of the mongol. Their simplicity, and sometimes the slowness of gesture, add to the impression of density and sincerity which emanate from it, making it particularly suitable to express the sacred and the religious.

Rhythm, sometimes difficult to acquire, can often, be manifested as very faithful. Creativeness here is not without variety and originality.

Tiring quickly is generally a common feature, but the mental deficient is capable of persevering to the end of his or her powers.

Finally, one is astonished at the extra-ordinary muscular strength and dexterity which some sufferers from oligophrenia possess.

2. *Psychological Conditionings.* We hear about the « weak ego » of oligophrenics, but what does the expression mean ? We also hear about the « weak ego » of the delinquent and the neurotic... The oligophrenic does not seem to us so easily influenced interiorly even if he or she acquiesces exteriorly. Their tenacity of will is often astounding, even tinged with rigidity.

Their simplicity, also, does not exclude a certain shrewdness. They are quite open to humour.

Their capacity for symbolization is remarkable. Perhaps the opinion of DUMAS deserves mention here, according to which « the symbol is born of difficulty in direct expression. » In that case, oligophrenics would be among the first prompted to symbolization. The paths of thought and speech being difficult for them, gesture, colour, music, being of more intuitive and affective order, would be all the more used by them to enter into contact with others, within the measure that this desire for communication has been aroused.

This can go as far as surprising « rituals, » like the little child who could neither read nor write, yet said to the priest or catechist : « Write down your name for me, » and then swallowed the piece of paper on which the name had been written... symbolism of identification and of communion ? Or the action of another, who would pull out one of his teacher's hairs and tried to plant it on his own scalp..., or the action of suddenly kissing the hand of some one they revere, the priest especially...

This spontaneity is one of the characteristics of the mentally deficient just as they prove themselves capable — much more than is usually imagined — of original creation and renovation. Unfortunately, the immense majority of mental defectives have been deprived, on principle, of means of expression, and also on principle, they have been too often reduced to the state of robots induced to repeat the same thing unendingly. If only the experiment were sincerely made — and some have done so with success — of giving the necessary material and initiative to mental defectives ! The creativeness and originality they can manifest would cause real surprise.

It is noticeable also that the initiative and originality of the mentally deficient is not only possible, but it is also « resistant » so to speak. This fits in with their resistance to accepting suggestion. We have noticed, during lessons of free expression, that several children, especially those extremely defective, were quite capable of following the expression of their neighbours, or of watching closely some bodily expression (on a given subject : « Make a gesture to show God our Father that you are praying to Him, » « Think hard of something you have in your hand, and which you want to offer to some one you love »), without copying the attitude of the others. They showed an extra-ordinary capacity of independent expression. Paradoxical as it may seem, the slightly defective seem to be much less « independent, »... as are many normal children.

Same experience with drawing. Here we are thinking of some who are severely defective, capable of drawing only a rudimentary « fellow »; yet they were able to respond to the catechist's invitation : « Show how you can say ' Glory to God ' with your hands... ». Each produced his own drawing, completely personal and alive in its rudimentary outline, without in any way seeking inspiration from his neighbour's production... Some will say it is because they are artistic ; that may be, but it also proves their capacity to create and to express their own personality when they turn towards God.

Their identification with adult life is not impossible. It will be expressed in naïve fashion, but there again it will be more « disinterested » in some way, in the growing girl who has extreme or medium mental deficiency, more than in a « normal » child of the same age. The former is more capable than the latter of admiring the beauty or costliness of her mistress' clothes, without any selfish reaction and without wishing to imitate, more or less clumsily, the style of dress or head-dress of the adult, or her way of speaking or walking. Exceptions, of course, can confirm this rule, but the exceptions are more likely to be found among the slight defectives.

3. *Religious Expression.* Repeating the plan we have already used several times, we can notice a few points concerning motivation, behaviour, form and content.

Motivation.

Contrary to what might be supposed from what we have just said, and taking into account certain theories — which are very attractive — about the narcissistic character of mental defectives, the emotional relationship seems to play a very important role for them. They are ready to give much in order « to please » their teacher or catechist, to do much in order « to please God. »[1] Care should be taken not to abuse this, but, as we have said, it can be used with discretion and prudence, especially on « great occasions. »

Oligophrenic children or adolescents express themselves for the joy of doing so and of expressing what they feel. They « live » it, and really re-live or truly anticipate it when they « re-present » it. If they like and often seek approval — the normal reaction of a subject often snubbed and humiliated, or approved insincerely to be got rid of — they can often do without it quite well. They are not unlike the small child, or the great artist, notably when in the religious domain.

They like to repeat and act over again what they have seen and experienced : liturgical acts (Mass, incensation, reading from the Missal), celebrations, for example, or just a visit to the church, a sacrament received or given to others in their presence (Baptism, Confirmation, Holy Eucharist). Or they may try to draw a cross, or paint the light of a candle or the carpet in the church, quite independently of the building, simply as a happy experience which they repeat.

Behaviour.

The behaviour of mentally deficient children, when it comes to expression, is generally marked by slowness. They need time to get started. They splash about first, or finger the end of the paintbrush or pencil, as if trying out their colours. They listen to notes on the piano one after the other, sometimes the same note for a long time. They unfold and stroke material before beginning to use it... Is not their slowness a little better than our precipitation in making use of all these riches ? In an excellent study, SÉGUIN has already spoken of this kind of « contemplation. »[2]

Expression will often come, like delayed action, at the end of a long maturation, at the moment when we, wearied or pressed for time, are ready to call out : « Come along now, time's up ! »

1. Ruth WINTERGEST drew attention to this in her remarkable thesis *Religiöse Erziehung des Geistesschwachen Kindes*, Zurich, 1945.
2. *Op. cit.*, p. 156

On the contrary, this is the exact « time » for the mentally deficient child or adolescent, and we cut down the tree, just when it is ready to bear fruit.

Even a certain sense of perseverance can be detected, but it is not constant, and more often than not, we find a surprising fecundity.

What is especially remarkable is the degree in which the mentally defective children put energy into their work. Their drawing, bodily expression, modelling, is an action lived, lived like a dream and better than a dream, lived like a marvellous reality.

There again, rationalists that we are, is it the mentally deficient child or adolescent who is in the wrong ? « Intellectus est quodam modo omnia, » wrote St. Thomas in his day. « In a certain way intelligence is all things. » Obviously, there is no question of losing perspective, but what we know, « represent » and express is certainly there in some way.

Form.

The expression of the mental defective, will always have something in its form that suggests the child or the primitive. When speaking of psychopathological expression in general, we pointed out the difference which must be established between these three types of expression.

The mental defective's form of expression shows this « realism » (in the childish and primitive sense) which we have just mentioned. It is a realness lived over again, or a dream which has passed into reality. Like the child's production it is without distance and without barriers, but at the same time it has a certain capacity for testing the real, in the adult sense of the word. Like the child and perhaps even more, the mental defective is relatively insensible to the principle of non-contradiction. To him a thing can quite well be black and white, possible and impossible at the same time... But there are nuances which he seizes more shrewdly than many normal adults, he « formulates » by juxta-position of intuitions, more or less shut off from one another, as the topographical figures by LEWIN show. [1] In this diversity, unity is difficult for him. It is slightly achieved around the dominant impression, the major interest invading the field of consciousness. At the same time it resounds in the affective life, hence the synchronism of the expression. The most appreciated element is brought out, enlarged, detached from the rest. We know that it passes into the front rank in the subject's life.

---

1. K. LEWIN, *A dynamic theory of personality*, McGraw, New York, 1935, p. 208.

This predominance of the emotional life and its evolution can be decidedly greater in this subject than that of intelligence. [1] It will appear in the predominance, richness, accuracy even, of the colours in contrast with the poverty of the design, and habitual absence of perspective. But it will stress, give dynamism, so to say, to the action, movement and their intentionality. At sight of some of their experiments, you are inclined to exclaim : « That is well captured ! » The dominant trait is stressed, like an excellent caricaturist ; colour appreciated is produced as in the impressionist school. We remember a severely mentally deficient child who spent some time among snow-capped mountains and then went straightway to Normandy. In two paintings, done one after the other but on the same day, he reproduced the two landscapes ; in one, the glittering blues and whites of snowy peaks in the sunlight, and in the other, the grey tints with delicately blended woodlands. Or some acutely defective adolescent girls who, after a pilgrimage to Chartres wanted to reproduce their impressions : there was the brilliance of stained-glass, spires soaring into the sky, the mysterious shadow of arches, and suddenly in one corner, a green square, the copper roofing of the apse...

We remember too, a big mongol boy whose canvases were exhibited in Paris recently, whose fidelity of tints managed to give his landscapes an astonishing depth and relief. He had achieved a real perspective, which almost contradicted the principle that perspective is inaccessible to the mentally defective. But his perspective is different from the more geometrical perspective of a subject normally developed, whose talent has been and can be trained.

This sensitivity to colour and this dynamism can be perceived in the expression of attitude and gesture whether drawn, plastic, or bodily reproduced. Posture is reduced to its essential trait, almost exaggerated, finalized in its trajectory, hence the amazing impression of truth.

As Isabel DIAZ ARNAL has shrewdly pointed out, the normal subject, especially as he grows, wants to multiply details and his drawing becomes confused. He is too logical and too rational as well. The mentally defective catches the essential with sheer simplicity. He expresses the causal connection quite crudely: « The very special portrayal of movement by the mentally deficient seems to us more expressive and complete than that produced by normal subjects... they reflect the idea of movement as the passage from essence to existence... The astounding thing about this repre-

---

1. We say indeed his « affectivity, » in the strong sense of the word.

sentation of movement which is so complete, is that the mental defective does not arrive at it through mental exercise or logical relation, but through life itself, through his own vital experience, his own existence. » Hence « the physiological normality of the mental defective's perception. » [1]

To our mind, these remarks are keenly interesting for religious expression. We think they explain the paradoxical sense of richness and the impression of truth contrasting with the barrenness of the design, modelling or gesture of the oligophrenic child or adolescent... The density too of some of their sayings, which are powerless to reveal their intimate wealth, but which seem to reveal so much in so few words.

Content.

Finally, what can be said of the content ? Everything can come into the mentally defective child's drawing. In one sense, everything is there. We must admit this, even if we cannot see it. From the point of view of expression, if not of art, the essential is that the subject really intended to put it there, and is persuaded, if only for a moment, that it is there.

Like the small child he can change his mind, at least from our point of view as an adult on-looker. The figure drawn, is at one moment his teacher, then it turns into himself while the teacher is the new person outlined at his side. A clumsy square was his house. Now it can turn into the church, or the tabernacle, and later on into « the book of the word, » or the altar. It matters little ; what is really interesting is that it evolves, and becomes something through expression...

Once we are on the plane of religious education, the most important thing is that a religious vitality and a deep religious sense are revealed. Religious sentiment of an intensity and evolution often far beyond the mental age, and sometimes beyond the actual age of the subject is evident. This fact is so striking, and remarkable in the measure that it is possible to work out verifications in such a domain as this, [2] it seems to argue in favour of a certain specificity of this religious sense in man. Even between two oligophrenic children, the less defective is not necessarily the more developed in this sense. Sometimes it is definitely the contrary,

---

1. *Op. cit.*, p. 77 and ff.
2. Among others, see the thesis by E. PAULHUS, *L'éducabilité religieuse des déficients mentaux*, Vitte, Lyon, 1962.

which in no way means that the religious sense grows in opposition to the intelligence of man.

We have in mind certain expressions, drawn, modelled, or produced in gesture by children markedly deficient, of « the widow's mite, » « Christ calming the storm at sea, » « the life of St. Clare, » of a child sleeping peacefully in its cot, of a priest with the thurible, of a wondering vision of the altar at Mass. Or again, we remember these attitudes produced in modelling clay or wire ; or the passing attitudes of the child in person : attitudes of humility, repentance, trust, adoration, offering, exultation or of profound peace. We remember a little girl who came into the chapel, thinking she was alone, going slowly and reverently up to the altar, bowing low and slowly raising her arms up towards the tabernacle, lowering them... and remaining in contemplation for such a long time. A wondering witness and seized with emotion, we dared not move from the recess of the confessional where we awaited a penitent... That little girl had given no bodily expression for several months. The catechist who had taught her had gone away. But the little one knew now how to pray without words, with a simple attitude, a simple gesture, telling God she loved Him with all that she was...

What Conclusions Can Be Drawn ?

First of all, there is no doubt, that the sincerity in all the expression of the mentally deficient should be a joy for us, and also perhaps the occasion for this salutary examination of conscience of which we have spoken above. We must say, all the same, that for the mental deficient, however simple and uninhibited he may be, as for other people, the « best » will probably never be expressed perceptibly. It will remain « the secret of the King... » and it is better so.

Let us remember, however, that the mentally defective child, perhaps more than any other inadaptive type, needs to develop the non-verbal means of expression. This is not to say that his education in speech or even writing should be neglected. God awaits a return of love from this human being, however simple in form, gesture or stroke of pencil. We can remember a big mongol girl, almost repulsive to look upon, whom one of our priests had patiently taught by gesture. We can still see her joy the day we asked her a few questions on the Mass, and she was able to answer quite simple and without a word... merely by the attitude of her arms.

Let us admit that expression from the mentally defective is different from ours, slower, more limited, sometimes reduced to a

« phrase-word, » but not less full of meaning and rich in real value. How much is sometimes contained in their gaze alone !

Above all, let us keep to the liberty, the spontaneity of this expression for these children and adolescents, as for all others. We should prefer their rudimentary figures with arms and legs coming out of a big head, of which they may tell us : « That's me in the chapel, » or even « That's Jesus in the crib » to this fine coloured ready-made picture which the child has only got to daub with red and blue. May God preserve us from seeking out easy ways and simple recipes, for making something pretty, at slight cost to ourselves.

Let us also accept the symbolic language of the mental defective. Let us talk to him in his language. We should have confidence in it, not in falling back to the level of small children — that would be merely artificial, and even dangerous, as much for the subjects as for ourselves — but in going beyond our own reasoning, to encounter the exceptional, and God as well at that level.

Let us believe in the exceptional child's sincerity, and his capacity. We would willingly go so for as to say his « totality » of engaging himself. He is all of a piece, and when he gives, he gives all. It has been said that he hardly knows how to lend. After all, the commitment of the whole being, which the religious undertakes, who vows his possessions, his body, his liberty, and life itself, is it not « expression » in the highest degree ? This full expression of the being itself, the mentally defective children can achieve in a surprising way.

Finally we must not forget that to these children we have to transmit a mystery, to teach them to adore a mystery which in-finitely transcends both us and them. As we have said elsewhere, from the poverty of our expression to the poverty of theirs, there are only degrees of incompetence. We are both in a deep community of situation as of destiny. That is true in all research into expression between masters and pupils. It is also true between the person called normal, even gifted, and the smallest defective child.

At the end of it all, he knows about as much, he says about as much to God, as we do. Perhaps it is he who has the most to teach us and to reveal to us. Perhaps he is our real master :

« Unless you become as little children... » are Our Lord's own words.

Who Wrote the Bible?

A Psychological Study of Religious Thinking Between 6 and 17 years

by Ronald J. GOLDMAN

Lecturer in Educational Psychology at the University of Reading, Great Britain [1]

Religious Thinking.

The purpose of this research has been to attempt to supply insights into the modes and patterns of thinking which children and adolescents bring to bear upon the religious teaching to which they are exposed daily in school, church and family. In order to understand the Bible, the Church, religious activities and their relation to life children must be able to grasp intellectually the central ideas expressed and implied in teaching. Teaching involves the communication of ideas in such a way as they can be understood by the learner.

This does not suggest that religion is a mere intellectual exercise, a philosophical puzzle to be put together in a rational and orderly manner. In the last resort religion is a mystery and speaks of matters and experiences which are incommunicable. This view is accepted by the investigator and has in fact been developed elsewhere (GOLD-

---

1. This article contains extracts from the Introduction and one chapter from a research, considerable for both extent and precision, undertaken four years ago with a view to revision of the Syllabuses of Religious Instruction in the state schools. This study in its entirety — announced for publication this summer (1964): *Religious Thinking from Childhood to Adolescence* (London, Routledge and Kegan Paul) — shows through which intellectual categories biblical stories are assimilated by children and adolescents, and determines the age (chronological and mental) at which these mental structures undergo readjustment which directs them towards adult functioning. In the chapter we publish, results seem particularly dependent on information received in class, and could therefore gain by the recommendations made by the author in his important conclusions. — Address: Department of Education, The University, Reading, GREAT BRITAIN (Editor's note).

MAN, 1959). Knowledge can be both intellectual and emotional. The feeling element involved in religious experience, the truths which come from identifying ourselves as in artistic appreciation, are as important and usually much more compelling than those truths which come from inductive and deductive logic.

Nevertheless, a teacher's major task is to communicate truths on an intellectual plane whereby thinking is engaged at as high a level as the ability of the pupil will allow. Religious truth must be compelling intellectually and not only emotionally, so that the whole man is involved. To hide behind emotional appeal, to avoid both answering and even raising intellectual problems about religion, is dishonest and ultimately unsatisfying.

General Design of the Research.

The design of the research was evolved after preliminary discussions with two groups of pupils, and a clinical interview method for individual pupils was standardised and administered to a pilot sample of 20 pupils. The content of this was the discussion of three *pictures* [1] to test out concepts of Church, Prayer and the Bible, and of three Biblical *stories* to test understanding of basic Biblical concepts : The Burning Bush, Crossing the Red Sea and The Temptations of Jesus.

Population.

This was then administered to a sample of 200 pupils representative of the school population aged 6 to 17 years, normally exposed to religious teaching under Agreed Syllabuses. The pupils were selected in the form of a stratified sample, so that intelligence, [2] sex, religious affiliation, religious behaviour and social background should be comparable from year to year.

---

1. The Complete analysis of the answers to the three pictures and five stories will be found in the volume in preparation : *Religious Thinking from Childhood to Adolescence* (London, Routledge and Kegan Paul, New York, Mac Millan, 1964).

2. As some of the Infant and Junior portions of the school population had been tested by the SLEIGHT Non-Verbal Intelligence Test this was used for estimating mental age with pupils up to 10 years of age. Beyond this age pupils had been tested by various MORAY HOUSE and N.F.E.R. tests; the highest I.Q. was taken as typical of each pupil. The criterion of mental age was recognized as only approximate and no pupil was selected as part of the sample where the school's estimate of his ability differed appreciably from that achieved in tests.

The responses of the pupils were scored by the investigator and independent judges, and with few exceptions, items showed a sufficiently high scorer reliability as to suggest objective assessment. The scores in most items were analysed in terms of a Guttman Scalogram analysis.

Picture 3 and the Questions on the Bible.

PICTURE 3 is a rather simple and rough representation of a child contemplating a mutilated Bible. Then four questions come in the interview as follows :

Q. 1. — What do you think the boy/girl is thinking ?
Answers may conveniently be classified as : anger — shock — disgust — regret — Its naughty — Its wicked.
Q. 2. — Does he/she think this because the Bible is different from other books ? What is so different about the Bible, what's so special about it, that he should think this way ?
Q. 3. — You can see from the picture its called « Holy Bible » (or : You yourself called it holy).
What is holy about it ? What makes it holy ?
Q. 4. — How did the Bible come to be written ?

The Interview Method.

Before assessing results against these criteria, we should reiterate that this third picture was used firstly to establish rapport at the outset of the interview, secondly, to partially disguise the personal nature of the information required, thirdly to assist the young and especially the dull pupil to respond to questions related to a specific situation rather than abstractions, and finally to elicit not attitudes but concepts of a specific type, that is, of Bible.

A problem implicit in the method used in this part of the research is the difficult one of verbalism. There are several aspects of this problem which are relevant including :

1) Children who hold concepts but cannot express them adequately due to poor verbal ability or personality difficulties. How far is the test merely one of verbal facility ?

2) Children who have linguistic fluency and poor concepts, but their verbal flow conveys insight of a level higher than the level they actually possess. How far can the child convey a higher ability than he actually possesses ?

3) Children who for various reasons wish to supply answers which are acceptable to the investigator. How far can the child consciously deceive ?

The question of deception, conscious or unconscious, was faced in the construction of the interview. First of all, by establishing good rapport and by stressing the fact that the questions were not a test for getting marks — « there are no right or wrong answers » — and all that was required was what the pupil thought, a conscious emphasis was made to minimize this factor. Secondly, the probing nature of the interview with its follow-up questions such as « What makes you think so ? » or « How do you mean ? » or « I don't understand ; can you put that in another way ? » penetrates behind the glib answer to the reasons behind the verbalisms. It is true that these reasons are couched in language, but it was discovered frequently that what looked like an advanced concept at first, when reduced to its essential rational elements was in reality very limited and childish. Thirdly, answers were assessed in terms of their content meaning, so that crudely expressed ideas were scored at the same level of insight as the same idea expressed in a verbally polished manner.

On the question of deception, Piaget (1929) typified five types of reaction revealed by clinical interview as answers at random, romancing answers, suggested conviction answers, liberated conviction answers and spontaneous conviction answers. The two latter are sought for by any interviewer who seeks to liberate ideas about problems already thought through or to evolve spontaneous thought about a problem obviously new to the child. The child who is unmotivated or cannot understand the questions will tend to provide random answers by mere association of words and here the problem is to motivate the child or to rephrase the question in such a way as to make it intelligible. The romantic and the suggested convicted answer are the deceptive answers and the methodology outlined above was evolved to meet these.

This raises the further question of adult teaching and the child repeating with real conviction what he has been taught. Here again, the scoring criteria would appear to penetrate this and the questioning in depth sought to constrain the child to go beyond what is learnt at the school level from adults and to justify the statements he makes.

This whole matter is discussed very fully by Piaget (1929) in his introduction to « The Child's Concept of the World. » In conclusion (p. 32) he points out that « if all the children of the same mental age arrive at the same conception of a given phenomenon, in defiance of the variations in their personal circumstances, their experience and the conversation they have overheard etc., this may be regarded as a prime guarantee of the originality of the conviction. » Whilst we consider this a somewhat sweeping generalization, if we substituted « most » for « all, » the argument would appear to be a valid one. Piaget makes the further point that as the child's convictions (here he appears to mean « concepts ») evolve to higher levels with age a sudden disappearance of concepts is not evident, but combinations or compromises of the new with the old takes place. Elsewhere, he describes this as the process of assimilation and accommodation. The fact that this process is visible with responses from numbers of children in sequence of age and ability, would seem to argue the rather fantastic view that children develop their ability to provide deceptive answers with increasing age in a uniformly rational manner so as to provide a scoring sequence, or that, in fact, the responses on the whole are valid « liberated » or « spontaneous » modes of thinking.

In the realm of religious thinking levels of understanding and the ability to verbalise them will tend to interpenetrate each other, especially with the advent of schooling. There will, naturally, be variations due to personality differences, but this is a problem common to all testing situations dependent upon language ability. In our test examples, it should be pointed out that they were deliberately designed in « situations » or « action » settings, both in picture and story form, to assist the normally inhibited and verbally limited child.

Statistical Analysis.

The sample of 200 subjects and the items of the test were so arranged that *scale analysis* could be applied to the data. The technique of scale analysis can be used with qualitative data and has been applied, in the main, to the measurement of attitudes and opinions.

The technique has been described by GUTTMAN (1944 and 1947), SOUFFER and GUTTMAN (1950), and PEEL (1959) has clearly outlined how it may be used to evaluate sequences of thought in relation to Piagetian-type data.

We would expect that, if levels of insight are related to mental age, the scores would move gradually from left to right, i.e. from lower scores to higher scores, so that the familiar parallelogram of scores would occur. In this case, the *reproductibility* can be said to be 100 %. However, as can be seen in TABLE I, the reproducibility is far from perfect. In other words, some children of low mental age score higher than some of those of superior mental age, and the ideal parallelogram does not occur.

To improve reproducibility it is legitimate to combine categories of scores.[1] Cutting lines are then inserted according to the frequency of each category, in the case of Q. 2/3 : at the 73d and 200th pupil. It will be seen that in each category there are some displacements or 'errors.' Thus (Table I) in relation to mental age, we have :

---

1. GUTTMAN, 1947, elaborates the reasons for this : « It has seldom been found that an item with four or five categories is regarded as distinct. One reason for this is the verbal habits of people... ; (they) may have essentially the same position in the basic continuum, but differ on an extraneous factor of verbal habits. By combining categories, minor extraneous variables of this kind can be minimized » (p. 256).

Category 1 has 29 errors in a frequency of 73 responses
Category 2 has 29 errors in a frequency of 127 responses

Total No of errors : 58   Total frequency : 200

The coefficient of reproducibility is then found by the formula :

$$\text{Coeff. of reprod.} = 100 \ (1 - \frac{\text{Total No. of errors}}{\text{No. of items} \times \text{No. of subjects}}) \ \%$$

$$= 100 \ (1 - \frac{58}{200}) \ \%$$

$$= 100 \ (1 - .29) \ \% = 100 \times .71 \ \% = 71 \ \%.$$

This coefficient of reproducibility has been obtained in dividing the scores in two categories (scores 0 1 2 versus scores 3 4 5 6). One finds (Table I) that the reproducibility is higher (80 %) with the scores combined in two other categories (0 1 2 3 versus 4 5 6), and still higher (90 %) with the scores combined in two other categories (0 1 2 3 4 versus 5 6). This corresponds to three different cutting lines (mental age), respectively: 10 year, 1 month — 13 years, 1 month — and 16 years, 7 months.

GUTTMAN, in scaling attitude questionnaires, says PEEL (1959) « insisted upon a minimum of 85 %. Guttman's condition is very stringent and not often met, and in this work (logical judgments) we might say that 75 % is a reasonable figure to take » (p. 94). The view is taken here that any coefficient of reproducibility which approaches or meets Peel's 75 % requirement is sufficient to justify the existence of *sequences in thinking*, based upon the scoring criteria given.

RESULTS FROM PICTURE 3 : CONCEPTS OF THE BIBLE

Questions 2 and 3 :

What makes the Bible a special kind of book ?

The picture evoked a fairly standard response in the pupils of shock at its condition, and the almost total reaction was that the children responsible were naughty. A few said it was naughty because no books of any kind should be treated in this way, but most conveyed particular concern that it was the Bible involved. However, all pupils in the discussion of the picture made quite clear that they regarded the Bible as a special kind of book. Questions 2 and 3 then naturally followed from this. The two questions were combined in one assessment.

Answers to Q. 2 only are scored, with Q. 3 acting as a statement which may enlighten the meaning of Q. 2. The most frequent response to the question « Why is the Bible holy ? » is « Because it is about God (or

Jesus) and he is holy. » But occasionally there is a response which gives
further insights.

Answers range from the grossly material, such as the external
appearance of the book, its price, its print, its special old language to
real insight into the contents of the Bible as the message of salvation
by which God was revealed. On the whole *all* answers tend to have « It's
about God or Jesus » and so this answer is discounted, in search of further
insight, into what makes the Bible a unique book.

Here are some examples of how the answers were scored :

SCORE 1

Very inadequate, very incorrect or irrelevant answers

« It's about God and Jesus » (and nothing more even after several sub-questions).
« It's about God and Jesus and it costs a lot of money. »
« It's a big book and it's got small print. »
« It's got no pictures in it. »

SCORE 2

Inadequate answers

« It's a church book. You take it to church. »
« It's got commandments in it » or « psalms. »
« It's got a New Testament and an Old Testament. »

SCORE 3

Fair answers

« It's true stories » (no definition of what is true).
« It's older. »
« It's got the teachings of Jesus » (unelaborated).

SCORE 4

Fairly good answers

« It teaches you good behaviour » or « Helps with problems. »
« It has original stories by eye witnesses. »
« It's about people who believed in God. »
« It has more meaning and truth than other books. »

SCORE 5

Good answers

« It's the original source book for other religious books. »
« It helps us to understand God's will. »
« It comes through men in revelation, visions, etc. »

Score 6

Very good answers

« It expresses the Christian Faith. »
Anything which shows the real meaning of Christ's mission.
A development of ideas in man's struggle for salvation.

Three dichotomous arrangement of categories yield high reproducibility, as can be seen below.

TABLE 1

Table of Errors and scalability for questions 2 and 3[1]

Criterion	Combined Categories		Total Error	% age Error	Coeff. of Reproducibility	Cutting Lines (Years)
	1	2				
	(012-3456)					
Frequency	73	127				
Chron. Age	30	30	60	30	70 %	9 : 8
Mental Age	29	29	58	29	71 %	10 : 1
	(0123-456)					
Frequency	130	70				
Chron. Age	27	27	54	27	73 %	12 : 6
Mental Age	20	20	40	20	80 %	13 : 1
	(01234-56)					
Frequency	173	27				
Chron. Age	13	13	26	13	87 %	14 : 8
Mental Age	10	10	20	10	90 %	16 : 7

All these produce a sufficiently high reproducibility to confirm the item's scalability and to show several possible observed sequences. The last series (combining 0 1 2 3 4 ; and 5 and 6) show very high reproducibility, the error indicating a not spuriously induced high reproducibility, especially on the criterion of mental age.

Three separate observed sequences can be observed.

1) Two observed stages, dividing about C.A.* 9: 8 and M.A.* 10: 1 up to which time irrelevant ideas such as colour and size are evident ; and after which time the Bible's truth, age and teaching content are seen as important.

---

1. The composition and meaning of the Tables 1 and 2 have been explained above (Editor's note).
* C.A. = Chronological Age; M.A. = Mental Age.

2) Two observed stages, dividing about C.A. 12: 6 and M.A. 13: 1. Before this time pupils see the Bible as 'unique' in irrelevant terms such as colour, size, age and as 'absolutely true' and as a teaching book. After this time, its content and message is the dominant emphasis of its uniqueness.

3) Two observed stages, dividing about C.A. 14 : 8 and M.A. 16 : 7, after which an accurate apprehension of the uniqueness of the Bible as an original source book of religion, of revealed insights into God's purpose and as the major book of Judaism and Christianity.

The three two-stage observed sequences present considerable overlap and from such high reproducibility coefficients we can infer the existence of three to four stages from the evidence.

Stage 1 : Childish concepts of physical appearance, principally size and colour.

Stage 2 : Concepts of veneration for the Bible as the only completely true book, the oldest book and a teaching book.

Stage 3 : Concepts dependent upon its teaching content in terms of helpfulness, eye witness accounts and its worth as more truthful and meaningful than other books.

Stage 4 : Concepts of an original source book of religion through revelation.

Stage 1 appears to terminate about C.A. 9: 8 and M.A. 10: 1 ; stage 2 about C.A. 12: 6 and M.A. 13: 1 ; and stage 3 about C.A. 14: 8 and M.A. 16: 7. The last stage is not too clearly identifiable but can be assumed from the data.

Question 4 : « How did the Bible come to be written ? »

If this question is answered fully it should cover both the authorship of the Bible and the purpose for which it was written. Most children required supplementary questions such as (« Who ? » i.e. Who wrote the Bible ?) and (« ALL the Bible ? » — or the Rest of the Bible ?) i.e. to see if the child has ideas of multiple authorship and distinguishes between Old Testament and New Testament. Sometimes, where the different testaments are implied in an answer, a further question (Old Testament ?) is asked, about the author(s) of the Old Testament.

Marking on the authorship and origins of the Bible record, namely, answers to « Who ? » Insight into the purpose « Why ? » boosts an answer by a point, if it is good. Very occasionally, a very good answer for the purpose of writing the Bible, boosts a score by two points.

A grading can be seen from crude to advanced thinking about the Bible, from seeing God or Jesus as the actual author, to one holy man writing it, then some religious people, then disciples, then disciples and prophets. Only late in the scores does recognition of oral tradition and eye-witness accounts combined occur (4 plus).

Below are illustrations and examples of how the scale was scored.

SCORE 0
D.k. (Don't know), or completely foolish
e.g. « A little girl, » « printers » or « the man who owns it. »

SCORE 1
Very inadequate, incorrect or irrelevant

« God, on His typewriter. »
« Jesus thought of the stories and God wrote them down. »
« A king or a queen. »
« The Vicar because Bibles are in his church. He loves Jesus. »

SCORE 2
Inadequate

One man, religious in some way, e.g. Stephen, a man requiring forgiveness, a disciple (unspecified).
« People long ago wrote it » (multiple authors but unelaborated).
« Some people who found old tablets of stone. »
— God or priests are authors « to further people's beliefs » e.g. : score one *plus* an insight into purpose of Bible.

SCORE 3
Fair

Answers which clearly show multiple origins by religious people who were either there at the time or inherited stories in some way.
« People who lived in Palestine where God and Jesus were. »
« The disciples » (no mention or implication of Old Testament).
« Peter, the disciple, wrote the New Testament » (vague idea of Peter as original source of Gospels).
« People who believed, like monks and nuns, wrote it down after. »
Where there is clearly confusion between Old Testament an New Testament (e.g. « Christians » writing the Old Testament).

SCORE 4
Fairly good

Stronger idea of eye-witness accounts and use of « hearsay, » and some oral tradition vaguely seen.
Old Testament and New Testament now distinguished with only slight confusion.
« Disciples and prophets wrote it. »
« Disciples wrote it (All ?) No, Moses wrote the rest. »

Score 5

Good

Use of eye-witness and oral traditions clearly seen and expressed.
Some ideas of the possible fallibility of the record.
Clear distinction between Old Testament and New Testament.
Need clearly seen for written record as time passed to avoid distortion of stories.

Score 6

Very good

« I presume God thought there ought to be some tangible means of explaining Himself without appearing, and to serve as a reference people could turn to.

(How ?) Used His prophets and leaders of His people — influenced or inspired them to do it — told them various things about the beginning of the world, commandments and ceremonial laws.

(New Testament ?) He led mainly the apostles to write the story of Christ's life. He got several to write it so there was more than one opinion. »
« The people who wrote it are inspired, not the Bible. »

Two trichotomies are possible combinations, the best reproducibility being shown below. Only 192 pupils were asked this item.

TABLE 2

Table of Errors and Scalability for Question 4

Criterion	Combined Categories			Total Error	% age[1] Error	Coeff. of Reproducibility	Cutting Lines (Years)
	1	*2*	*3*				
	(012 - 34 - 56)						
Frequency	61	101	30				
Chron. Age	12	26	14	52	27	73 %	9:3 and 14:6
Mental Age	14	24	10	48	25	75 %	9:7 and 15:8

[1] (Calculated error on 192 pupils)

The reproducibilities approach the 75 % requirement being more marked on the criterion of mental age than on the criterion of chronological age. The item is thus scalable and an observed sequence of three stages is clearly demonstrated. These stages are :

Stage 1 : The Bible is written by God, one powerful person or a very religious man. It is regarded as a unitary composition (Up to about C.A. 9: 3 and M.A. 9: 7).

Stage 2 : Some concepts of the multiple authorship of the Bible are seen as based upon eye-witnesses or hearsay accounts, but the concepts are somewhat confused with frequent untenable generalizations (Up to about C.A. 14: 6 and M.A. 15: 8).

Stage 3 : Composite authorship seen clearly without confusion ; and inspiration rather than accuracy is regarded as its dominant character (from about C.A. 14: 6 and M.A. 15: 8).

Summary of Results.

1. Concepts of the Bible as a unique book can be seen in Questions 2 and 3. These items were combined due to the repetitious verbalisms, such as « It's God's book, » « It's holy » and « It's about God and Jesus, » used by most pupils.

Three stages could be inferred, in the growth of understanding in what the uniqueness of the Bible consists.

1) Childish concepts of physical appearance.

2) Veneration as the ' true ' and ancient book, used by teachers.

3) Concepts based upon its content as true (not necessarily in a literal sense), helpful and rooted in historical fact.

A fourth stage is possible, that of the Bible as an original source book of religion through revelation, which, of course, may be included in the latter part of stage 3. Stage 1 appears to terminate about C.A. 9: 8 and M.A. 10: 1, stage 2 about C.A. 12: 6 and M.A. 13: 1 ; stage 3 about C.A. 14: 8 and M.A. 16: 7.

2. Concepts of the origins and authorship of the Bible seen in Question 4, yield clear indications of *three observed stages.*

1) Concepts of unitary authorship, by God, a powerful or very religious person.

2) Concepts of multiple authorship based upon eye witness or hearsay accounts but frequently confused.

3) Concepts of multiple authorship seen without confusion. Inspiration rather than accuracy is regarded as its dominant character.

Stage 1 appears to terminate about C.A. 9: 3 and M.A. 9: 7, and stage 2 about C.A. 14: 6 and M.A. 15: 8.

3. The age boundaries are regarded only as rough indicators of changes in quality of thinking due to many displacements. Despite this, however, it is the sequences and stages which are seen as significant.

4. Since there are only two items, one trichotomous and one dichotomous and the dichotomous frequency is 130-70 we may combine the two items. On the criterion of chronological age there

are 106 errors and a coefficient of reproducibility of 73 %. On the criterion of mental age the total errors are 88 with a coefficient of reproducibility of 77.5 %. This appears to indicate the two Bible picture items as a single scalable universe, with the dominant variable being progress in conceptual thinking about the nature and authorship of the Bible.

GENERAL CONCLUSIONS AND COMMENTS

As the major source book of religious teaching it is important for us to understand how pupils regard the Bible, for it obviously influences their judgments and thinking process when using Biblical material. Since we have examined concepts of the nature, the origins, the authority, veracity and relevance of the Bible, it will be useful to summarize and relate them at this point (even if some of them are not fully reported in this article. — Editor's note).

Practically all children regard the Bible as « special » if not unique. *Questions 2-3* show that up to about M.A. 10 : 0 children are limited by concepts of a physical nature such as the size, colour or print of the book, and up to about M.A. 13 : 0 it is venerated as an ancient book, containing the truth (usually literal truth) and often felt to be so because of the authoritative statements of powerful adults, parents, teachers and preachers. After this, the Bible is seen as « special » or unique because its truth is « helpful » or true to experience and is an expression of truth as a historic fact. M.A. 13 : 0 (C.A. 12 : 6) appears to be a significant boundary in thinking here.

Question 4 (« How did the Bible come to be written ? ») shows a similar boundary as in the uniqueness of scripture. Up to about M.A. 9 : 7 (C.A. 9 : 3) the Bible is conceived as written directly by God (« on His typewriter ») or by a powerful religious person, Jesus or a prophet (« God dictated it and Jesus took it down ») some children even citing the vicar or Enid Blyton. [1] Generally the Bible is the result of a single author's efforts. After this multiple authorship based upon eye-witnesses or reporting is grasped, but there is still much confusion to about M.A. 15 :8 (C.A. 14 : 6). This latter age boundary appears to mark the end of confusion about multiple authorship by most pupils when Scripture is recognized as inspired literature rather than literally accurate.

---

1. Enid Blyton is a prolific English writer of children's books, very popular with the young.

Concepts of the authority of the Bible as « true » in relation to all three stories (used in other parts of our research) tend to show belief in it because of external authority (« God, or Jesus wrote it, » « It's written down, » « My mummy, the vicar, teacher, said it's true ») about M.A. 11 : 0 (C.A. 10 : 6). It is true after this age for most pupils because its subject matter is God and Jesus, or the words themselves sound true. Only later M.A. 15 : 0 (C.A. 14 : 0) is it true because it is based upon eye-witness accounts or its consistency with other sources. At this time pupils tend to see its authority in terms of how it speaks to human experience, not in terms of externally induced authority. This is roughly substantiated by crude Yes/No answers which reveal a basic literal stage to about C.A. 12 : 11, an intermediate, partly critical, stage from about 12 : 11 to 14 : 11 and a fully critical stage about C.A. 15 : 0 onwards. Qualitative answers tend to show an awakening of this kind in some cases before the twelfth year. It is probably that they are becoming critical about certain aspects of the Bible some time before they consciously recognize their own emerging criticisms.

Acceptance of the written word, of course, is not confined to the Bible since there is a fairly wide conviction, not limited to school pupils, that the printed word is true because it has attained the prestige of being printed. When, to this, is added the weight of associations with God, divine authority and many adults, it is not surprising that literalism persists until well into the secondary school years. Is it because the beginnings of criticism of the Bible comes in the early, difficult years of adolescence, that pupils will swing to an extremely critical position towards the end of their secondary schooling ? Do they become hostile to religion because they recognize childish patterns of thinking as inadequate and are not offered a satisfactory intellectual alternative to literalism ? LOUKES (1961) discovered among secondary school leavers frequent complaints of « childish » religious and biblical teaching.

On the possible relevance and occurrence of the three Bible stories, in any form, it was seen that children up to M.A. 10 : 0 (C.A. 9 : 6) tended to have « isolation-in-time » concepts of the stories as having happened long ago and as not relevant to today since God has died, run out of breath, considers us too naughty or similar reasons. Not until about M.A. 13 : 2 (C.A. 12 : 6) does a « relevance-for-today » concept emerge in most pupils. The Exodus escape story is particularly limited in general transfer to today, probably because of the startling and dramatic physical event of the parting of the sea. No pupil, incidentally, draws the conclusion that God saves us in any spiritual sense but only in approximately identical modern situations, such as when people are escaping from criminals, God will stop the criminals somehow. The rough age boundary of M.A. 13:2 indicates, however, an awareness that if God is alive and omnipresent then historical consistency demands the possibility of His continued activity in the world of men. Unless this view is acceptable then no relevance can be seen, and yet much teaching tends to reinforce « isolation-in-time » concepts in relation to the Bible by emphasizing the Holy land, where these particular events appeared to happen to special holy people, wearing holy clothes, in a special holy period of history. Many pupils, even after the age boundary mentioned, betray the tendency to isolate the events in much the same way as a fly trapped in a piece of amber, sealed off from the outside world. The remedy is not the moral, implanted artificially at the end of a Scripture lesson, nor a vague parallel drawn up in modern time. Relevance must be a thorough-going assumption on the part of the teacher so that the Bible event seen is explored in human and spiritual terms common to ancient and modern times. There is evidence from « Teenage Religion » again, that pupils are bored and exasperated by much religious teaching, simply because it is not relevant to them.

Pupils, in our view, must be helped to pass through this stage and weaned towards a more critical view of the Bible. A prerequisite for any course which involves the use of Biblical material with older children would appear to be some systematic examination, exploration and discussion of such questions as « What is the Bible ?, » « How did the Bible begin ?, » « In what way is the Bible true ?, » « Can we trust the Bible » and others. As concepts of what is the nature and inspiration of the Bible affect all other concepts of what it contains, a new emphasis appears to be necessary. Lessons of this nature need not be abstract theological talk but active exploration and research into the text to provoke the important questions such as, « Is this true ?, » « Can it be true in more ways than one ?, » « What do we mean by true ? »...

*

*   *

It is evident from the Biblical concepts reviewed that no real awareness of the nature of the Bible is grasped until well into the secondary school course, and even here the Bible is regarded as authoritative in a strongly literal sense. It appears that pupils are not aware often of the possibility of a critical but reverent approach to Scripture. Concepts of the nature and authorship of the Bible are extremely confused until middle-adolescence. There would appear to be a need for parts of the religious education syllabus to deal with the whole approach to the Bible as « true, » as « inspired, » and as « revelation. » There is no reason why this could not be provided for late Juniors or early secondary school pupils in a suitable form. There is a need for children, as they enter into a more detailed study of Biblical history, especially the Old Testament, to have a clearer frame of reference within which they can interpret what they read.

BOOKS MENTIONED

GOLDMAN, R.J. (1964) *Religious Thinking from Childhood to Adolescence* (London, Routledge and Kegan Paul; New York, Mac Millan).

GOLDMAN, R.J. (1959) « What is Religious Knowledge ? » *National Froebel Foundation Bulletin*, N° 117.

GUTTMAN, L. (1944) « A Basis for Scaling Qualitative Data », *Am. Soc. Review*. Vol. 9, 2, 139-150.

GUTTMAN, L. (1947) « The Cornell Technique for Scale and Intensity Analysis », *Educ. and Psych. Measurement*. Vol. 7, 247-280.

LOUKES, H. (1961) *Teenage Religion*. London, SCM Press.

PEEL, E.A. (1959) « Experimental Examination of Piaget's Schemata Concerning Children's Perception and Thinking, and a Discussion of their Educational Significance », *Brit. J. Ed. Psych.*, XXIX, Part 2, 89-103.

PIAGET, J. (1929) *The Child's Conception of the World*. London, Routledge and Kegan Paul.

SOUFFER, S.A. and GUTTMAN, L. (1950) « Measurement and Prediction », in *Studies of Social Psychology in World War II*. Volume I, Princeton University Press.

The Burning Bush

The Symbolic Implications of a Bible Story among Children from 5-12 Years

by Christian VAN BUNNEN, S.M.A.

Priest of the African Missions of Lyons [1]

I. METHOD

We cannot reach directly a child's religious affectivity, still less its relation with God. Its feelings are only accessible in the measure in which it expresses them (if possible) or betrays them outwardly.

Since it is impossible to put the subject in a real situation which would cause the feelings we wish to analyse, our method is to suggest an *imaginary* one which may induce him to translate his reactions directly or indirectly. An imagined object can arouse real sentiments. That is the principle at the base of projective methods. Starting from a suggested idea we may be able to obtain some information about the subject's spontaneous affective representations. Let us imagine an encounter with God and see how the child interprets or reconstructs the behaviour of the person favoured with the grace. The chances are that the child will *project* his own feelings on to the person, or even identify himself with that person as if he had been in the same situation.

For our research we chose two theophanies from the Old Testament.

1. Father Christian VAN BUNNEN, teaching in Kikwit diocese (Congo-Leo), gives us this extract from his research for his Licenciate in Education (Louvain University, 1960) undertaken under the direction of Professor A. VERGOTE: *Recherches psychologiques sur le symbolisme religieux*. His method and reflections on the results seem to us particularly interesting. Born at Uccle, November 14, 1932, the author joined the Society of African Missions, and took his Licenciate in Theology at the Catholic Faculty in Lyons in 1957, being ordained priest the same year. After specialized studies at Louvain, he went out as a missionary, and was director of the secondary school at Gungu (September 1960). The troubles in South Kwilu forced him to leave Gungu on January 30, 1964. — Address in BELGIUM : 13, Zonnelaan, Alsemberg (Editor's note).

The first, which we analysed more fully was the story of the call of Moses (Exodus III, 1-6). God comes to Moses, manifesting himself in a sign : the miraculous fire of the burning bush. Fire is also a fairly universal image of the Divinity, a privileged symbol of the sacred.

The second story was that of Jacob's dream at Bethel (Genesis XXVIII, 10-19). Jacob meets God in a dream. To commemorate this vision, he erects a pillar in the place where « God dwells. » This article concerns the first story only.

We adopted the process of *individual* interviews. The process takes up much time, and excludes many subjects which statistics would welcome. In this light it is inferior to questionnaires which can be dealt with collectively, but it is the best way with children who cannot yet write easily. Besides that, it has several advantages ; the children can be observed closely, they have less communication with one another, we can see whether the question is understood, it can be repeated or explained if need be, etc.

As well as the questionnaire we had intended at first to make use of the method employing personal drawing. [1] It is a well-known technique for projection in child psychotherapy. [2] But we soon perceived that it was very hard to find a method of interpretation with objectively applicable exact criteria. We made the children draw, however, asking them to draw how they liked the story they had just heard. It was chiefly to give them something to do which would interest them and make the interview easier and less formal. Absorbed in their work, they noticed less that we wrote down their answers. With a few exceptions, they were quite ready to do this.

Here is the first story with the main questions (those which were used in the results analysed in this article).

THE BURNING BUSH

Moses was a shepherd. One day when he had led his flocks into the mountain, he saw a big flame in a bush. Moses looked hard ; the flame was burning, but it did not destroy the branches of the bush. Moses said to himself : « That is strange ! I must go nearer and see why the flame does not burn up the bush. » He went nearer to see better. Then he heard God's voice calling from the bush : « Come no nearer ! Take off

---

1. As Father A. Godin, S.J., did over the sacrifice of Isaac. Cf. *Lumen Vitae*, X (1955), no. 1, pp. 74-79, « Isaac at the stake. »

2. See, for example, S. Morgenstern, *Psychanalyse infantile*, Denoël, Paris, 1957, and Mme Dolto, « *L'interprétation psychanalytique des dessins au cours des traitements psychothérapiques*, in *Psyche*, III, no. 17 (March 1948).

*your sandals, for you are standing on holy ground. I am God.» So Moses
hid his face so as not to see God.*[1]

  II. *What would you do if God suddenly appeared before you?*
 III. *Would you be glad? Would you be afraid?*
  V. *What does flame make you think of?*
 VI. *Why did God appear under the form of fire?*
VII. *Was the fire Moses saw the same as the fire you know? What
       was special about it?*
VIII. *What would you have done if you had seen fire like that?*
 IX. *What did Moses do when he saw it?*
 XI. *Why did God not want Moses to come near the bush?*
XII. *What did Moses do when he heard God's voice?*
XIII. *What would have happened if Moses had gone too near the bush?*
XIV. *Why did Moses have to take off his sandals?*
XVII. *Why did Moses hide his face?*
XIX. *What would have happened if Moses had looked?*

Population.

We questioned 295 children, boys and girls ; 192 for the
« Burning Bush » and 103 for « Jacob's Dream. » They ranged
from the last year in Kindergarten to Grade VI primary, and were
taken almost exclusively from Catholic French-speaking schools in
the Brussels area. Ages ranged from 5 to 12 years. The proportion
of boys and girls and the numbers from each School grade are
about equal.

II. SOME RESULTS

A. Feeling of fear and feeling of transcendence

Experience of the sacred, according to the classic description by
R. OTTO,[2] is marked by an affective polarity of attraction and
fear ; the sacred is both « tremendum » et « fascinans. » Do children
perceive this ambivalence of feeling in presence of God or of symbols which manifest Him ?
Answers which reveal this ambivalence explicitly are very rare.[3]

---

1. To arrange this text, we followed Mme H. LUBIENSKA DE LENVAL, *L'éducation du sens religieux*, Paris, Spes, 1946, p. 38.
2. *Le Sacré*, Payot, Paris, 1949.
3. Ex. : q. VIII : « I would have approached with fear » (girl, 12, grade VI),
q. XIX : « He would have been struck with wonder and frightened » (girl, 8,
grade III).

Joy is not often the immediate answer. Fear is mentioned more often in the spontaneous answers, but without significant co-relation with age ; its frequence in each school grade does not help to decide whether fear in presence of the sacred is a feeling which increases or decreases with age, at least in following out our questions II, VIII, XVII.

We also asked an explicit question which forced out an answer : III. *Would you be glad ?... Would you be afraid ?* To the first query, almost all replied « yes. » This quasi-unanimity betrays conformism in the reply, so teaches us nothing ; it was simply intended as a contrast to the second query. This one, on the contrary, revealed a significant tendency in the division of YES and NO according to age. From the Kindergarten (here joined to Grade I) to Grade VI we obtained the following percentages :

FEAR	*K. and G. I*	*Grade II*	*G. III*	*G. IV*	*G. V*	*G. VI*
YES... a little !	8 %	21 %	44 %	47 %	70 %	69 %

The proportion of YES increases gradually with age. The younger the child, the steadier the negation. As the age rises, they recognize more and more that they would be afraid, or at least, they are less confident.

What does this frequency curve indicate ? Do the answers NO betray absence of religious experience, a barely awakened sense of the sacred ? Or do they simply reveal lack of self-analysis ? Comparison with certain types of answers to other questions may help us. We notice an increase with age of the sense of religious *reverence* due to God, of the feeling of His *transcendence*, of the idea of ' *tremendum* '.

II. *If God appeared to me*, « I would kneel down... I would adore Him... » etc.
    From the Kindergarten 24 % to Grade V : 70 %.

VI. *God chose fire to manifest Himself* : « to show His power, strength, to frighten... » etc.
    From Grade III : 14 % to Grade VI : 47 %.
    (Three-quarters of these answers come from Grades V and VI).

XIV. *Moses had to take off his sandals* : « out of reverence, » etc.
    From Kindergarten and Grade I : 0 to Grade VI : 39 %.

XVII. *Moses hid his face* : « because he was afraid of God..., because God is (very, too, so) great, powerful... » etc.
    From Grade I : 23 % to Grade VI : 66 %.

May we not conclude from observing this constant progress under its various aspects, that for question III (*Would you have been afraid ?*) the parallel mounting of the frequency of the answers YES also comes from growth in the sense of the sacred, of the feeling of the distance which separates man from God ? We cannot really know whether the curve of division for the answers YES and NO to question III proves a change in depth, a true affective evolution; we only reach verbal manifestations. But in any case, this curve proves a change with age in the reaction to a suggested idea of God, to a manifestation of His transcendence. The younger ones who protest NO seem to resist a feeling they find inacceptable, or else to be unwilling to contradict their first statement that they would be glad. The others who admit YES have understood that in presence of Him who surpasses us infinitely, fear would be quite normal and to be admitted, and quite compatible with happiness and joy. The regular drop in the answers NO to question III seems to come from this implicit reasoning. That there should be a component of fear and alarm in the soul confronted with the sacred is considered more and more as natural. The ambivalence characterizing the sense of the sacred becomes clearer with age.

In a word, prudence prevents our assuming that we really reached the children's affectivity through these replies, their religious attitude. Nevertheless, we can notice evolution in their way of evoking God, and of deciding the behaviour His presence demands.

With the younger ones, God is like grown-up people, their parents. They react in His presence as they would before a kindly, fatherly, human creature : they must be good, well-mannered, at ease when they know it is He.

With age, the idea of God's transcendence, power and greatness, develops more and more. They gradually grasp that God is Almighty and awe-inspiring, perhaps the avenging Judge. They feel less and less at ease in His presence. They even fear direct contact with Him. They find it quite normal that the soul He encounters should fear, in spite of feeling attraction and joy. Besides this, they are much more influenced by culture as to describing behaviour in presence of the sacred, as we shall see.

B. - The action of kneeling

In the questions on reaction in presence of the sacred, answers suggesting the action of kneeling down were very frequent. They mounted with age like a kind of stereotyped pattern, settled by culture (suddenly lessened in Grade VI).

Kneeling down	Kindergarten and I	Gr. II	Gr. III	Gr. IV	Gr. V	Gr. VI
II. *What would you do if God suddenly appeared to you ?* (60 times = 32 %)	13 %	25 %	38 %	37 %	68 %	33 %
XII. *What did Moses do when he heard God's voice ?* (44 times = 24 %)	4 %	18 %	13 %	32 %	35 %	44 %

This increase with age of the idea of kneeling down is also found in questions VIII (« *What would you have done if you had seen fire like that ?* ») and IX (« *What did Moses do when he saw it ?* »), but with much lower figures (5 % and 8 % respectively).

Confining ourselves to questions II and XII, we got 130 answers : « I would kneel down. » They came from 85 different subjects (44 % of the total population). Divided into their school grades, they present the following results :

GRADE	NUMBER OF SUBJECTS replying : " kneel down „		FREQUENCY OF ANSWERS : " kneel down „	
Kindergarten	1	6 %	2	2 %
Grade I	4	13 %	6	5 %
Grade II	13	46 %	16	14 %
Grade III	14	48 %	17	14 %
Grade IV	13	46 %	24	21 %
Grade V	21	75 %	38	34 %
Grade VI	19	69 %	27	25 %

Therefore it can be noticed that the same subject gave the same answer of kneeling down to the questions II and XII in many cases. As these two questions are similar, one (question II) concerning the child, and the other, Moses (question XII), an interesting confirmation of the *correspondence* between the answers supplied in both cases can be noticed.

The X^2 or coefficient of association is very significant : 39 (21,6 being the threshold of probability at the .01 level). It is remarkable that the value of X^2 comes chiefly from the association between the answers « knelt down » : *12.* This shows a clear tendency among the subjects to attribute to Moses an attitude which they imagine for themselves personally in evoking God's presence. Would we speak of a projective answer here (to question XII) ? Is it not rather verbal stereotype ? At any rate, the re-grouping obtained through the two questions, widely separated in conversation with each child. seems to us worthy of note.

Here is a table of these correspondences (marked in percentages) :

Q. II. What would you have done if God suddenly appeared before you ?

		Don't know	Knelt down	Prayed- Adored	Others
XII. What did Moses do when he heard God's voice ?	Hid face	0,5	2	0,1	0,4
	Knelt	3,6	12	0	4
	Stood still, obeyed, took off sandals,	1,7	0,2	0,3	2
	Others	0,1	5	0,1	7

$$S \frac{(O - E)^2}{E} = 39$$

(Prob. : .01 > 21,6)

We point out that the idea of *kneeling down* is so vividly imagined that Moses is described as doing so, whereas the text nowhere suggests it, but even the contrary : Moses hid his face — no mention of his position — and wished to approach... The strength of this idea appeared also in the drawings we obtained. Whenever Moses was drawn, he was kneeling in 62 % of the drawings by children of 8 to 12 years (under 8 years, the « fellow » drawn is often so sketchy that it is hard to see whether he is standing or kneeling). Here again we found a highly significant X^2 : 14,7 (Probability .01 > 6,6) between the « kneeling » drawings and the answers « knelt » for question II.

Therefore, *association between evocation of the sacred and kneeling down increases with age.* It is probable that this mental persistence is an effect of education, a gesture learnt through influence of environment. As to its slight lessening in the Sixth Grade (in which some subjects were nearly 13), we can hardly determine

whether this was due to mere chance on the beginning of a curve
of decline (the summit then being in the Fifth Grade), possibly
due to the critical spirit and reaction against convention common
to adolescence.

C.   The Symbolism of Fire.

In the Bible, fire is a privileged sign of the presence of God.
It accompanies many theophanies. [1] The symbolism of fire, however, is not exclusive to the Bible. The history of religions shows
that it is fairly universal. Several properties of fire make it suitable
for this symbol value : it frightens, fascinates, is alive, it shines...

In our narrative of the burning bush, the religious symbolism of
the fire was stressed by a prodigious aspect : the flame was im-
material, not consuming the matter affected, burning without need
of being sustained. This detail was clearly brought out in our text.

In spite of that, many of the children (30 %) thought it could
have burnt Moses. Blinded by the idea of the material (or perhaps magical) danger associated with fire, they miss the *sign* value
of that mysterious fire, and interpreted the attitude of Moses as a
reaction of prudence or self-defence. Here are the frequencies of
this type of answer :

Frequencies

XI. *Why did God not want Moses to come near the bush ?*
« So that he would not be burnt... »   32

XIII. *What would have happened if Moses had gone near it ?*
« He would have been burnt... »   46

XIV. *Why did Moses have to take off his sandals ?*
« So as not to be burnt... »   7

XVII. *Why did Moses hide his face ?*
« Because he was afraid of the fire... »   17

XIX. *What would have happened if Moses had looked ?*
« He would have been burnt... »   14
                                                        _____
                                                          116

---

1. Cf. for example, Exod., XIII, 22; XIX, 18; XXIV, 16; Ezechiel, I, 27-28.

Thus we find that 116 answers to these five questions agree in meaning. They came from 59 subjects. In fact, 23 answered only one question in this sense, 21 answered 2 questions, 10 answered 3, 4 answered four, and one answered all 5 in the same sense.

Dividing the 59 subjects and their 116 answers into their respective school grades gives the following table :

Grade	Number of Subjects answering in this sense to one or to several questions		Frequency of answers in this sense		Average : answers by subjects
Kinder :	12	60 %	28	28 %	2,3
I	15	50 %	41	28 %	2,7
II	8	28 %	14	10 %	1,7
III	9	31 %	13	9 %	1,4
IV	8	28 %	10	7 %	1,2
V	4	14 %	5	3½ %	1,2
VI	3	10 %	5	3½ %	1,3

It will be noticed that the number of *subjects* giving the « danger of burning » type of answer, as well as the total number of *answers* in this sense, gradually diminishes with age. The burning of the bush is perceived less and less as a material fire, dangerous because it burns, or as a magic power full of menace, and the attitude of Moses is less and less interpreted in this light. Does not this curve reveal progress (with age) of the aptitude of seeing beyond the immediate content or the first affective appearances, to approach a vision of things in their function as *signs* ? It could at least express this negatively, by the gradually lessened frequency of purely material evocations.

To verify this conclusion, the counter-proof should be applied, by observing, in each question, which answers advance with age instead of diminishing.

We did this, and calculated the coefficients of association between the types of answer from one question to another. Here is a summary of this analysis in table form :

Q. XI. Why did God not want Moses to come near the bush ?

« Because he would have been burnt. »
— Answer varying from 50 % to 3 %. *

« Because it was holy ground. » (or any answer suggesting reverence for the sacred).
— Answer varying from 14 % to 87 %. *

Q. XIII. What would have happened if Moses had gone too near ?

« He would have been burnt... »
— Answer varying from 56 % to 11 %. *

« He would have sinned, disobeyed... would have been punished » etc.
— Answer varying from 7 % to 50 %. *

Q. XVII. Why did Moses hide his face ?

« Because he was afraid of the fire. »
— Answer varying from 10 % to 4 %. *

« Because God was there. » (or any answer manifesting a religious attitude).
— Answer varying from 23 % to 66 %. *

Q. XIX. What would have happened if Moses had looked ?

« He would have been burnt. »
— Answer varying from 24 % to 0. *

« Nothing. » « He would have been dazzled. » etc.
— Answer varying from 3 % to 38 %. *

The answers which show a frequency increasing with age are those which implicitly took the flame of the burning bush as a vision or the manifestation of a presence, demanding a religious and moral attitude.

In short, we may say that *to a diminution of answers dominated by a fear of life* (« being burnt »), *there corresponds a progress with age of the frequency of answers showing a better perception of the flame's symbolic function.* An increasing number of children implicitly see in Moses' actions (standing still, removing his sandals, hiding his face) the expression of a religious attitude (reverence, humility, fear), and therefore, pay more attention to the transcendent Presence manifested by the flame, than to the physical or magic danger of fire. Contact with the sacred, not danger of fire, determines Moses' behaviour. At least, this progress is perceptible in the majority of children over 11.

---

* The first percentage is that of Kindergarten and Grade I together; the second is that of Grade VI. — The coefficients of association (X^2) are significant as follows : between XI and XIII, $X^2 = 77$; between XI and XVII, $X^2 = 18$; between XIII and XIX, $X^2 = 46$. Alone, the association between XVII and XIX does not reach the .01 level of significance.

It seems justifiable to speak of progress in sensitivity to religious symbolism, of aptitude in approaching the sacred through signs, by getting beyond the first representations. This progress seems possible for most children at about 11-12 years, given a favourable education.

CONCLUSION

By way of conclusion we will try to sum up the principal differences in the answers to our questions between the first and last groups of children according to age ; on one hand, of children of 5-6 years, and on the other, children of 11-12.

5-6 Years

In the flame of the burning bush, many of the smallest children saw the *physical or magic danger* of fire more than the value of a sign. They judged the movements of Moses from the stand-point of danger from fire, neglecting certain details in the story, although quite explicit (Questions XI, XIII, XVII, XIX). Their imagination seemed to be filled with a certain affective idea of fire « that burns » (V) and their attention absorbed by it. Before the burning bush the wrong kind of behaviour would have meant an immediate immanent punishment : « You would get burnt. » This idea is special to the youngest and tends to disappear with age.

10-12 Years

In the Fifth and Sixth Grades, certain answers become more and more predominant, and manifest several tendencies :

1) The oldest children in our inquiry have the sense of distance from God, of *reverence* for the sacred (XI, XIV, XVII) much more spontaneously. This religious attitude usually shows in one way : that of kneeling down (II, XII). This uniformity in expression is not surprising ; it is the result of the children's increasing culture or socialization, in keeping with their age, which has taught them the attitudes and behaviour suitable for a given situation, according to the cultural norms of their social group. Kneeling down is an attitude associated with prayer, contact with the sacred, in our, but not in all, cultural traditions.

2) The sense of God widens. At 10-12 years old, they see more clearly than at 6, certain divine attributes. God is felt to be the *Tremendus*, the Almighty who can inspire fear (III, VI, XVII). Fear is admitted as a component and normal quality in the state of soul before God (III). The ambivalence of feelings inspired by the sacred is grasped better.

3) With progress in age, we note the children's progress in capacity to see the *symbolic* value of things and of acts. The fire

of the burning bush is better appreciated as a sign, a vision. It is no longer perceived as a physical danger or magical power, against which protection is needed, but as a heaven-sent manifestation calling for religious behaviour (XI, XII, XIV, XVII).

The symbolic significance of certain acts as expression of an interior attitude is also understood more easily (XIV, XVII).

4) Had Moses approached or looked, he would have infringed a divine stipulation or would not have behaved as he should. He might have incurred reproach or punishment from God, but he would not have « been burnt. » The behaviour of Moses is judged as possibly being an offence against God, with moral consequences only, no longer as a silly thing to do or the violation of a taboo, leading to an immanent and spectacular reprisal. This proves, we consider, more personalist *moral* conceptions at this age.

5) We notice, in general, a progress in critical judgment, which is quite normal, and a capacity to retain all the facts of the story to interpret one of the details. The older children are more faithful to the text (VII, XI), and do not set off into fanciful additions as the smaller ones sometimes do.

From a catechetical point of view therefore, the story of the *Burning Bush* can be grasped in its symbolic value, by most children of 11-12 years old, provided that it is told and explained in accordance with the observations we have just given. *

---

* It is interesting to know that the educational insight of the best ' caté-chètes ' in France are reaching exactly the same conclusion. In the quite new *Directoire de Pastorale Catéchétique* (published in the review *Catéchèse*, Paris, January 1964, N° 14), we read: « For children aged 7... religious instruction for this first cycle cannot use the working instruments planned for the next cycle » (article 80, p. 42). « After 9 years of age... priority should be given to Biblical scenes and stories, words and attitudes of the people in them, and generally speaking, to the events of the salvation story » (article 90, p. 45). In a study by R. GOLDMAN (Reading University, England) concerning the *Burning Bush*, lists of answers are given which were obtained in personal interviews with 200 children and adolescents, with their classification and frequency according to natural age and to mental development: *Religious Thinking from Childhood to Adolescence* (London, Routledge and Kegan Paul, announced for this summer 1964). The part concerning children (6-12 years) is summarized in *Studies in Education* (London, Evans Brothers, 1963): « *Children's Spiritual Development* », pp. 167-206 (by R. GOLDMAN). Study of the answers from most of the children suggests that it is difficult to expect this story, told collectively, to be grasped by a group of children under 10, according to the significance of its religious symbolism. — Needless to say, there are some children, even younger, who show a precocious facility to grasp this kind of story in its symbolic and spiritual significance. Some teachers maintain that this depends on the educational climate the children lived in before. It would be extremely interesting to supply an objectively convincing proof of this, and to describe accurately the nature of this catechetical climate. (Editor's note).

The Idea of God

Its evolution between the ages of 11 and 19

by Pierre Babin, O.M.I.

Professor of Religious Pedagogy at Lyons, Paris and Ottawa

In order to study in a systematic and exact manner the notions of God in the minds of French adolescents, it seemed useful to institute a large-scale enquiry among them. In proceeding thus, a double object was pursued : that of giving due weight to the law of the many, whilst further giving objective consideration to the manifold variety of individual views.

The questionnaire given to the young people to answer did not call only for information about « their God » but also for a general picture of their religious mentality. In this article we shall in fact confine ourselves to analysing certain aspects of the replies to the first question of the enquiry, a question immediately concerning the idea of God. Very often, however, the teams to whom the task of interpretation was entrusted, make reference to the totality of the replies in a given protocol, in order to bring out the better, in the light of the context, the exact sense or meaning of such and such a statement about God. No one can claim to be able to unravel the mystery of man's personal relationship with God. Indeed it is not only unfathomable but absolutely unique in each one of

---

1. Our readers will find here the first English translation of some of the results of a very extensive enquiry carried out in France into the evolution of the idea of God in youthful minds. Two thousand young men and young women there reply, *inter alia,* to the question : « What does God mean to you ? » The investigation was analysed by a team working at Lyons under the direction of Père P. Babin at the *Centre de Recherche de Psycho-pédagogie religieuse.* The complete account of this investigation (method, results, both quantitative and qualitative, commentaries and conclusions) has just been published in French in a volume of 320 pages : *Dieu et l'adolescent.* Editions du Châlet (Paris, 8, rue Madame (VIme) and Lyons, 36, rue du Trion (Vme), 1963). — Author's address : Centre de Recherche de l'Ecole Franco-Canadienne, Sainte-Foy-les-Lyon (Rhône), France (Editor's note).

us. It is, however possible to see a reflexion of God in certain forms of human expression and by that means also to obtain some idea of the ways in which man normally apprehends God and by which God Himself « becomes incarnate » in man throughout the ages.

Such was our objective in respect of these young people between the ages of 11 and 19.

I. THE ENQUIRY : PRELIMINARY REMARKS

To Whom Was the Enquiry Addressed ?

This enquiry was directed to young people of different social backgrounds, ages and sex. They all attended schools, secondary public, secondary private, or technical. The technical school could be public or private.

The numerous replies have been sorted into groups of 100, as shown in the following table :

AGE GROUPS	SECONDARY SCHOOLS		TECHNICAL SCHOOLS
	PRIVATE	PUBLIC	(PRIVATE & PUBLIC)
PRE-ADOLESCENTS (P.A.)			
Boys 12-13	100	100	100
Girls 11-13	100	100	100
ADOLESCENTS (A)			
Boys 14-15	100	100	100
Girls 14-15	100	100	100
OLDER ADOLESCENTS (G.A.)			
Boys 16-18	100	100	100
Girls 16-19	100	100	100

1,800 replies have thus been submitted to analysis. In order that this relatively small number might have a representative value, we have made a point of obtaining a variegated collection ; thus the enquiry has been carried out in different regions and towns : Paris, Lyons and the centre, Marseilles, Champagne, the North, Brittany, the Bordeaux region, the Central Plateau, etc.

Why Was the Question about God Thus Worded?

Was question No. 1 : « *What does God mean to you ?* » intentionally phrased in a banal and anodyne manner ?

We had in fact pointed out that in the case of young people, questions too evocative and too direct (such as that put in a German enquiry : « If God were to appear to you, what do you think He would look like ? ») cause reactions of silence or of embarrassment.

On the other hand, questions that were too mathematical in character, even if easy to deal with, met with replies that were devoid of interest and ambiguous in meaning. We think of a questionnaire by Watson where the children were asked to classify certain phrases in order of interest. Experience has moreover revealed that the meaning attached to these phrases by certain children or groups is different.

In a similar test we noted that the expression « God-Confidant » is taboo to certain adolescents not because they object to the idea that it is intended to convey but because of the expression itself which is spurned by their class of society. On the other hand the same phrase is regarded as perfectly in order by adolescents of a different *milieu*. We can judge by this fact to what an extent certain results may be misleading if we claim to be able to appraise statistically by the words used the objective meaning of the idea.

We have heard the objection raised that, given the meaning of the word « God » in the precise context of this or that civilization — that of France for instance — the question thus put forward has led to a rather stereotyped type of answer, having reference less to the God of revelation than to the idea of the Divine in general.

To which we would wish to say three things in reply. First, if in a country of Christian traditions, the meaning of the word « God » had thus lost its revealed sense, this state of things would but confirm on a yet larger scale the findings of the enquiry. Secondly, the attentive perusal of the replies shows us clearly that the word « God » has not led to a stereotyped reply about the Divinity of philosophers and professors, but to personal replies about a Being in relation with mankind. Finally soundings carried out in Protestant circles have shown us that, in a milieu culturally identical with that of Catholics, the word « God » at once leads to replies on the God of Jesus Christ.

In What Sense Can We Speak of ' Adult Faith ? '

As we shall often have occasion to speak of religious realities (which, for a Christian, are supernatural realities) in connexion with psychological realities, such as for example, ' adult faith ' we are anxious to explain exactly what we mean by this phrase. Having in view the scope of our present study, it has seemed to us better to opt for a clear distinction rather than for some ambiguous statement.

Let us explain ourselves by an example. A small child, baptized, confirmed, communicant, normally expresses his religious life in what we call a (psychologically speaking) childish way of behaviour, i.e. incomplete, egocentric, dependent on parents' example, etc. On the religious level then, what would the word *adult* signify ?

a) If we used the word *adult* to denote the plenitude of a person's *sacramental ' situation ' in the Church*, we would then say that the child mentioned above was an adult, even if he were only five years old. The analogy is fully valid, but would be of little use to us in the present study and is too ambiguous on account of the risk of confusion with the psychological realities to which constant reference must be made. This manner of speech, somewhat sacramental and canonical in character, will not be adopted here.

b) If we used the word *adult* to denote the completeness of *the subject's response to the call of God*, we should be entitled to say that a child of seven years is an adult believer in the measure in which his adhesion to God is full and entire on the subjective level. But what would be the objective criterion of such a reality ? And why make use here of a phrase with so definite a psychological meaning ? One would prefer rather to speak here of holiness. This manner of using the word « adult » will then also not be ours.

c) If we use the word *adult* to describe that grown-up state of responsibility and freedom in which the life of faith is normally expressed, we could certainly no longer apply it to a child of seven years. This manner of employing the word corresponds however with useful meaning and with a reality recognized by psychology. Such then will be our manner of speech, without prejudice either to the sanctity or to the situation in regard to the Sacraments, of the persons about whom we make use of this word. [1]

II. THE IDEA OF GOD
IN THE THREE PERIODS OF ADOLESCENCE

A First Reading.

A first reading of the results of the enquiry make abundantly clear the existence of one group of ideas which are prevalent in pre-adolescence and another group of ideas which characterize later adolescence, these being entirely contrary to one another in meaning and tendency.

---

1. We could doubtless find another possible sense for the word *adult* by drawing inspiration from the words of St. Paul about the « full stature » of Christ. We have not dwelt here on this meaning which expresses an eschatological conclusion and seems, in fact, to include in itself all the other interpretations.

These two groups of ideas correspond to the titles given to God : in the first case these titles express an idea of God that is more objective, more external to the ego, possibly more derived from schooling : the Divine Spirit, Creator, Trinity. God is spoken of in the third person : as « He. » The reference here is to God in Himself.

In the second case, however, the titles given to God express a more subjective idea of God, more subjective, that is to say, one that is closely related to the tendencies or psycho-sociological needs of the adolescent : God-Confidant, Guide, Ideal, Friend, Model, God as Mystery, Life and Light. God is spoken in the first person : « I »; « My God. » Here the reference is to *God in relation with man.*

To us, the progress of youth from pre-adolescence to later adolescence coincides with an evolution in the adolescent idea of God ; it seems that those concerned advance from knowing God in a somewhat school-childish way, in accordance with what they have been taught, to knowing Him in a more personal manner and as a result of experience.

Evolution of the Idea of God According to Age.

The TABLES given below have been drawn up on the basis of a percentage derived from the 1,800 replies received. They aim at placing in relief the process of evolution indicated by drawing attention to the ideas which are most common in the pre-adolescent period as also to those which are dominant in late adolescence.

Some ideas seem to be partially in abeyance during the adolescent period : these have been noted in a third table.

A.   *Ideas which grow in strength and become dominant in late adolescence*

GOD	PRE-ADOLESCENCE	ADOLESCENCE	LATE ADOLESCENCE
Great-Powerful	18 %	25 %	28 %
Guide-Ideal	19 %	22.5 %	26.67 %
Confidant	4 %	12 %	13 %
Mystery	3.65 %	4.65 %	5.35 %
Life-Light	0.35 %	1.35 %	1.65 %

B.   *Ideas which weaken after pre-adolescence*

GOD	PRE-ADOLESCENCE	ADOLESCENCE	LATE ADOLESCENCE
Spirit	32 %	21 %	14 %
Creator	34 %	30 %	28 %
Mercy	10 %	7.5 %	6.5 %
Trinity	1.35 %	1.35 %	0.5 %

C.   *Ideas which weaken temporarily at adolescence*

GOD	PRE-ADOLESCENCE	ADOLESCENCE	LATE ADOLESCENCE
Father-Love	59 %	53 %	58 %
Eternal, Just, Perfect } *Qualities*	25.5 %	16.53 %	19 %

One must not of course exaggerate the significance of these figures : the divergencies are often slight. It is more illuminating to peruse the completed questionnaires attentively as this enables us to deduce better the character and direction of the children's ideas at such and such an age. We can see the two key-groups come clearly into shape : the *God-in-Himself* group and the *God-in-relation-to-us* group, the latter much obsessed by subjective needs. Let us note that, looking at things from the point of view of statistics, *no* one *idea* is dominant among adolescents (14-15 years). This is a conclusion of interest as it proves that this age is essentially a time of transition, a passage. We thus go abruptly from one *plus* to one *minus* or *vice-versa*. The sense of evolution is continuous and the phenomena of puberty have their influence without striking a discordant note on the general trend towards maturity.

True, the third group records a decline in certain ideas at the time of adolescence but this on the whole is of little importance. The ideas of this third group transform themselves according to circumstances into an objective or subjective interpretation : we must then avoid applying to them any interpretations that have been defined *a priori*. Only perusal of the documents can decide what meaning should be read into them.

III. THE IDEA OF GOD
IN THE MINDS OF BOYS AND GIRLS

1. PRE-ADOLESCENCE.

A school-child mentality
is uppermost in the replies,
but those of the boys show more spontaneity.

The boys, like the girls, give replies which, taking them all in all, are somewhat impersonal, very similar to the teaching received from the catechism : « Invisible being, All-Powerful, Whom we are bound to obey... Father. » We find however, among the boys, more replies of a personal character, spontaneous, affective, sometimes expressed in a charmingly unsophisticated manner. « He loves me well and, I too love Him well... »; « I should like to behave as God's boy. »

The banal character of the girls' replies must not however make us oblivious of the deep inner life of the best among them. True, they reply to the enquiry like « good pupils, » content merely to repeat what they have been taught ; but direct contact with pre-adolescent girls reveals that this docility can perfectly well be combined with a real knowledge of God, with personal reflexion and with genuine religious experience. In fact they find it decidedly difficult to put their deepest thoughts into words, fearing to commit themselves unduly by their replies.

Boys, more impulsive, more independent of their surroundings, detach themselves more easily from their educational background and from accepted ideas. The greater mental and affective elasticity of girls inclines them to repeat precisely what they have learned, even if only thereby to give pleasure to their teachers.

Among boys : predominance of the moral
aspect and insistence on purity.

The girls seem to be much less aware than the boys of the existence of an objective moral order, founded on God's own precise will.... The boys, on the other hand, connect very closely with their idea of God that of a moral obligation.

The mention of a God, « the Master who commands, » « who sees me, » « whom I must obey » is demonstrably more frequent on the part of boys than on that of girls. The proportion resulting from a total of 1,800 answers (900 boys, 900 girls) is as follows : Girls, 19.21 % — Boys 23.53 %.

A boy makes this characteristic pronouncement : « When we separate ourselves from Him, we feel that He is reproaching us. »

Some of their replies stress the logical need for reciprocity in love. « We must make sacrifices because He makes them for us. »

A considerable number of them display a kind of astonishment or admiration in face of the mystery of the Godhead.

« To my mind, God is a Spirit, who possesses very great power and who would wish that all things created by Him should be perfect, should deserve Paradise : that is why He exhorts them to do good. »

« God is an unknown Being Whom I endeavour to please and Whom I try to love deeply (in which effort I am not always successful). »

« He manifests Himself by means of the voice of conscience. »

It is very striking to note that the Divine Purity which is never mentioned by the girls, seems to have a real fascination for many of the boys :

« Pure and beneficent Spirit... »

« God is a pure Spirit, without any body, hence immortal. We start off with a pure spirit, with the body it becomes more or less a slave. Purity is the image of all virtues. »

That God is so often considered as an absolute value « in purity » and as « One who demands that we should be pure » seems to suggest, amongst other things, how hard the struggle for purity is already proving for them. The fact that many of the pre-adolescents are seeking in God the strength they need to aid them certainly seems to confirm this.

From the girls : insistence on the
fatherly care of God and on His goodness.

In their replies the girls frequently insist on the spiritual nature of God. They also feel an over-all and trustful certitude of God's goodness.

« God is a Father who is interested in His creatures, who takes care of each one. »

We can then lean on Him, count on Him, rest affectionately in Him. He protects and loves. Christ our Saviour is seen by many of them as the proof of this love.

« God loves us and has given us His Son to atone for our personal sins. »

The pre-adolescent girl sees God in relation with her *ego*. This relationship of trust, brought into being by the goodness of God the Father, will evolve into a relationship of confidence, more personal and more egocentric, which is characteristic of adolescence. We may note that, while some pre-adolescent girls speak already of « telling their grief » and their difficulties to God, the same expressions are not found among the boys before the age of about 16 years.

To sum up, despite a phraseology which, here and there, is still very school-boyish, we note *more dynamism* in the boys. They count on God to help them reach their goal : « He leads me by the hand. » The girls, on the other hand, seem more *static*, seeking in God an affective security, a support, the goodness of God causing them to trust in Him before later on giving Him cause to trust in them.

From a statistical point of view, the percentages obtained for the « Purity-Love-Goodness » conception of God serve to confirm what we have been saying : Boys 51 % — Girls 63 %.

Age Groups	Boys	Girls
Pre-Adolescence	67	51.65
Adolescence	45	62.35
Late Adolescence	41	75

2. ADOLESCENCE.

Feeling of Insecurity,
more intellectual in character in the boy.

The replies to the enquiry reveal, in boys and girls alike, the existence of a period of insecurity, of instability. There is but little difference in the ways in which they express their doubts, sometimes even their agnosticism or refusal to accept God.

The boys will say : « One cannot attain to Him by thinking » ; « What we know about God is very vague and undefinable. »
The girls on the other hand say : « A mysterious being who alone knows what ends he has in view. » « A very exalted and mysterious stranger. »
Here and there, we find a searching attitude, a sense of mystery, sometimes of doubt, expressed. « Perhaps I know the definition of God too well to be able to know Him well, » said one boy. « God stands for something very good to me, » writes a girl, « but I am not altogether sure of His existence, for that would be too good to be entirely true... »

On the whole it would seem that a stronger need for intellectual certainty is felt by the boys than by the girls.

For Boys :
the God who strengthens us in temptation.

In the state of spiritual and mental disarray through which adolescents commonly pass, the idea of relations with a personal God differs as between boys and girls, even though both alike call Him Father. The boys seem to seek in God a source of strength, a bastion of defence to which they can cling.

« God is the great pillar, that is, the starting point of our religion. »
« God is a leader. »
« God is a dictator who governs his Kingdom justly and worthily. »

Such words as « combat, » « putting to the test, » « struggle » appear constantly. « Father who has placed on this earth in order to put us to the test, » « Companion in the fight, » « Giver of the graces we need for the combat. »

The principal difficulty with which the average boy of that age is faced is moral in character. It is the struggle to remain faithful, despite the temptations (constantly mentioned) to yield to surrounding influences and, above all, to give way to impurity. God will often be called a « Father » but the idea of a Father's goodness is frequently linked with that of « pardon. »

« Like the prodigal son, we can count on His mercy. »

« God is a Father who, when we are tempted, puts us back on to the right road. »

« Father to whom one commends all one's efforts. »

« I can sense His presence when I feel that I have offended Him. »

Girls too seek strength and security from God, but they approach Him from a different angle.

For Girls :
search after a sure and consoling Presence.

For girls indeed the principal difficulty lies not so much in the permanent danger of moral falls as in *a lack of emotional satisfaction*. They are conscious of an emotional void which they seek to fill. That is why God appears to them as the Confidant in whom their *unfulfilledness* can find a refuge.

« God is for me a living being whose presence and superiority one can feel, a living being whom one cannot always understand very well, but whom one is longing to find. »

The dominant characteristic in their replies is undoubtedly their stress upon a God who is in relation with the individual *ego* a God « who understands me, » « who can love me, » « who, when I am in distress comes to my rescue. » The adolescent girl hopes to be rid of her emotional loneliness : thus it is that she frequently joins to the word « Father » words with such shades of meaning as « protector, » « friend, » « confidant. »

The following extracts are typical :

« God is the only person on whom one can rely entirely, even in desperate situations. »

« God is He to whom I have recourse in all my difficulties and sufferings and who imbues me with strength. »

« A friend who is at the same time full of understanding, and exigent, intransigent. »

« A Father who keeps me constantly in sight. »

« A Father who helps me. »

« A Father who desires my happiness. »

One notion of God which attracts a certain number of these girls seems distant, alarming, mysterious :

« For me, God is a being whom I love deeply but who veils himself from me. »

« A father, certainly, but somewhat inaccessible, whom we must love without seeming to be able fully to understand Him. »

Faith, hope and charity seem very difficult virtues to these young people in their obscurity of soul. Feeling no fervour, having no desire to pray, not feeling as though their prayers had been heard, all these are stumbling blocks for a great number of them.

On the other hand they are very much alive to any signs which God conveys to them in their personal life. Thus one of them (15 ½) wrote after having had her prayer granted : « It is no longer possible to disbelieve after this, now it is graven on my mind for good... »

In the girls :
a new sense of God's presence in the Universe.

Finally, we should note, in the girls, an acute symbolic sense.

« We feel His presence in a place of beauty » (mountain or sea). « He seems present to me in all that I see, in nature, in the Universe, everywhere ! »

In her desire to « feel, » in her rapturous sense of a Presence, the adolescent girl is looking for a sphere in which her emotional nature will be at ease. One of them confesses :

« It is now only out of doors that I can bring myself to pray a little... Liturgy, sacraments, mean nothing to me... »

Certain of the expressions they use are almost pantheistic but one needs of course in each particular case to divine the true meaning hid under words which may well express more than is intended, verbal exactitude not being their strong point.

Among the boys' replies on the other hand, one finds but very rarely expressions such as the following :

« God for me means the woods, the flowers, the animals, in short, nature and all that I see. »

To sum up, whilst the boy seeks *his safety* in loyalty to a leader, in a power which will help him to pull himself together and to come through a difficult period, the girl seeks the remedy for her disquiet and for her emotional dissatisfaction in the desire to be understood and loved, also in the feeling of a presence that satisfies ; her notion of God is thus strongly coloured by her condition of mind.

3. *LATE ADOLESCENCE.*

In the girls, interest in religion
is more common and is expressed with greater ease.

Older adolescents, boys and girls, try to justify their acceptance or rejection of God by rational reflexion. They all tend to think out anew the great problems of life in a more personal manner.

The replies show that a deep interest in religion is commoner among the girls than among the boys. That is due no doubt to their more receptive and affectionate nature, directed towards « another. » The boy is self-sufficient and in more danger of falling into the temptation of Prometheus.

The dominant ambition of a boy of that age is to find himself a place in the sun, to see realized the ideal picture that he paints of himself in his mind. Rare are the expressions denoting a personal relationship with God. The crises that he has to face have to do above all with the impossibility of attaining complete success or of making the best use of his experiences.

Where the girls are concerned we note a regard to their attitude towards God, a certain lessening of emotionalism which often finds an outlet elsewhere, and leaves the intellect freer. The idea of God as confidant is less to the fore than during the preceding period. On the other hand, the boys, who express this idea less frequently than the girls, are apt to do so, if at all, in late adolescence and not in adolescence like the girls. Does this mean that the experience of emotional confusion comes later to them ?

Intellectual crises concerning Faith :
more general in character in the boys,
more personal and existential in girls.

It is significant that a good number of older adolescents make no reply to the question : « *What does God mean to you ?* » or reply simply : « An unknown quantity. »

Sometimes irony, doubt or scepticism make their appearance, together with a striving after original replies, lapidary formulae, trenchant in character and often definitely heterodox. In this spirit, we find boys writing :

« I do not believe in God any longer, God is the creation of man. » « An embarrassment when one loves a gay life. » « God, that is when I am a *chic* comrade. » « An enigma, a power. Everything. »

The girls for their part say :

« God is a goal to be sought anew for He has been misrepresented by men. » « God is a philosophy, the only one of any value, which each of us must seek to recreate for himself. »

In numerous cases we observe a progressive alienation from the Church, doubtless a reaction against everything that smacks of authority.

« Christian or Hindoo God ? What matter ? The main thing is to seek Him in good faith » (Boy).

At this age, we find reflected in these youthful minds all the religious ideas which are in the air, popularized by literature, radio, cinema. The influence of their own social *milieux* is here predominant.

What seems to be an essential distinction between boys and girls in this crisis of « re-thinking » their Faith is that the boy does so in more intellectual, more abstract terms, in universal categories : the girl in a more personal fashion, in more existential categories.

« Re-thinking » the Faith.

If it is undeniable that a majority among older adolescents undergo a crisis of an intellectual kind, the most faithful among them, boys as well as girls, feel the need to be put in possession of serious reasons for belief. Provided that they find themselves in a well-endowed educational milieu, they achieve a just, profound and personal notion of God. But here we are undoubtedly dealing with only a small *élite*. For those :

« God is a Father who has created us out of love and who has given His Son to redeem us. God is a Father who cares for us all the days of our life and in whom we can have perfect confidence » (Boy — 16 years).
« A Father for whom each one of His sons is irreplaceable » (Boy — 20 years).
« God is the Father of all men whom He has loved to the point of giving us His Son to save us; who is Truth and who guides us in our workaday life of every day so that we may try to do as He does » (Girl — 18 years).
« He is the Father, Sovereign, Creator and Master of all. He has complete power over us and fills us with gifts and graces » (Girl — 18 years).
« It is clear that God is a pure and infinite Spirit, that is what we have always been taught. He is for me too comfort, hope and consolation. He helps me every day to love Him, understand Him and serve Him » (Girl — 17 years).

To sum up, at the period of late adolescence, we note, among boys and girls alike, a need of coherence and of harmony between the revealed fact and the deepest instincts of the human subject, between « what I have been told about God » and « my subjective aspirations. » This work of securing coherence and harmony, a sort of quest in the field of apologetics must also be carried out on the subjective level. The following datum is confirmed by experience drawn from catechetical work among the older adolescents : when we approach them with a very abstract apologetic, little concerned with their own problems, we satisfy them as little as we convince them.

The coherence of which they are in search is not to be found on the level of abstract and impersonal ideas. Their concern is not to assure agreement between God and reason, but rather between God and their subjective needs. What they discover about God must link up with what they experience, their need to feel happy, secure and emotionally satisfied.

The course of this « re-thinking » will thus be different in boys and girls, whilst retaining the same general significance. With boys, the problem of God is thought out anew in connexion with the individual and social success of his *ego* ; with girls, in connexion with the flowering of a personal « other »-ward relation, with the felt presence of God.

4. CONCLUSION.

A boy, in the course of the evolution of his affective life, sees God above all as a support in the warfare he has to wage, as the great friend who will help him to become a man.

Girls prefer to see God as the One who watches over them, who interests Himself in them. Before being in their eyes the « Confidant » who comforts them and shares all with them, God is for them the « Father » who protects and who upholds. Everything in their psychology can be reduced to a question of affective relationship with « another. » To be understood and loved, this is for them an indispensable condition for development and self-surrender. Thus they seem more disposed than boys to understand that the Christian attitude is a response to the antecedent love of God.

Boys are tempted to make use of God as someone who will aid them to construct their ego, to realize the ideal image which they make of their own personalities. In extreme cases, God might be confused here with the ideal image of the boy himself. His conception of God thus appears to be dynamic but *utilitarian*.

Girls, for their part, are tempted to seek in God for that presence which is necessary to them for their affective development. Hence a view of God that is more static than that of the boys but less egocentric and utilitarian.

Boys, like girls, project upon the Absolute their profound subjective needs.

IV. GENERAL OBSERVATIONS

After having compared the replies obtained from boys and girls of the three periods of adolescence, both in the milieu of the free schools and in that of the public schools ; after having analysed certain features peculiar to the replies of a hundred young Protestants (predominance of God as Saviour and of biblical themes), Père Babin presents his psycho-pedagogical comments on the three specific characteristics of Christianity as lived by young people. The following lines constitute an abridged version of the most important chapter of Père Babin's work (Editor's note).

1) The *naturality* of the religious instinct is a form of mentality and expression in accordance with which the idea of God and the sense of His Presence appear as the final stage of a progression from

man towards God. Relationship with God here appears as a relationship motivated essentially by the experiences and needs of men, no explicit mention being made of the revealed doctrine of the One God in Three Persons. This word ' naturality ' (even « hyper-naturality » where adolescents are concerned) is not necessarily a pejorative term : such an attitude, under wise direction, can free young people from being unduly conditioned by their family and scholastic surroundings and can enrich the fervour of their Christianity by enabling them to develop their natural religious impulses in various ways.

2) The *egomorphism* of the idea of God formed by these young people reveals itself in their express preference for certain words (« Confidant » — « Pure » — « Ideal »). From this it is clear that the relationship with God which these young people cultivate is profoundly imbued with subjective factors. Indeed God tends, in the minds of these adolescents, to take the form of the EGO. This egomorphism can assume a variety of forms, determined deep down by the psycho-sociological conditions of the subject's personality. But its characteristics are generally speaking to be found in a *pseudo-pantheism* (which, in its positive aspect, means an acute addiction to symbols and symbolism) and in *idealization*, ultimately emotional, intimist and compensatory, of which the positive value may consist in the acquisition of a personal realization of the mystery of salvation.

3) *Ethnicality*, sometimes known as moralism, shows that the religion of numerous pupils, especially from the free schools, is characterized by a predominance of moral imperatives which run the risk in certain cases of outclassing the genuinely religious realities of relationship with God. The subjective exigencies of realization take precedence of the personal appeal expressed historically in Jesus Christ and addressed to all sinners. Spontaneous action tends to be preferred to contemplation and the response to grace. Ethicality, more than the other two specific notes here dealt with, appears to derive in large measure from the teaching received and from the kind of authority under which the questioned pupils have been educated.

These three characteristics illustrate well both the relativity and the importance of this period of specific sensitivity through which the young must pass. Important increases of knowledge regarding all that is involved in the idea of God can thus be acquired : a sense of God's immanence and of His personal Alliance with man. Other acquisitions of knowledge concern more the manner of our relationship with God : access to an individual vocation, to a reflexive conscience. to the autonomy of the human personality in its relations with God.

The line of evolution towards adult status already appears in embryo in the maturer attitude of older adolescents. We have pointed out the signs already visible in those of this age-group of a return to a more responsible idea of God, one more in conformity with the dictates of reason and the requirements of a given social group. The following seem to us to be the two main trends of evolution towards the adult period :

a) *Social and Church-ward Trend.* The young adult is about to enter progressively into a course of activity in God's name. This involves him in an historical situation whereby, little by little, he will be willing to give his life to God's service.

b) *Objective orientation.* After having made the discovery of God, a man will enter more and more into relations with Him which will be true to all the objective dimensions of a Revelation. His thought and his life will enter into the Trinitarian dimension of the Mystery of God. But before that there will be a long road to follow before youth is ended, consisting above all in perfecting the life of personal union with Jesus Christ and in purifying and stabilizing the acquisitions gained during adolescence.

*
*   *

Except for extreme youth and perhaps old age is there a time of life which is at once as rich in treasures and as dangerous as the adolescent period in the matter of entering upon the knowledge of the True God ? It is a period that is rich because of the powerful appeal to lead a full life which springs from the flowering of our human nature. A period that is rich also as a result of the new possibilities opening out before the adolescent who is called upon to sweep away the primitive caricatures and false images of God which are still dormant within him. A period of ambiguity as a result of the dangers that beset the adolescent of becoming imprisoned by his natural surroundings or of being led into deviations by a human nature weighed down through sin.

We have described the adolescent as God has willed him to be, in order that, through this struggle and through this painful growth, he may eventually become, having overcome his difficulties, an adult in the Faith.

Religious Attitudes
of Educated Young Catholics
in the Same School Year

by Miss Joan B. Brothers

*Research Fellow at the Department of Social Studies,
University of Durham (England)* [1]

The psychology of religious crises or conversions is perhaps more interesting at first sight than the study of those who persevere in the religious beliefs in which they were brought up. Nevertheless, it is more than probable that the same kinds of phenomena of doubting and conviction which are experienced in conversion or loss of faith are to be found at some point in the lives of those who remain attached to their religious faith. It is with the religious views and experiences of a group of educated young adults, brought up as Roman Catholics and nearly all of whom still practised their religion, that this article is concerned. The investigation in question was predominantly a sociological one, aiming to describe how institutional change in the educational sphere has been instrumental in altering the social structure and as a consequence the social organization of Roman Catholicism in an English city, Liverpool. But convinced that to come to an understanding of a social situation,

1. Born at Liverpool, England, 1938, Dr. Joan Bernadette Brothers received her degrees : B.A. Honours, Social Science, Liverpool University, 1959; Ph.D., Liverpool, 1962. The research for this degree, on the consequences of grammar school education for the social structure and organization of Roman Catholicism, is being published by Liverpool University Press, Spring, 1964, under the title, *Church and School. A Study of the Impact of Education on Religion.* Other publications include : 'Grammar School versus Parish,' *The Clergy Review*, XLVIII, 9 (1963), 566-575, and Perception in Socio-Religious Research,' *Sociologia Religiosa*, VII, 9-10, 65-70. She has also carried out research on the assimilation of a group of Irish immigrants. In 1962, she was appointed as Research Fellow of the University of Durham, where she is engaged on research into the social organization of the university. Miss Brothers is editing a reader on the sociology of religion, and is also engaged on a book on sociology for the Catholic Social Guild, Oxford. — Address : 52, Caldwell Road, Allerton, Liverpool 19, Great Britain. (Editor's note).

it is necessary to take into account not only observable behaviour but also attitudes, values and opinions, [1] thus considering factors more usually associated with the functions of a psychologist, the investigator was concerned to discuss some of the more profound elements of the religious mentality underlying the situation being studied.

The religious development of adolescents has deservedly been given considerable attention, [2] but the experiences of early adulthood are also of particular importance, especially in the lives of those whose intellectual development is fostered by formal education beyond the average age. [3] Experiences at universities and colleges are likely to be of tremendous importance in shaping the religious life, particularly when the young people in question have been educated in denominational schools, keeping them apart from the wider society up to that time. It is with young men and women who have been for the most part successful in their higher education and training and who were about to settle into their chosen professions that the present investigation was concerned. [4]

Respondents' Backgrounds.

By intensive interviews with 42 young men and 42 young women in their early twenties who had three years earlier completed their secondary education in Catholic grammar schools in the city of Liverpool, this inquiry included information on their religious development since leaving school. [5] Nearly half were university students or had just ended their studies at university, while a further 29 %, almost all girls, had attended Catholic Teacher Training Colleges,

---

1. This methodological position is discussed by the writer in 'Perception in Socio-Religious Research,' *Sociologia Religiosa*, VII, 9-10 (1963), 65-70.

2. See *Lumen Vitae*, passim.

3. See, for instance, P.N. DE VOLDER, 'Inquiry into the Religious Life of Catholic Intellectuals,' *Journal of Social Psychology*, XXVIII, 1 (1948), 39-56, and E.N.P. NELSON, 'Patterns of Religious Attitude Shifts from College to Fourteen Years Later,'*Psychological Monographs*, LXX, 2 (1957), 274-285.

4. The material on which this article is based has been taken from a forthcoming book entitled, *Church and School. A Study of the Impact of Education on Religion.*

5. Interviews were carried out with all those who had completed the course in the nine Catholic secondary grammar schools in Liverpool in a particular year and who were still resident in the city; after the necessary eliminations had been made, there were eighty four young people in this research group, an equal number of each sex.

and were either teaching or intending to teach in Catholic schools. Others were student apprentices in industry, and nearly all had trained in some way for a profession after leaving school at about the age of eighteen or nineteen. Only two, one of each sex, were married at the time of the investigation.

It is important to stress that they came from a wide variety of socio-economic backgrounds, for the main emphasis of the research was upon analysing the consequences of educational innovations which were giving many of them opportunities to become socially mobile. Very few, incidentally, were of British origin, the majority being of Irish descent, or in a few cases the children of families from continental Europe.

Method of Inquiry.

The material described in this article forms part of a much larger investigation, and the interview schedule used (which was semi-structured) involved about two hundred questions, the interviews lasting on average from an hour to an hour and a half or more. All the interviews were carried out by the writer, and answers and comments were noted verbatim ; respondents were encouraged to enlarge on their statements wherever possible. The questions on religious beliefs were deliberately placed in the middle of the interview, to allow plenty of time for *rapport* to be established. Questions were asked about family background, school experiences and the like, and then about the final years at school ; these led to a discussion on religious lessons at that period. Since those who were interviewed tended to hold strong opinions on these lessons, they had already given considerable indication of their attitudes towards Catholicism, and the topic of religious beliefs was easily introduced into this context and met with a ready and full response. The following questions were then put directly :

Do you think that people change their ideas about religion after leaving school ? In what ways ?

Do you think you have yourself ? In what ways ?

Do you think Catholics have any need to study their religion after leaving school ? Why ? On what lines ?

What in your experience are the main reasons why some Catholics stop going to church ?

Respondents were then encouraged to elaborate what they had said as much as possible. It must be strongly emphasized, however, that in describing some of the religious experiences of these young men and women, use has been made not simply of the answers to these open questions, but also of the frequent and detailed references which were made by respondents in answer to other questions throughout the interview ; without this deeper knowledge, the answers to the above questions would not have been sufficient.

It is important to note that no direct questions were put about religious practice, not simply because of the usual biases which creep into replies of this kind, but chiefly because of the results of a pilot inquiry which revealed that educated young Catholics of this type strongly objected to being asked about religious practice on the grounds that this was an intrusion into a private sphere, a view the writer is inclined to share ; a person who wishes to conceal his own opinions and behaviour can give an evasive answer in speaking of religious attitudes, but questions on church attendance require a direct reply. However, the majority of those who were interviewed appeared to take the matter of church attendance for granted and referred to it casually as they talked. A handful who either rejected the Church's teaching or who were doubtful of its validity were surprisingly ready to state their own position.

Preliminary Remarks.

It was noticeable how willing the majority were to talk freely about their religious views,[1] and in this context it is worth noting that the writer had herself attended one of the schools included in the inquiry and thus belonged to the same community.[2] Before discussing their religious opinions these young people were, in fact, concerned to place the interviewer in the in-group. Brought up in homes where at least one parent was a Catholic, and then educated in Catholic schools, some of them subsequently in Catholic colleges, and all of them with close Catholic friends, they were deeply conscious of their status as members of a minority group, and were defensive about ' letting down the side.'[3]

---

1. Cf. J.J. BYRNE, *A Study of Student Problems in Catholic Men's Colleges.* Washington, 1957.

2. Cf. G.E. LENSKI and J.C. LEGGETT, Caste, Class and Deference in the Research Interview,' *American Journal of Sociology*, LXV, 5 (1960), 463-467.

3. Cf. C. K. WARD, Some Aspects of the Social Structure of a Roman Catholic Parish,' *The Sociological Review*, N.S., VI, 1 (1958), 75-93.

The interviewer's familiarity with the situation[1] made them willing to discuss their views and feelings freely ; at times they would add comments such as 'You'll know what I'm talking about,' and it was clear they felt at ease in criticizing Catholicism in the presence of someone belonging to the in-group.

Before discussing religious opinions, it is important to note first of all the relationship between religious *beliefs* and *practice* in the eyes of these young men and women. For them the major religious issue was not so much whether they attended church, but whether or not they accepted the beliefs of Catholicism. If they believed, they went to church; for them the matter was as simple as this. On the other hand, the converse way of thinking, that if one did not believe one did not go to church, did not necessarily apply ; one young man, for instance, went to church when he was at home to conceal from his family the fact that he was an agnostic, to save hurting them.

Changes in Religious Beliefs.

The question of *changes in religious beliefs* was approached obliquely first of all, by asking respondents if they considered that other people changed their views on religion after leaving school, but the personal element was very evident in many replies, some referring to their own experiences immediately. Others, however, related accounts of people they knew, usually former class mates, nearly always in terms of Catholics who had received a similar education. Although *18 %* could not think of ways in which people changed their ideas, and a few more spoke in purely personal terms, the remainder gave complex statements of opinion, in which certain elements can be distinguished.

1. Nearly *a quarter* referred to Catholics becoming more critically disposed as a result of contact with non-Catholics ; such replies drew attention to the difficulties which young Catholics might encounter on leaving an environment largely composed of people of similar ideas to move in a wider milieu. *Great emphasis* was invariably placed in this kind of answer *upon the impact of environmental factors on religious beliefs*. A typical answer of this sort, coming from a university student, was :

It all depends on what they do after leaving school. If they're in constant contact with the Church, I don't think their basic ideas will change at all. If

---

1. Cf. A. Spitzer, Aspects of Religious Life in Tepoztlàn,' *Anthropological Quarterly*, XXX, 1 (1957), 1-17.

they drift away, their ideas *will* change. They'll think it's a whole great fairy story. It depends on the will. If you're weakwilled, you'll be led anywhere.

2. Another important point which emerged was that *a high value was placed* by those who were interviewed *upon the faith of a person who had experienced doubts and overcome them.* The kind of faith that had been tested, they thought, was superior to the traditional 'simple peasant faith.' Examples of this kind of reply were :

You meet people who come up with problems. Sometimes it alters your own views on religion. Sometimes a person's faith weakens, but sometimes it's strengthened. You begin to search. It's a testing point, standing on your own feet.

Well, at school, you accepted everything everybody told you. When you leave, you have doubts. You weigh things up and see why you believe them, not just because you're told in class.

3. References were also made to Catholics either *becoming more interested in their faith or losing it* altogether as a result of such periods of examination of beliefs. One person put it this way :

People either improve greatly or drop off. It all depends on the company you go with. You think more. You just jog along at school.

Such people were emphatic in stating that there was ' no in-between stage,' and this conclusion was certainly mirrored in the answers on changes in personal beliefs. Their education, it seems, led them, after a period of consideration and perhaps doubting, to either complete acceptance or rejection of Catholicism.

4. *12 %* of the replies to this point suggested that people became much *more tolerant* in their approach towards the views of other people, and this was echoed in answer to the next question, which was concerned with changes in their own beliefs since leaving school. One person put it this way :

I've always held these things on faith. I'm beginning to see the reason for many of them. I'm less dogmatic in my approach. I used to snap down on arguments. Now I can see where they fall down.

5. Whereas only *18 %* thought that others did not change their views, as many as *58 %* reported that their own beliefs were still basically the same. Some who had said that they had not changed in their basic convictions then went on to make comments or

reservations. *A fifth* of the replies described how people had grown *more interested in Catholicism* and found it more important and more relevant to their lives after leaving school. A typical remark, coming from a university student, was :

> When I was at school I didn't take religion seriously. I went to church and I said my prayers. But now I don't go to church as often as I used to, but religion is now much more personal. I realize it's a serious matter.

6. *13 %* referred to becoming *more critical of Catholic beliefs* and there were some who described how they had experienced a period of doubt or indifference which was followed by increased interest and appreciation. Going to university or taking a job in industry was the first personal contact for many with non-Catholics, and often it came as a shock to realize how sincere and firm such people could be in their views. One young man described his experiences at university in the following terms :

> I was very lax at university. I went to Mass every week, that's all. I was going round with atheists and I got the impression that to have a religion was to be in a minority of one. Then I met a Catholic who was living a far better life than me. That made me feel ashamed and made me practise with more fervour.

7. There were remarkably *few who had stopped believing altogether*, though a handful reported *doubts* of a more serious nature than those already described. One of them, a recent graduate, put it this way :

> I believe a good deal less now, but I wasn't very strong at school. It's just in general. I always had doubts about the Catholic faith. I was never answered satisfactorily. I don't move in Catholic circles to support my ideas. I've heard more convincing viewpoints. I wouldn't say I didn't believe. I'm more in a quandary... I don't think it's because I left school, it's just a natural development.

There were also *two young men* who went out of their way to make it clear that they no longer regarded themselves as Catholics (though in the eyes of the Church they were still members) : interestingly, they were still in close contact with Catholic friends from school. It was noticeable in this context that the views of those who were wavering in their faith or who had lost it were well known to their friends. Although one or two were understandably evasive in describing religious difficulties, the rest talked remarkably freely about their religious experiences and doubts.

Leaving the Church.

1. Respondents' opinions as to *why people stopped going to church* gave more opportunities for *projection*. What is particularly interesting is that although some had reported experiencing difficulties over belief, comparatively few, *13 %*, gave this as a factor in causing Catholics to stop attending church. The predominating response was that *laziness* and *indifference* were the main reasons, and answers expressed strong rejection towards Catholics who lapsed from their faith. As many as *40 %* included laziness in their answers, most of them giving it as their first suggestion, while a similar response came from the *17 %* who gave indifference as the chief reason. It was emphasized that most people stopped going gradually rather than deliberately deciding not to go. Typical replies were :

Laziness is the main thing. Also being fairly weakwilled. Then they're influenced by the strongwilled. I'm convinced that laziness is at the bottom. Also, if they're away from home, there's no one to remind them. Some have a simple faith and don't think of reasons, and they're inclined to give up, too.

I think it's purely and simply that they get into an attitude of couldn't-care-less. I don't think they say, 'I'm not going.' It's just a gradual falling off. They don't give any thought to it — that's the problem. They've that many other things to do that religion takes about tenth place in their lives.

2. Environmental factors featured in *41 %* of the answers, often revealing *hostile or defensive attitudes towards the milieux* in which the respondents lived or worked. It was apparent that these young men and women often found it *hard to maintain minority beliefs*, and they emphasized the supportive role of the company one kept (a point repeatedly emphasized by the schools). One person summed up the point about environmental factors by explaining why people stopped going to church in the succinct remark, ' Because they meet someone that doesn't go. '

3. A more sympathetic approach was to be found when *moral problems* were included, as they were in 18 % of the answers, individual instances often being cited. Only one person suggested the traditional reason of resentment against a priest, [1] while a hand-

---

1. It may be added in this context that these young people distinguished plainly between the priest and the priesthood in a way earlier generations of Liverpool Catholics do not always appear to have done. (In another part of this investigation, Liverpool pastors were also interviewed.) Thus, while they re-

ful considered that some stopped going in reaction against religious teaching in school, a point some of their head teachers, interviewed in another part of the investigation, had predicted.

Study of Catholicism.

The seriousness of respondents' attitudes towards religion was echoed in discussing whether they considered it desirable *to study their religion after leaving school.* Their answers stressed the necessity of studying in order to be able to discuss religious matters intelligently ; an example of this kind of reply was :

Definitely, definitely. Most of them — a great many — seem to forget what they've learned. *Me,* for instance ! When you're in factories, there are lots of non-Catholics... All these ideas have an effect. You tend to get rather lax. You should study the things you come up against every day, questions you get asked. But in the forefront of one's mind should be the importance of going to Mass and the Sacraments.

In answering this question, *defensive attitudes towards the wider community* became very apparent once again. It was plain that the apologetical approach which they had learned at school, where the religious course in one of the final years was devoted to a syllabus largely influenced by Counter-Reformation theology, had left its mark. They had grown to expect criticisms and attacks upon their religion, and it would be interesting to investigate in a later inquiry how far the self-fulfilling prophecy operates in response to these expectations. It is worth noting that this religious course was probably to some extent responsible for the ideas which some held about the nature of the Church, as being predominantly a *spiritual* union of the faithful ; the notion of a *social* community within the Church made very little impact on their lives, as the analysis of behaviour in relation to parochial and other Catholic activities revealed.

Conclusions.

Thus, while in some ways these young people were more ready to come to terms with their environment, expressing a better under-

---

served a basic respect for the priesthood, they were often highly critical of individual men; but at the same time, the actions of such men did not cause scandal for them.

standing of the values of other people, and a greater willingness to believe such people were sincere, in other ways they saw themselves as a distinct group which had to maintain its beliefs and values in the face of constant opposition. With such views, it is not surprising that the analysis of their friendship patterns revealed how closely they associated with other Catholics of a similar education. Their answers emphasized the importance of their values and beliefs to their own lives, and stressed the necessity for accepting them on rational grounds rather than because they had been taught to hold them.

It seems worthwhile adding a further point, based upon the findings of the rest of the investigation, of which the material and inquiry described here formed only a section : it appears that the period of life described by these young people in their early twenties was the decisive one in their adulthood. Many had experienced doubts and hesitations, but most had solved them one way or another by this age. Nearly all settled into their professional careers very soon afterwards, and marriage followed for a considerable number before long. It was noticeable that a high proportion were married not simply in a Catholic church, but to someone either belonging to the same community as they did or to another one rather like it. The descriptions they gave of their religious experiences since leaving school, then, related directly to their behaviour and attitudes later on.

Bibliography of Reviews and Periodicals in Religious Psychology

Journal for the Scientific Study of Religion. Official Journal of the Society for the Scientific Study of Religion (2000 members). Editor: Professor Prentiss L. Pemberton (Colgate Rochester Divinity School). 2 volumes (of 140 pages) a year: $5.00. Subscriptions: Professor James Dittes, 409 Prospect Street, New Haven, Connecticut 06511 U.S.A.

The review publishes technical researches and methodological or phenomenological reflections at a high standard of scientific demands. Clarity, precision, perfect presentation, full bibliographical studies; no other review at present attains this scientific standing. Open to all works of merit, interconfessional, it is (slowly) becoming international in both collaborators and surveys.

Journal of Religion and Health. Published by the Academy of Religion and Mental Health (International). Editor: George C. Anderson (Academy), Harry C. Meserve (Journal). 4 numbers (90 pages) a year: $5.00. Subscriptions: 16 East 34th Street, New York, New York 10016 U.S.A.

The review publishes chiefly theoretical or descriptive articles on the relations between religion and psychiatry, moral values and sciences of human conduct. A few (too few) articles give the results of scientific researches, or good excerpts from case studies. First-class collaborators, excellent presentation, copious and good book reviews. Interconfessional, not very international, the review is a crossroads of all kinds of opinion, with predominance of a religion primarily understood as an experience, and even (at least among some contributors) supposed to serve mental health.

Archiv für Religionspsychologie. Published by Vandenhoeck und Ruprecht, Göttingen.

The reappearance of this series, interrupted after Volume VI in 1936, under the energetic efforts of Professor W. Keilbach (general secretary to the Internationale Gesellschaft für Religionspsychologie) is an event which could have a great influence over the development of works on the psychology of religion in Europe.

Insight. Quarterly Review of Religion and Mental Health. Four numbers a year (48 double pages, large size): $5.00. Subscriptions:

St. Anthony Monastery, 3140 Meramee Street, Saint Louis, Missouri 63118 U.S.A.

This review was started in the summer, 1952, by Father Fintan McNamee, Franciscan, president of the Academy for Religion and Mental Health at Saint Louis (U.S.A.), psychological adviser and member of the therapeutic staff at the State Hospital of Saint Louis.

Review of Religious Research. Quarterly. Editor: Frederick A. Shippey. Three numbers (of 60 pages) a year: $3.00. Subscriptions: Dr. Yoshio Fukuyama, P. O. Box 228, Cathedral Station, New York, New York   10025 U.S.A.

Published by the Religious Research Association since the summer, 1959, and greatly improved in presentation since Volume V, No. 1 (Fall 1963).

Religious Education. Published by the Religious Education Association (Herman Wornom, General Secretary). Six numbers (of 90 pages) a year: $8.50. Subscriptions: 545 W. 111th Street, New York, New York   10025 U.S.A.

The best review, interconfessional, for teachers of religion. A regular report gives the results of theses (even unpublished) having incidence in psychopedagogy of religious education.

The Psychological Record. Two volumes, about 80 pages, a year: $3.00. Subscriptions: Managing Editor, American Catholic Psychological Association, Department of Psychology, Boston College, Chestnut Hill, Massachusetts   02167 U.S.A.

A new review, appearing twice a year, containing the best psychological works and conferences at the annual congress of the American Catholic Psychological Association (W. Bier, S.J., Executive Secretary).

Archives de Sociologie des Religions. Two volumes a year, each of about 200 pages, have appeared since January 1956. 22 French francs: Centre National de la Recherche Scientifique, 13 quai Anatole-France, Paris VII, France.

Besides a generous and very precise bibliographical bulletin, this series is the only one in French that regularly gives works in the psychology of religion of really scientific standing.